The Economics of Race and Crime

Edited by

Margaret C. Simms and Samuel L. Myers, Jr.

Routledge
Taylor & Francis Group
LONDON AND NEW YORK

First published 1988 by Transaction Publishers

Published 2019 by Routledge
2 Park Square, Milton Park, Abingdon, Oxon OX14 4RN
52 Vanderbilt Avenue, New York, NY 10017

First issued in hardback 2019

Routledge is an imprint of the Taylor & Francis Group, an informa business

ISBN 13: 978-1-138-53538-1 (hbk)
ISBN 13: 978-0-88738-755-5 (pbk)
ISSN: 0034-6446

Contents

ABOUT THE AUTHORS

Frontier Authors

Richard B. Freeman, Ph.D., is a professor of economics at Harvard University (Cambridge, Massachusetts) and director of labor studies at the National Bureau of Economic Research.

David H. Good, Ph.D., is an assistant professor in the School of Public and Environmental Affairs at Indiana University (Bloomington).

Richard McGahey, Ph.D., is Deputy Commissioner for Policy and Research for the New York State Department of Economic Development.

Dario Melossi, Ph.D., is an assistant professor of sociology at the University of California (Davis).

Samuel L. Myers, Jr., Ph.D., is director of the Afro-American Studies Program at the University of Maryland (College Park).

Llad Phillips, Ph.D., is a professor of economics at the University of California at Santa Barbara.

Maureen Pirog-Good, Ph.D., is an assistant professor in the School of Public and Environmental Affairs at Indiana University (Bloomington).

William Sabol is a faculty research associate in the Afro-American Studies Program at the University of Maryland (College Park).

Harold L. Votey, Jr., Ph.D., is a professor of economics at the University of California at Santa Barbara.

Landmark Authors (affiliation at time of original publication)

W.E.B. Du Bois was one of the first blacks to receive a Ph.D. from Harvard University and was a professor at Atlanta University.

Gunnar Myrdal was a Swedish economist at the University of Stockholm, who later received a Nobel Prize for his work on racial issues and on welfare economics.

Thorsten Sellin was a professor at the University of Pennsylvania.

W.F. Willcox was a professor at Cornell University and chief statistician of the Census Bureau.

Monroe Work was director of the Department of Records and Research at Tuskegee Institute.

PREFACE

At least once a year, the *Review of Black Political Economy* publishes a special issue that focuses on a topic of importance to blacks. Over a year ago Sam Myers agreed to develop a special issue on "Blacks and Crime," in conjunction with Jack Votey. In spite of a very busy schedule during his first year as director of the Afro-American Studies Program at the University of Maryland, Sam kept his commitment to the *Review*. The result, while unique in some respects, continues the *Review's* long tradition of presenting empirical and theoretical work that represents various views on a given subject. Because of the widespread interest in the topic, a decision was made to make the volume available to a broader audience in the form of a book. We are thankful to the University of Maryland for the support that allowed us to do this.

In his introduction to the volume, Myers recounts the origins of the volume, summarizes the important points that are made in each article, and provides the analysis that links these seemingly disparate articles together. He has done an excellent job of pulling together a set of landmark articles that have not been generally known or available to the group of scholars who have developed an interest in the "causes" of crime. He has also pushed researchers who are currently doing work in the area of blacks and crime to present their work in a variety of arenas for debate and for the enlightenment of those of us who are not working in the "vineyards" of economics and crime. This volume is just one of his efforts, but one that, hopefully, will expand the parameters of the debate.

Like all efforts of this magnitude, there are a number of people whose contributions must be acknowledged. I would like to extend a special thanks to Sam Myers for his work as guest editor of the *Review*, without whom the volume would not have been possible. In addition to Sam, the *Review* is grateful to Jack Votey for his assistance in laying out the scope of the volume. Although he was not able to serve as a coeditor when the final work had to be completed, his intellectual insight and thoughtful consideration were helpful in the early stages. Last, but certainly not least, I would like to thank Deborah Taylor for the assistance she provided both to Sam and to me in compiling documents, cajoling authors, and typing tables.

Margaret C. Simms

INTRODUCTION

Samuel L. Myers, Jr.

This volume is unusual in several respects. First, it tackles the issues of crime and the economy—arguably important to students of black political economy, but too often absent from the pages of both alternative and mainstream journals alike. Second, it reflects an emerging intellectual tension within scholarship on race and crime, in a manner that makes the readings seem more like a debate than a standard collection of articles. Third, at first glance it may not appear to be about *Black* political economy at all. Several of the articles make no pretense of attempting to explain black crime or to explain why blacks account for nearly fifty percent of the inmates in the United States' federal and state prisons. Instead, these apparently aberrant works seek to shed new light on crime and economy in a broader and, in one instance, international and comparative perspective, in hope of stimulating subsequent research on blacks and crime.

But the unique feature of this volume is its attempt to resurrect several classic writings by and about blacks on the elusive topic of criminal justice and economics. Some of the works that can be termed landmark articles are unknown to the current generation of researchers in economics and crime; these include W.E.B. Du Bois' famous examination of crime in Philadelphia and Booker T. Washington's peculiar indictment of drugs and alcohol (discussed later in this introduction) as the causes of black crime. Important precursors to modern (or neoclassical) economic models of crime are omitted due to space constraints; these include Adam Smith's often rambling lectures on jurisprudence with his singular emphasis on the use of police for the protection of life and property, as well as Bentham's underappreciated essay on why and when criminals do not respond to the just invented principles of pleasure and pain. The intention for bringing the few old and dusty writings on blacks and crime off the shelf is to expose the current generation of researchers to the antecedents of the ongoing tensions underlying scholarly endeavors to uncover the mystery of economy and crime.

ORIGINS OF THIS VOLUME

This project has its origins in a series of discussions that University of California, Santa Barbara economist Harold Votey and I began nearly a decade ago. We were both working away at refinements of our respective models of criminal behavior. Votey and his long-time collaborator Llad Phillips were reconciling their earlier work on labor markets and crime with the then dominant Beckerian analysis of deterrent effects of punishment. I was challenging the conventional deterrent model and was arguing within the rational choice framework that not only might not punishment reduce crime, it might even increase optimal participation in illegal activities.[1] We realized that important precursors to the rational model of crime existed among economic writers during the previous centuries. Bentham, Beccaria, Smith, and others could be found to be enunciating exactly (or nearly exactly) the same broad theorems now attributed to Becker, Ehrlich, and like-minded modern writers. What we did not know then was that economists of an earlier era, who embraced some of the racialist perspectives prevalent in the turn-of-the-century academic thought, had sketched out some of the reasoning that now pervades much of the conservative criminal justice literature. Our original intention was to produce a volume that brought together past and current writings on what economists had to say about crime. Through a fruitful interchange over the years, the result was several collaboratively organized sessions at various meetings of the American Economic Association and the Western Economic Association.

Something else happened as well. Both of us became more and more interested in looking closely at quality microdata in order to understand peculiar aspects of criminal justice processes. My concern was with racial discrimination in punishment. I examined several aspects of differential treatment of black and white offenders and found the need for better measures of pre-prison and post-prison employment and crime outcomes. Phillips and Votey examined the paths to crime from school and work among youthful offenders and found the need for reliable measures of unreported criminal behavior. The obvious and conspicuous racial discrimination in parole release rates and in time served uncovered in the data I examined led me and my collaborator, William Sabol, to ask how that discrimination came about historically. The barely obvious and inconspicuous difference in crime between blacks and whites uncovered in Phillips and Votey's data led them to ask what role if any is played by labor market and family variables wherein prominent racial divergences are registered. And so, in the quest for answering different questions, we have come to the recognition of what discussant Richard McGahey calls, "The problems at the Tower of Babel."

As our original research agendas began to diverge, so too did the conceptualization of what historical evidence was pertinent for the understanding of contemporary criminal justice policies. William Sabol, an intellectual historian by predilection, uncovered several gems of black history in the tomes of Harvard's Littauer Library. Black writers like W.E.B. Du Bois and Monroe Work were using their newly invented tools of social history to unlock not the mystery of why blacks were criminal but of why the criminal justice system was so black. Individual specific models, becoming increasingly prevalent at the turn of the century, were deemed inadequate for explaining how the convict lease systems, the prison farms, and the whole evolution of penitentiaries in America somehow evolved into a predominately black repository for the outcasts of society. Unfortunately, few modern economic or criminological writers, even those like Thorsten Sellin (an admirer of Du Bois) have given more than passing recognition to the pioneering contributions of these black scholars. More recent classics, such as that by Gunnar Myrdal, can be faulted as well for doing too little justice to the scholarship of blacks, except that in the case of Nobel-laureate Myrdal, most of the analysis was actually based on the previous writings of the black sociologist and criminologist, Guy Johnson. Nonetheless, Myrdal's interpretation of the selective evidence raises some interesting paradoxes when viewed from the window of the late 20th-century applied econometrician.

Upon reading the classic works of turn-of-the century black writers, along with other often forgotten treasures by early "radicals," Sabol and I began in earnest the task of reviewing how prisons became so black. This effort was stimulated principally by a nagging concern about the National Academy of Sciences' errant conclusion that while there may be some discrimination in some places and some times against some criminals, there was no systematic discrimination against blacks.[2] The emphasis needed to be shifted to understanding why and how the outcomes of the criminal justice system came about. These efforts resulted in a new historical data set on crime, race and employment from 1850 to 1980.

Phillips and Votey, in turn, were shifting their attentions to the National Longitudinal Survey of Young Americans, which promised to reveal insights into self-reported criminal involvement and economic factors. They sought to extend the rational choice model to include such social and behavioral factors as schooling, family background, and early labor market experiences. As such, their work breaks new ground that exposes both the promise and the limits of neoclassical economic models of crime.

While Votey's and my research paths were taking divergent routes, we continued to envision a volume of landmark and frontier articles on crime and economics. This is the end-product of that vision. We organized and arranged two separate panels of papers, one at the Western Economic Association meetings in San Francisco, in the summer of 1986, and the other at the American Economic Association meetings, winter 1986. The nontechnical versions of the WEA papers appear in *Contemporary Policy Issues* (Fall, 1987). The revised technical versions of the WEA papers, the AEA papers along with some insightful comments on them, and selections from five landmarks on race and crime are all included here.

LINKS BETWEEN PAST AND PRESENT

The first series of articles are landmarks in that they have important seeds of current thinking about crime and economics. They also help to underscore the tensions between research focused on why blacks are so criminal and on how the criminal justice system is so black. Witness the diverging perspectives of economist Walter Willcox and criminologist Thorsten Sellin:

Willcox writes:

> A large and increasing amount of negro crime is manifested all over the country. This raises a problem pressing with weight upon the States where negroes are numerous. The causes may be grouped as defective family life, defective industrial equipment and ability in comparison with their competitors, increasing race solidarity among negroes, and increasing alienation from the whites.[3]

While Sellin intones:

> The literature dealing with the social problems of the Negro is filled with statements which in no uncertain terms accuse the Negro of ex-

> cessive lawlessness. They have charged him with failure to appreciate, or utilize, the freedom which his emanicipation from slavery gave him. They have accused him of filling our prisons with dangerous criminals, because his inferior mentality and primitive emotions made it impossible for him to develop the self-control or the conformity to standards of conduct which life in a civil society demands. . . . [S]tudents of Negro criminality . . . have arrived at the general conclusion . . . that the Negro commits more crimes than the white. . . . [C]onsidering the poverty of our source material, such a conclusion requires considerable modification.[4]

When American Economic Association stalwart, Walter Willcox, read his infamous paper on "negro crime" before the American Social Science Association, the then-Chief Statistician of the Census Bureau sought to do more than summarize the alarming disproportionality of imprisonment and crime among blacks in the South. Reinforcing his conclusions by allusion to what blacks themselves had to say at the 1898 Hampton Negro Conference, Willcox, then secretary of the young organization called the American Economic Association and destined to become the 17th president of the primary organization of economists in America, sought to uncover the falsehoods he thought were being propagated by the Northern apologists for the Negro's condition in America. For example, writing in the tone of the time—a time during which William Baumol asserts American economists were governed by "loose standards of evidence" and often made pronouncements "based on no more than personal conviction"[5]—Willcox exclaims after summarizing the Northern liberal's claim that blacks were somehow discriminated against in the Southern criminal justice system:

> To meet these objections to the entire satisfaction of the person raising them would probably be difficult or impossible, and so, for the sake of my argument, let me for a moment admit their validity. If one thinks they furnish an adequate explanation of the large number of negro prisoners in the South, he may be asked whether they also lie in the North. Does it take less evidence to convict a negro here, or is a negro's sentence for the same offense likely to be longer? Such a claim has never to my knowledge been raised. Yet in the Northern States, in 1890, there were twelve white prisoners for every ten thousand whites, and sixty-nine negro prisoners to every ten thousand negroes. . . . These facts furnish some statistical basis and warrant for the popular

> opinion, never seriously contested, that under present conditions in this country a member of the African race, other things equal, is much more likely to fall into crime than a member of the white race.[6]

Willcox's racist persuasion did not prevent him from exposing an altogether uncovered myth: that the racial disproportionality of prisons was purely a southern phenomenon. This is a theme that arises in the Myers–Sabol paper.

Progressive criminologist, Thorsten Sellin, in contrast, who as recently as 1976 was denouncing the racism of the South and the penal institutions that evolved after emancipation to reenslave blacks, steadfastly holds to the enlightened view in the above quotation that the criminal justice statistics tell us less about why or whether blacks are more criminal than whites and more about how justice is administered differentially. Votey and Phillips are uniformly skeptical about the existence of "unexplained" racial differentials in crime. They would argue that the observed racial differentials in criminal involvement are due to differentials in economic opportunities and not, as Sellin implies, racial discrimination in the criminal justice system.

Sellin, nevertheless, in failing to see the unequal justice in the North, also fails to put to rest the fallacy of Willcox's argument. This leaves the door open for conclusions like those of Blumstein that perhaps blacks are more criminal after all. The tension between the search for causes of crime and the examination of the outcomes of the criminal justice process evident in writings by economists and criminologists writing more than a half-century ago is evident still, and emerges as the unifying force behind this unusual volume.

The principal tension in the historical papers and in contemporary ones as well is the tension between attempts to explain black crime and attempts to explain blacks' status in the economic or political system. Votey and his coauthor have been working mainly on how people make choices. This has implications for differences in crime by race. Increasingly the more sophisticated models show that blacks are not more criminal than whites even though conventional econometric results show that race is a powerful independent explanatory variable in the supply of crimes. But why is race so significant? Because blacks are more criminal? Or because blacks lack economic opportunities? Du Bois in his earliest work on crime in Philadelphia struggles with this dilemma, even though he, like most other classical writers is left to wade through arrest statistics to reach his conclusions. Phillips and Votey, in contrast are blessed with a superior data set, a superior model, and an unquestionably superior estimation methodology. It is surprising, then, that the result is the relatively low explanatory power of the economic specification of individual criminal behavior.

Myers and Sabol, for their part, are more concerned with how blacks end up where they are. They are concerned with imprisonment and the process by which prisons blackened in America following the Civil War. Their work does not provide a full-fledged nor adequate test of the racial discrimination hypothesis that Willcox rejects, nor is it free of the data bias alluded to by Sellin. Indeed, the omission of any measure of actual criminal participation in their model of business cycles and not crime but punishment leaves open the possibility that Willcox's thesis about industrial competition and black crime—detailed below—is correct after all. For all that it is worth, the Myers and Sabol article does nevertheless exonerate Willcox on the score of North-South variations in racial disparities in imprisonment, but not by using a Marxian analysis as McGahey claims in his comments.

Thus there are two trends in the contemporary articles that appear in this volume. One is the attempt to push microeconometric modeling as far as it will go to explain criminal behavior under the basic hypothesis that while official data show greater criminal involvement among blacks than whites, the real culprit is opportunities, broadly defined. Another is the attempt to see more macroscopically the process of imprisonment as a form of labor market equilibrating device. Blacks and whites do experience different criminal justice outcomes, in this view, but not simply because blacks are more prone to crime. Both the historical and the contemporary papers unveil this microeconomic vs. macrosociological tension. The result is a collection that will raise many new questions about what we know or think we know about crime, criminal justice, and the economy.

THE LANDMARK ARTICLES

The essays are arranged to evoke a sense of tension between the microeconomic and the macrosociological perspectives. The first essay, for example, provides excerpts from Du Bois's *The Philadelphia Negro*. In the selection from his chapter on the Negro criminal, Du Bois establishes, using the arrest statistics, the greater involvement of blacks in crime from the earliest days of their existence in Philadelphia. Accepting this racial disproportionality in crime, he then turns to a compelling account of how it, and the resulting racial disproportionality of imprisonment came about. Du Bois plainly sees the inferior legal status of the Negro as the most important factor contributing to his overrepresentation in prisons.

Following chronologically is Willcox's elaborate thesis that industrial competition between whites and "inferior" blacks reduced blacks' wages and thus contributed to their criminality. Added to this is the interesting contention that racial pride and solidarity fuels the sort of lack of respect for law and order that prevents the functioning of a true democracy. Willcox's analysis is useful not only for the glimpse it provides of how leading economists of the early 20th century viewed blacks, but also for its apparently accurate account of how blacks—or at least black intellectuals—viewed themselves. To make his point that blacks accepted the public view of their disproportionate participation in crime, Willcox quotes from the proceedings of the 1898 Negro Conference at Hampton Institute. We find in the brief excerpts from the Du Bois-edited ninth Atlanta Conference proceedings, which follow Willcox, similar admissions of the greater criminality of blacks as compared to whites and the need for educated blacks to curb the "excesses" of the black masses.

Monroe Work's 1913 article in the *Annals* comes next. It was published when he was located at Tuskegee Institute. He undoubtedly had been influenced by Du Bois (he was a contributor to the Atlanta volume in 1906) and also by Booker T. Washington, the principal of Tuskegee at the time. Washington published a paper called "Negro Crime and Strong Drink" in the *Journal of Criminal Law* (Vol. 3, 1912-13 pp. 384-92) in which he concluded, following a descriptive examination of the impacts of prohibition on black crime:

> Although the data presented above is inconclusive, yet when all the facts are considered, strong drink, I believe, is one of the chief causes of Negro crime in the South. It appears that where prohibition has really prohibited negroes from securing liquor their crime rate has been decreased.

Almost exactly these same words are echoed in Work's conclusion, although it seems much out of place, given the emphasis throughout on the racial injustices that preceded the rise of black imprisonment, suggesting an editorial addition that might have been at the insistence of Washington, Work's boss at the time.

The landmarks conclude with Thorsten Sellin's brief remarks on social science research and Negro crime and excerpts from Myrdal's *American*

Dilemma, wherein the absence of black political power is offered as the cause of black crime.

The early writings, as illustrated in our selection, reveal a great degree of disagreement, some of which continues into the present. It is useful, when moving on to the frontiers, to consider what we have learned from that controversy and what questions, if any, have been resolved by more recent research. Most people would argue that the nature of black-white differences in society have been evolving. It seems useful to inquire how this evolution has modified the terms of the debate.

THE FRONTIER ARTICLES

The article by Richard Freeman raises an important issue that has received much less attention than it deserves. He raises the question of the feedback effect of crime participation on employment of black youths. It is conducted very much in the tradition of behavioral choice models as used in the study of the labor market behavior of individuals. It takes the extent of black participation in crime as a given.

The approach reflects a difficulty with quality empirical research in economics. Incorporating all the complexities of a problem in a single equation estimation process is difficult and not always appropriate. What Freeman is telling us in his introduction is, in effect, that there is a problem of simultaneity; yet, he utilizes a single equation approach to make his point. And the evidence he presents suggests strongly that indeed simultaneity may be a crucial aspect of the crime-employment nexus.

The work of Good and Pirog-Good makes heroic headways in the direction of combining the microeconomic models of crime and employment to answer the questions raised by Freeman. It represents an ingenious advance in the formulation of a model to estimate simultaneously participation in work, crime and other activities. The approach effectively circumvents the most severe criticism of the use of simultaneous estimation techniques in crime participation research—that such estimation calls for the arbitrary exclusion of variables in the set of explanatory variables in order to achieve identification of key parameters. The research explicitly estimates separate relations for blacks and whites so that there can be no question as to whether parameters might differ between blacks and whites. This specification is chosen because of the a priori racial differences in labor markets and racial disparities in arrests.

Unfortunately, the measure of criminal participation is arrests, and as

Sellin warns us, this may mar the interpretations of the results. Nevertheless, the authors find confirmation for what Du Bois suspected all along: that criminal involvement among blacks is intimately linked to labor market outcomes.

The next article by Phillips and Votey, originally presented as three separate papers represents one piece of a continuum of research attempting to explain the involvement of youth in crime, within a framework that incorporates effects of deterrence measures, economic opportunities or their lack, investment in education, and a host of factors that reflect moral compliance with law. What is immediately apparent about this work is that, except for the third section, no race variable is included. And when race is included, it is found to be statistically insignificant. This modeling decision was intentional. Phillips and Votey adopt a broad range of measures to attempt to explain crime, that are specific to individuals. If crime differs by race, in their view, it is because the choice set differs between the races and not that there are individual differences between blacks and whites in the manner that Willcox envisions them.

Next follows the Myers–Sabol article referred to earlier and an important contribution by a sociologist working in the vineyards of business cycle theory. Dario Melossi's research provides a splendid comparison with Myers and Sabol's synthesis and an excellent test of Sellin's and Rusche and Kirchheimer's models of imprisonment. In these two articles the argument is made that punishment serves a social control function. Mellosi uncovers such a function in times-series data for Italy, and Myers and Sabol find it in the United States. These results add new fuel to the heated debate over whether unemployment or economic cycles cause crime. Both reveal that the operational mechanism that links economic cycles to crime is not criminal participation as conventionally conceived. It is imprisonment.

Two sets of comments conclude the volume—one by Llad Phillips and the other by Richard McGahey. Although McGahey limits his remarks to the four studies he discussed at the American Economic Association meetings, the assessment of the state of research on crime and economics is valuable. And while McGahey seems to exaggerate the importance of Karl Marx in some of the analysis, he is fair enough to note the failings of the neoclassical model in the rest. Thus, the tension between the first two perspectives finds a critic suggesting a third, institutional approach to economy and crime problems.

WHAT HAVE WE LEARNED?

If the reader is left with an erie sense that the state of affairs of social science research on race and crime is no better now than it was in 1900, then an important objective will have been achieved. There are now many more unanswered questions than Sellin and Willcox believed were there to be asked. For example, in the work of Freeman and Votey and Phillips there seem to be indications that churchgoing and other measures of personal values exhibit strong statistical impacts on employment and crime outcomes. Is this simply the empirical counterpart of the cries by the conventioneers at the Ninth Atlanta Conference? Or, is it a quirk in the data, a twist in the selection bias phenomenon that now is beginning to plague all users of microdata sets where certain segments of the population—like young black males—somehow withdraw nonrandomly?

Or, for another example, if the imprisonment process of the reconstruction era served to restructure southern labor markets, precisely what is it about contemporary labor markets that would lead to the nearly tripling of the black incarcerated population between 1970 and 1986? If the business-cycle theory is to wash, it must explain why imprisonment continues on its upward spiral during the end of the 1980s when unemployment is on a downward path.

Hopefully, the readers of the *Review* will be stimulated by the combination of historical and contemporary essays provided herein, and that through such stimulation, new and challenging directions on race, economy and crime will emerge.

NOTES

1. Samuel L. Myers, Jr., "Rehabilitation Effects of Punishment," *Economic Inquiry* Vol. 18 (July 1980), pp. 353-66.
2. See Blumstein et. al for a critique of the statistical methodology upon which the NAS results were based. See also Myers, "Methods of Measuring and Detecting Discrimination in Punishment," *Proceedings of American Statistical Association* (December, 1985) and . . . *Journal of Quantitative Criminology.*
3. W. F. Willcox, "Negro Criminality," *Journal of Social Science*, December, 1899, Vol. 37, p. 97 (reprinted in this volume).
4. Thorsten Sellin, "The Negro and the Problem of Law Observance and Administration in light of Social Research," in Charles S. Johnson, *The Negro In American Civilization*, 1930, pp. 443-444 (reprinted in this volume).
5. William J. Baumol, "On Method in U.S. Economics a Century Earlier," *American Economic Review* Vol. 75, No. 6 (December, 1985), p. 3.
6. Willcox, op. cit. p. 78.

THE NEGRO CRIMINAL

W.E.B. Du Bois

From his earliest advent the Negro, as was natural, has figured largely in the criminal annals of Philadelphia.[1] Only such superficial study of the American Negro as dates his beginning with 1863 can neglect this past record of crime in studying the present. Crime is a phenomenon of organized social life, and is the open rebellion of an individual against his social environment. Naturally then, if men are suddenly transported from one environment to another, the result is lack of harmony with the new conditions, lack of harmony with the new physical surroundings leading to disease and death or modification of physique, lack of harmony with social surroundings, leading to crime. Thus very early in the history of the colony, characteristic complaints of the disorder of the Negro slaves is heard. In 1693, July 11, the Governor and Council approved an ordinance, "Upon the Request of some of the members of Council, that an order be made by the Court of Quarter Sessions for the Countie of philadelphia, the 4th July instant (proceeding upon a presentment of the Grand Jurie for the bodie of the sd countie), agt the tumultuous gatherings of the Negroes of the towne of philadelphia, on the first dayes of the weeke, ordering the Constables of philadelphia, or anie other person whatsoever, to have power to take up Negroes, male or female, whom they should find gadding abroad on the said first dayes of the weeke, without a ticket from their Mr. or Mris., or not in their Compa, or to carry them to gaole, there to remain that night, and that without meat or drink, and to Cause them to be publickly whipt next morning with 39 Lashes, well Laid

---

This article is excerpted from W.E.B. Du Bois's *The Philadelphia Negro*, which was originally published in 1899 for the University of Pennsylvania. These excerpts are from an edition published by Kraus-Thomson Organization Limited, Millwood, N.Y. in 1973.

on, on their bare backs, for which their sd. Mr. or Mris. should pay 15d. to the whipper," etc.[2]

Penn himself introduced a law for the special trial and punishment of Negroes very early in the history of the colony, as has been noted before.[3] The slave code finally adopted was mild compared with the legislation of the period, but it was severe enough to show the unruly character of many of the imported slaves.[4]

Especially in Philadelphia did the Negroes continue to give general trouble, not so much by serious crime as by disorder. In 1732, under Mayor Hasel, the City Council "taking under Consideration the frequent and tumultuous meetings of the Negro Slaves, especially on Sunday, Gaming, Cursing, Swearing, and committing many other Disorders, to the great Terror and Disquiet of the Inhabitants of this city," ordered an ordinance to be drawn up against such disturbance.[5] Again, six years later, we hear of the draft of another city ordinance for "the more Effectual suppressing Tumultuous meetings and other disorderly doings of the Negroes, Mulattos and Indian servts. and slaves."[6] And in 1741, August 17, "frequent complaints having been made to the Board that many disorderly persons meet every ev'g about the Court house of this city, and great numbers of Negroes and others sit there with milk pails and other things late at night, and many disorders are there committed against the peace and good government of this city." Council ordered the place to be cleared "in half an hour after sunset."[7]

Of the graver crimes by Negroes, we have only reports here and there which do not make it clear how frequently such crimes occurred. In 1706 a slave is arrested for setting fire to a dwelling; in 1738 three Negroes are hanged in neighboring parts of New Jersey for poisoning people, while at Rocky Hill a slave is burned alive for killing a child and burning a barn. Whipping of Negroes at the public whipping post was frequent, and so severe was the punishment that in 1743 a slave brought up to be whipped committed suicide. In 1763 two Philadelphia slaves were sentenced to death for felony and burglary; petitions were circulated in their behalf but Council was obdurate.[8]

Little special mention of Negro crime is again met with until the freedmen under the act of 1780 began to congregate in the city, and other free immigrants joined them. In 1809 the leading colored churches united in a society to suppress crime and were cordially endorsed by the public for this action. After the war, immigration to the city increased and the stress of hard times bore heavily on the lower classes. Complaints of petty thefts and murderous assaults on peaceable citizens now began to increase, and

TABLE 1
Commitments to Eastern Penitentiary by Race, 1829-1854

Years	Total Commitments	Negroes	Percent of Negroes	Percent of Negroes of Total Population
1829-34	339	99	29.0	8.27 (1830)
1835-29	878	356	40.5	7.39 (1840)
1840-44	701	209	29.8	7.39 (1840)
1845-49	633	151	23.8	4.83 (1850)
1850-54	664	106	16.0	4.83 (1850)

in numbers of cases they were traced to Negroes. The better class of colored citizens felt the accusation and held a meeting to denounce crime and take a firm stand against their own criminal class. A little later, the Negro riots commenced, and they received their chief moral support from the increasing crime of Negroes. A Cuban slave brained his master with a hatchet, two other murders by Negroes followed, and gambling, drunkenness and debauchery were widespread wherever Negroes settled. The terribly vindictive insurrection of Nat Turner in a neighboring state frightened the citizens so thoroughly that when some black fugitives actually arrived at Chester from Southampton County, Virginia, the Legislature was hastily appealed to, and the whole matter came to a climax in the disfranchisement of the Negro in 1837 and the riots in the years 1830 to 1840.[9]

Some actual figures will give us an idea of this, the worst period of Negro crime ever experienced in the city. The Eastern Penitentiary was opened in 1829 near the close of the year. The total number of persons received here for the most serious crimes is given in the next table. (See Table 1.) This includes prisoners from the Eastern counties of the State, but a large proportion were from Philadelphia.[10]

Or to put it differently, the problem of Negro crime in Philadelphia from 1830 to 1850 arose from the fact that less than one-fourteenth of the population was responsible for nearly a third of the serious crimes committed.

These figures however are apt to relate more especially to a criminal class. A better measure of the normal criminal tendencies of the group would perhaps be found in the statistics of Moyamensing, where ordinary

TABLE 2
Commitments to Moyamensing Prison by Race, 1836-1855

Years	Total White Prisoners Received	Total Negro Prisoners Received	Percent of of Negroes of Total Prisoners	Percent of Negroes of Total Population
1836-45	1164	1087	48.29	7.39 (1840)
1846-55	1478	696	32.01	4.83 (1850)

cases of crime and misdemeanor are confined and which contains only county prisoners. (See Table 2.)

Here we have even a worse showing than before; in 1896 the Negroes forming 4 percent of the population furnish 9 percent of the arrests, but in 1850 being 5 percent of the population, they furnished 32 percent of the prisoners received at the county prison. Of course there are some considerations which must not be overlooked in interpreting these figures for 1836-55. It must be remembered that the discrimination against the Negro was much greater then than now: he was arrested for less cause and given longer sentences than whites.[11] Great numbers of those arrested and committed for trial were never brought to trial, so that their guilt could not be proven or disproven. Of 737 Negroes committed for trial in six months of the year 1837, it is stated that only 123 were actually brought to trial; of the prisoners in the Eastern Penitentiary, 1829 to 1846, 14 percent of the whites were pardoned and 2 percent of the Negroes. All these considerations increase the statistics to the disfavor of the Negro.[12] Nevertheless, making all reasonable allowances, it is undoubtedly true that the crime of Negroes in this period reached its high tide for this city.

The character of the crimes committed by Negroes compared with whites is shown by the following table, which covers the offences of 1359 whites and 718 Negroes committed to the Eastern Penitentiary, 1829-1846. (See Table 3). If we take simply petty larceny, we find that 48.8 percent of the whites and 55 percent of the Negroes were committed for this offence.[13]

Negro Crime Since the War

Throughout the land there has been since the war a large increase in crime, especially in cities. This phenomenon would seem to have suffi-

TABLE 3
Offences of Prisoners in Eastern Penitentiary by Race, 1829-1846

Kinds of Crimes	White Number	White Percent	Negroes Number	Negroes Percent
Offences vs. the person	166	11.4	89	12.4
Offences v.s property with violence	191	13.1	165	22.9
Offences vs. property without violence	873	59.8	432	60.2
Malicious offences vs. property	22	1.5	14	2.0
Offences vs. Currency and forgery	167	11.5	7	1.0
Miscellaneous	40	27.0	11	1.5

cient cause in the increased complexity of life, in industrial competition, and the rush of great numbers to the large cities. It would therefore be natural to suppose that the Negro would also show this increase in criminality and, as in the case of all lower classes, that he would show it in greater degree. His evolution has, however, been marked by some peculiarities. For nearly two decades after emanicipation, he took little part in many of the great social movements about him for obvious reasons. His migration to city life, therefore, and his sharing in the competition of modern industrial life came later than was the case with the mass of his fellow citizens. The Negro began to rush to the cities in large numbers after 1880, and consequently the phenomena attendant on that momentous change of life are tardier in his case. His rate of criminality has in the last two decades risen rapidly, and this is a parallel phenomenon to the rapid rise of the white criminal record two or three decades ago. Moreover, in the case of the Negro there were special causes for the prevalence of crime: he had lately been freed from serfdom, he was the object of stinging oppression and ridicule, and paths of advancement open to many were closed to him. Consequently, the class of the shiftless, aimless, idle, discouraged and disappointed was proportionately larger.

In the city of Philadelphia, the increasing number of bold and daring crimes committed by Negroes in the last ten years has focused the attention of the city on this subject. There is a widespread feeling that something is wrong with a race that is responsible for so much crime and that strong remedies are called for. One has but to visit the corridors of the public buildings when the courts are in session to realize the part played in law breaking by the Negro population. The various slum centres of the colored criminal population have lately been the objects of much philanthropic effort, and the work there has aroused discussion. Judges on the bench have discussed the matter. Indeed, to the minds of many, this is the real Negro problem.[14]

That it is a vast problem a glance at statistics will show;[15] and since 1880 it has been steadily growing. At the same time, crime is a difficult subject to study, more difficult to analyze into its sociological elements, and most difficult to cure or suppress. It is a phenomenon that stands not alone, but rather as a symptom of countless wrong social conditions.

The simplest, but crudest, measure of crime is found in the total arrests for a period of years. The value of such figures is lessened by the varying efficiency and diligence of the police, by discrimination in the administration of law, and by unwarranted arrests. And yet the figures roughly measure crime. The total arrests and the number of Negroes is given in the next table (See Table 4) for thirty-two years, with a few omissions.

We find that the total arrests in the city per annum have risen from 34,221 in 1864 to 61,478 in 1894, an increase of 80% in crime, parallel to an increase of 85% in population. The Negroes arrested have increased from 3114 in 1864 to 4805 in 1894, an increase of 54% in crime, parallel to an increase of 77 percent in the Negro population of the city. So, too, the percentage of Negroes in the total arrests is less in 1894 than in 1864. If, however, we follow the years between these two dates, we see an important development: 1864 was the date bounding the antebellum period of crime; thereafter the proportion of Negro arrests fell steadily until, in 1874, the Negroes came as nearly as ever furnishing their normal quota of arrests, 3.9 percent from 3.28 percent (1870) of the population. Then slowly there came a change. With the centennial exposition in 1876 came a stream of immigrants, and once started, the stream increased in speed by its own momentum. With this immigration, the proportion of Negro arrests arose rapidly at first as a result of the exposition—falling off a little in the early eighties, but with 1885 rising again steadily and quickly to over 6% in 1888, 6.4% in 1890, 7% in 1893, 8.5% in 1895, 9% in 1896. This is, as has been said before, but a rough indication of the amount of crime for which the Negro is responsible; it must not be relied on too closely, for the number of arrests cannot in any city accurately measure wrongdoing save in a very general way; probably increased efficiency in the police force since 1864 has had large effect, and yet we can draw the legitimate

TABLE 4
Arrests in Philadelphia, 1864-96

Date	Total Number Arrested	Total Negroes Arrested	Percentage of Negroes
1864	34,221	3,114	9.1
1865	43,226	2,772	6.3
1869	38,749	2,907	7.5
1870	31,717	2,070	6.5
1873	30,400	1,380	4.5
1874	32,114	1,257	3.9
1875	34,553	1,539	4.5
1876	.....	.....	....
1877	44,220	2,524	5.7
1879	40,714	2,360	5.8
1880	44,097	2,204	4.98
1881	45,129	2,327	5.11
1882	46,130	2,183	4.73
1883	45,295	2,022	4.46
1884	49,468	2,134	4.31
1885	51,418	2,662	5.11
1886	.....	.....	....
1887	57,951	3,256	5.61
1888	46,899	2,910	6.20
1889	42,673	2,614	6.10
1890	49,148	3,167	6.44
1891	53,184	3,544	6.66
1892	52,944	3,431	6.48
1893	53,297	4,078	7.11
1894	61,478	4,805	7.81
1895	60,347	5,137	8.5
1896	58,072	5.302	9.1

conclusion here that Negro crime in the city is far less, according to population, than before the war; that after the war it decreased until the middle of the seventies and then, coincident with the beginning of the new Negro immigration to cities,[16] it has risen pretty steadily.

The Causes of Crime and Poverty

A study of statistics seem to show that the crime and pauperism of the Negroes exceeds that of the whites; that in the main, nevertheless, it follows in its rise and fall the fluctuations shown in the records of the whites (*i.e.*, if crime increases among the whites, it increases among Negroes, and *vice versa*, with this peculiarity: that among the Negroes the change is always exaggerated—the increase greater, the decrease more marked in nearly all cases). This is what we would naturally expect: we have here the record of a low social class, and as the condition of a lower class is by its very definition worse than that of a higher, so the situation of the Negroes is worse as respects crime and poverty than that of the mass of whites. Moreover, any change in social conditions is bound to affect the poor and unfortunate more than the rich and prosperous. We have in all probability an example of this in the increase of crime since 1890; we have had a period of financial stress and industrial depression. The ones who have felt this most are the poor, the unskilled laborers, the inefficient and unfortunate, and those with small social and economic advantages. The Negroes are in this class, and the result has been an increase in Negro crime and pauperism; there has also been an increase in the crime of the whites, though less rapid by reason of their richer and more fortunate upper classes.

So far, then, we have no phenomena which are new or exceptional or which present more than the ordinary social problems of crime and poverty—although these, to be sure, are difficult enough. Beyond these, however, there are problems which can rightly be called Negro problems: they arise from the peculiar history and condition of the American Negro. The first peculiarity is, of course, the slavery and emancipation of the Negroes. That their emancipation has raised them economically and morally is proven by the increase of wealth and co-operation and the decrease of poverty and crime between the period before the war and the period since; nevertheless, this was manifestly no simple process. The first effect of emancipation was that of any sudden social revolution: a strain upon the strength and resources of the Negro, moral, economic and physical, which drove many to the wall. For this reason, the rise of the Negro in this city is a series of rushes and backslidings rather than a continuous growth. The second great peculiarity of the situation of the Negroes is the fact of immigration. The great numbers of raw recruits who have from time to time precipitated themselves upon the Negroes of the city and shared their small industrial opportunities, have made reputations, which, whether good or bad, all their race must share; and finally whether they failed or succeeded in the strong competition, they themselves must soon prepare to face a new immigration.

Here then we have two great causes for the present condition of the

Negro: slavery and emancipation with their attendant phenomena of ignorance, lack of discipline, and moral weakness; immigration with its increased competition and moral influence. To this must be added a third as great—possibly greater in influence than the other two, namely the environment in which a Negro finds himself—the world of custom and thought in which he must live and work, the physical surrounding of house and home and ward, the moral encouragements and discouragements which he encounters. We dimly seek to define this social environment partially when we talk of color prejudice—but this is but a vague characterization, what we want to study is not a vague thought or feeling but its concrete manifestations. We know pretty well what the surroundings are of a young white lad or a foreign immigrant who comes to this great city to join in its organic life. We know what influences and limitations surround him, to what he may attain, what his companionships are, what his encouragements are, what his drawbacks.

This we must know in regard to the Negro if we would study his social condition. His strange social environment must have immense effect on his thought and life, his work and crime, his wealth and pauperism. That this environment differs and differs broadly from the environment of his fellows, we all know, but we do not know just how it differs. The real foundation of the difference is the widespread feeling all over the land, in Philadelphia as well as in Boston and New Orleans, that the Negro is something less than an American and ought not to be much more than what he is. Argue as we may for or against this idea, we must as students recognize its presence and its vast effects.

At the Eastern Penitentiary where they seek so far as possible to attribute to definite causes the criminal record of each prisoner, the vast influence of environment is shown. This estimate is naturally liable to error, but the peculiar system of this institution and the long service and wide experience of the warden and his subordinates gives it a peculiar and unusual value. Of the 541 Negro prisoners previously studied, 191 were catalogued as criminals by reason of "natural and inherent depravity." The others were divided as shown in Table 5.

This rough judgment of men who have come into daily contact with five hundred Negro criminals but emphasizes the fact alluded to—the immense influence of his peculiar environment on the black Philadelphian; the influence of homes badly situated and badly managed, with parents untrained for their responsibilities; the influence of social surroundings which by poor laws and inefficient administration leave the bad to be made worse; the influence of economic exclusion which admits

TABLE 5
Causes of Crime Among Negroes at Eastern Penitentiary

(a) Defects of the Law	
Laxity in administration	33
Unsuitable laws for minor offenses	48
Inefficient police	22
License given to the young	16
Inefficient laws in regard to saloons	11
Poor institutions and lack of institutions	12
	142
(b) Immediate environment:	
Association	53
Amusements	16
Home and family influences	25
	94
(c) Lack of training, lack of opportunity, lack of desire to work	56
(d) General environment	6
(e) Disease	16
(f) Moral weakness and unknown	36
	114

Negroes only to those parts of the economic world where it is hardest to retain ambition and self-respect; and finally that indefinable, but real and mighty, moral influence that causes men to have a real sense of manhood or leads them to lose aspiration and self-respect.

For the last ten or fifteen years, young Negroes have been pouring into this city at the rate of a thousand a year; the question is then what homes they find or make, what neighbors they have, how they amuse themselves, and what work they engage in. Again, into what sort of homes are the hundreds of Negro babies of each year born? Under what social influences do they come, what is the tendency of their training, and what places in life can they fill? To answer all these questions is to go far toward finding the real causes of crime and pauperism among this race.

Color Prejudice

Incidentally, throughout this study, the prejudice against the Negro has been again and again mentioned. It is time now to reduce this somewhat indefinite term to something tangible. Everybody speaks of the matter, everybody knows that it exists, but in just what form it shows itself or how influential it is few agree. In the Negro's mind, color prejudice in Philadelphia is that widespread feeling of dislike for his blood, which keeps him and his children out of decent employment, from certain public conveniences and amusements, from hiring houses in many sections, and in general, from being recognized as a man. Negroes regard this prejudice as the chief cause of their present unfortunate condition. On the other hand, most white people are quite unconscious of any such powerful and vindictive feeling; they regard color prejudice as the easily explicable feeling that intimate social intercourse with a lower race is not only undesirable but impracticable if our present standards of culture are to be maintained; and although they are aware that some people feel the aversion more intensely than others, they cannot see how such a feeling has much influence on the real situation or alters the social condition of the mass of Negroes.

As a matter of fact, color prejudice in this city is something between these two extreme views. It is not today responsible for all or perhaps the greater part of the Negro problems, or of the disabilities under which the race labors. On the other hand, it is a far more powerful social force than most Philadelphians realize. The practical results of the attitude of most of the inhabitants of Philadelphia toward persons of Negro descent are as follows.

As to getting work: No matter how well trained a Negro may be or how fitted for work of any kind, he cannot in the ordinary course of competition hope to be much more than a menial servant. He cannot get clerical or supervisory work to do, save in exceptional cases. He cannot teach, save in a few of the remaining Negro schools. He cannot become a mechanic, except for small transient jobs, and cannot join a trades union. A Negro woman has but three careers open to her in this city: domestic service, sewing, or married life.

As to keeping work: The Negro suffers in competition more severely than white men. Change in fashion is causing him to be replaced by whites in the better paid positions of domestic service. Whim and accident will cause him to lose a hard earned place more quickly than the same things would affect a white man. Being few in number compared with the whites, the crime or carelessness of a few of his race is easily imputed to all, and the reputation of the good, industrious, and reliable suffer thereby. Because Negro workmen may not often work side by side with white workmen, the individual black workman is rated not by his own efficiency but by the efficiency of a whole group of black fellow workmen which may often be low. Because of these difficulties which virtually increase competition in his case, he is forced to take lower wages for the same work than white workmen.

As to entering new lines of work: Men are used to seeing Negroes in inferior positions; when, therefore, by any chance a Negro gets in a better position, most men immediately conclude that he is not fitted for it, even before he has a chance to show his fitness. If, therefore, he set up a store, men will not patronize him. If he is put into public position, men will complain. If he gain a position in the commercial world, men will quietly secure his dismissal or see that a white man succeeds him.

As to his expenditure: The comparative smallness of the patronage of the Negro and the dislike of other customers makes it usual to increase the charges or difficulties in certain directions in which a Negro must spend money. He must pay more house rent for worse houses than most white people pay. He is sometimes liable to insult or reluctant service in some restaurants, hotels and stores, at public resorts, theatres and places of recreation, and at nearly all barbershops.

As to his children: The Negro finds it extremely difficult to rear children in such an atmosphere and not have them either cringing or impudent. If he impresses upon them patience with their lot, they may grow up satisfied with their condition; if he inspires them with ambition to rise, they may grow to despise their own people, hate the whites, and become embittered with the world. His children are discriminated against, often in public schools. They are advised when seeking employment to become waiters and maids. They are liable to species of insult and temptation particularly trying to children.

As to social intercourse: In all walks of life, the Negro is liable to meet some objection to his presence or some discourteous treatment, and the ties of friendship or memory seldom are strong enough to hold across the color line. If an invitation is issued to the public for any occasion, the Negro can never know whether he would be welcomed or not. If he goes he is liable to have his feelings hurt and get into unpleasant altercation; if he stays away, he is blamed for indifference. If he meet a lifelong white friend on the street, he is in a dilemma. If he does not greet the friend, he is put down as boorish and impolite; if he does greet the friend, he is liable to be flatly snubbed. If by chance he is introduced to a white woman or man, he expects to be ignored on the next meeting, and usually is. White friends may call on him, but he is scarcely expected to call on them, save for strictly business matters. If he gain the affections of a white woman and marry her, he may invariably expect that slurs will be thrown on her reputation and on his and that both his and her race will shun their company.[17] When he dies he cannot be buried beside white corpses.

The result: Any one of these things happening now and then would not be remarkable or call for especial comment, but when one group of people suffer all these little differences of treatment and discriminations and insults continually, the result is either discouragement or bitterness or over-sensitiveness or recklessness. And a people feeling thus cannot do their best.

Presumably the first impulse of the average Philadelphian would be emphatically to deny any such marked and blighting discrimination as the above against a group of citizens in this metropolis. Every one knows that in the past color prejudice in the city was deep and passionate; living men can remember when a Negro could not sit in a street car or walk many streets in peace. These times have passed, however, and many imagine that active discrimination against the Negro has passed with them. Careful inquiry will convince any such one of his error. To be sure, a colored man today can walk the streets of Philadelphia without personal insult. He can go to theatres, parks, and some places of amusement without meeting more than stares and discourtesy; he can be accommodated at most hotels and restaurants, although his treatment in some would not be pleasant. All this is a vast advance and augurs much for the future. And yet all that has been said of the remaining discrimination is but too true.

It goes without saying that most private schools, music schools, etc., will not admit Negroes and in some cases have insulted applicants.

Such is the tangible form of Negro prejudice in Philadelphia. No one who has with any diligence studied the situation of the Negro in the city can long doubt but that his opportunities are limited and his ambition circumscribed about as has been shown. There are of course numerous exceptions, but the mass of the Negroes have been so often refused openings and discouraged in efforts to better their condition that many of them say, as one said, "I never apply—I know it is useless." Beside these tangible and measurable forms, there are deeper and less easily described results of the attitude of the white population toward the Negroes: a certain manifestation of a real or assumed aversion, a spirit of ridicule or patronage, a vindictive hatred in some, absolute indifference in others. All this of course does not make much difference to the mass of the race, but it deeply wounds the better classes, the very classes who are attaining to that to which we wish the mass to attain. Notwithstanding all this, most Negroes would patiently await the effect of time and commonsense on such prejudice did it not today touch them in matters of life and death, threaten their homes, their food, their children, their hopes. And the result of this is bound to be increased crime, inefficiency, and bitterness.

It would, of course, be idle to assert that most of the Negro crime was caused by prejudice; the violent economic and social changes which the last fifty years have brought to the American Negro, the sad social history that preceded these changes, have all contributed to unsettle morals and pervert talents. Nevertheless, it is certain that Negro prejudice in cities like Philadelphia has been a vast factor in aiding and abetting all other causes which impel a half-developed race to recklessness and excess. Certainly a great amount of crime can be without doubt traced to the discrimination against Negro boys and girls in the matter of employment. Or to put it differently, Negro prejudice costs the city something.

The connection of crime and prejudice is, on the other hand, neither simple nor direct. The boy who is refused promotion in his job as porter does not go out and snatch somebody's pocketbook. Conversely, the loafers at Twelfth and Kater streets and the thugs in the county prison are not usually graduates of high schools who have been refused work. The connections are much more subtle and dangerous; it is the atmosphere of rebellion and discontent that unrewarded merit and reasonable but unsatisfied ambition make. The social environment of excuse, listless despair, careless indulgence, and lack of inspiration to work is the growing force that turns black boys and girls into gamblers, prostitutes, and rascals. And this social environment has been built up slowly out of the disappointments of deserving men and the sloth of the unawakened. How long can a city say to a part of its citizens, "It is useless to work; it is fruitless to deserve well of men; education will gain you nothing but disappointment and humiliation?" How long can a city teach its black children that the road to success is to have a white face? How long can a city do this and escape the inevitable penalty?

For thirty years and more, Philadelphia has said to its black children: "Honesty, efficiency and talent have little to do with your success; if you work hard, spend little, and are good you may earn your bread and butter at those sorts of work which we frankly confess we despise; if you are dishonest and lazy, the State will furnish your bread free." Thus the class of Negroes which the prejudices of the city have distinctly encouraged is that of the criminal, the lazy and the shiftless; for them the city teems with institutions and charities; for them there is succor and sympathy; for them Philadelphians are thinking and planning; but for the educated and industrious young colored man who wants work and not platitudes, wages and not alms, just rewards and not sermons—for such colored men Philadelphia apparently has no use.

NOTES

1. Throughout this chapter, the basis of induction is the number of prisoners received at different institutions and *not* the prison population at particular times. This avoids the mistakes and distortions of the latter method. (Cf. Falkner: "Crime and the Census;" Publications of the American Academy of Political and Social Science, No. 190). Many writers on crime among Negroes (e.g., F.L. Hoffman, and all who use the Eleventh Census uncritically) have fallen into numerous mistakes and exaggerations by carelessness on this point.
2. Pennsylvania Colonial Records, I, 380-91.
3. See Chapter III and Appendix B.
4. Cf. "Pennsylvania Statutes at Large," Ch. 36.
5. "Watson's Annals," I. 62.
6. Ibid.
7. Ibid., pp. 62-63.
8. "Pennsylvania Colonial Records," II, 275; IX, 6; "Watson's Annals," I, 309.
9. Cf. Chapter IV.
10. Reports Eastern Penitentiary.
11. Average length of sentences for whites in Eastern Penitentiary during nineteen years, 2 years 8 months 2 days; for Negroes, 3 years 7 months 14 days. Cf. "Health of Convicts" (pam.), pp. 7,8.
12. Ibid., "Condition of Negroes," 1838, pp. 15-18; "Condition of Negroes," 1848, pp. 26, 27.
13. "Condition of Negroes," 1849, pp. 28, 29. "Condition of Negroes" 1838, pp. 15-18.
14. "The large proportion of colored men who, in April, had been before the criminal court, led Judge Gordon to make a suggestion when he yesterday discharged the jurors for the term. 'It would certainly seem,' said the Court, 'that the philanthropic colored people of the community, of whom there are a great many excellent and intelligent citizens sincerely interested in the welfare of their race, ought to see what is radically wrong that produces this state of affairs and correct it, if possible. There is nothing in history that indicates that the colored race has a propensity to acts of violent crime; on the contrary, their tendencies are most gentle, and they submit with grace to subordination.'" Philadelphia *Record*, April 29, 1893: Cf. *Record*, May 10 and 12; *Ledger*, May 10, and *Times*, May 22, 1893.
15. Except as otherwise noted, the statistics of this section are from the official reports of the police department.
16. Cf. Chapters IV and VII.
17. Cf. Section 49.

NEGRO CRIMINALITY

Walter F. Willcox

The number of prisoners in the United States was reported at the last census, showing those of African descent and those of pure white blood. In the Southern States, there were six white prisoners to every ten thousand whites and twenty-nine Negro prisoners to every ten thousand Negroes.[1] This seems to indicate that the liability of an American Negro to commit crime is several times as great as the liability of a white. But those who are unwilling to admit this inference sometimes urge that the judicial system of the South is almost entirely in the hands of the whites and that it is not administered with impartiality to the two races. They claim that a Negro is convicted on the average upon less evidence that is required to convict a member of the dominant race, that, if found guilty, he is less likely to escape prison by paying a fine; and that, if both are imprisoned, the Negro is likely to receive a longer sentence for a like offense. To meet these objections to the entire satisfaction of the person raising them would probably be difficult or impossible, and so, for the sake of my argument, let me for the moment admit their validity. If one thinks they furnish an adequate explanation of the large number of Negro prisoners in the South, he may be asked whether they lie also in the North. Does it take less evidence to convict a Negro here, or is a Negro's sentence for the same offense likely to be longer? Such a claim has never to my knowledge been raised. Yet in the Northern States, in 1890, there were twelve white prisoners to every ten thousand whites, and sixty-nine Negro prisoners to every ten thousand Negroes. In our own State of New York, the Negroes, in proportion to their numbers, contributed over five times as many as the whites to the prison population. These facts furnish some

---

This article was originally published in the *Journal of Social Science*, No. 37, 1899 by the American Social Science Association.

statistical basis and warrant for the popular opinion, never seriously contested, that under present conditions in this country a member of the African race, other things equal is much more likely to fall into crime than a member of the white race. This is the unanimous opinion of the Southern whites and is conceded by representative Negroes. Thus, among the resolutions adopted by the Negro Conference at Hampton, Va., in July, 1898, was the admission that "the criminal record of the colored race in all parts of the country is alarming in its proportions."[2]

The Negro prisoners in the Southern States to ten thousand Negroes increased between 1880 and 1890 twenty-nine percent, while the white prisoners to ten thousand whites increased only eight percent.[3] Here, again, to the obvious inference that crime is increasing among the Negroes much faster than among the whites, the same objection is sometimes raised, namely, that prejudice against that race is so influential in the South as to invalidate the argument. The same appeal as before to the figures for the North and West constitutes a convincing reply to any such contention. In the States where slavery was never established, the white prisoners increased seven percent faster than the white population, while the Negro prisoners increased no less than thirty-nine percent faster than the Negro population. Thus the increase of Negro criminality, so far as it is reflected in the number of prisoners, exceeded the increase of white criminality more in the North than it did in the South. To bring the facts home, I may add that for New York State in 1880 there were sixteen white prisoners to every ten thousand white population; and in 1890 the proportion has risen to eighteen. But the Negro prisoners of the State in 1880 were seventy-seven, and in 1890 one hundred to every ten thousand Negroes. These figures serve to show both the higher rate and the more rapid increase of Negro criminality, and in both respects New York is a fair type of the conditions elsewhere in the country. In these figures one finds again some statistical basis for the well-nigh universal opinion that crime among the American Negroes is increasing with alarming rapidity.[4] In further support of this conclusion, I may quote the concession of the Negro who is perhaps doing as much as any member of his race to throw light upon its present condition. Professor Du Bois, of Atlanta University, in a recent address before the Negro Academy, said: "The Negro Academy ought to sound a note of warning that would echo in every black cabin in the land.[5] Unless we conquer our present vices, they will conquer us. We are diseased, we are developing criminal tendencies, and an alarmingly large percentage of our men and women are sexually impure."

Let us grant then that there is a large amount and a rapid increase of

Negro crime in the United States. This gives rise to a serious practical problem—How may this amount be reduced, or at least the increase checked? The answer to that largely depends upon the answer to a more theoretical question, which will define my theme this morning—What are the causes of Negro crime? If those causes can be detected and removed or counteracting causes set at work, the practical problem will have been advanced towards solution.

The criminal is one who refuses to obey the laws of the community in which he lives. Such obedience to the law in the face of temptation is not an instinct or birthright but a product of training, and in the great majority of instances that training is obtained in the family. The primary cause of crime, therefore, is defective family life and training. Hence, crime is most common during the years after a child has passed out of the control of the family and while he is finding himself ill-adapted by his past training to the new sphere of life. In proportion to population of the same age, the prisoners between twenty and thirty are much more numerous than those of any earlier or later age period;[6] and, if the date of committing the first crime could be ascertained—and that is the important time—the juvenile character of our criminal population would appear yet more clearly. This youthfulness in comparison with the population outside is characteristic of all classes of prisoners, but pre-eminently of the Negroes[7]—a fact which tends in a measure to confirm the frequent statement that Negro criminals spring especially from the rising generation. If that be so, a further increase of Negro criminality in the future is probable, and this probability renders the situation still more serious.

Under the slavery regime, the Negro had a feeble family life, much of the responsibility for the proper rearing of the family falling upon the master. The emancipated slaves have not been able in a single generation of freedom to develop or to imitate that family life which it has cost the whites many centuries to acquire. The difficulty is the more serious because today the conditions of civilized life do not foster the family virtues as they have done in the past. The white race is living on its inherited capital of family organization and responsibilities; the Negroes have no such capital, but must acquire it, and that speedily, if the race is to survive.

What is the most effective safeguard against crime that the family furnishes the son or daughter? Not education, not even direct moral or religious training. The Negro and the injudicious among his friends too often look on education and religion as fetiches, that is, something external, the possession of which guarantees the possessor a charmed and happy life here or hereafter. In distinction from these, the most effective safeguard against crime which parents can offer to their children is the desire and ability to support one's self by legitimate industry. A formal education is subsidiary to this; it is important mainly because it increases the avenues through which self-support is possible. If ever it serves to decrease the desire for self-support, it is to that extent baneful. If ever it decreases the recognized avenues for self-support by arousing the belief that certain lines of legitimate industry are degrading and therefore inadmissible, it is to that extent baneful. This may give a standpoint from which to judge the difficult question of Negro education. If the Negro family on the average is far less effective than the white, the education provided for Negro children should aim frankly to supplement the shortcomings of their family life and reduce their temptations to crime by increasing their desire and ability to live by legitimate industry. Probably the best means by which to reach and reenforce the family life of the Negroes is a school system which frankly sets this up as its aim.

A closely related series of causes for Negro crime may be grouped as industrial. Under the compulsory cooperation of slavery, little competition between the two races was possible. Manual labor in many pursuits, notably those of agriculture, was deemed by the whites servile and degrading. Since the war, this motive for the white man to avoid fieldwork or other forms of manual labor had diminished in importance, and he has gradually entered upon tasks which before the war were closed to him by the pressure of social sentiment. In ceasing to be master he has become competitor, and to the presssure of this competition not a little Negro crime must be attributed.

Hence it is no digression to invite your attention for a few moments to some evidence of the increasing competition between the two races. The staple crops upon which the Negroes were occupied before the war were probably cotton, tobacco, sugar, and rice. In 1860 the great mass of the work in the cotton fields was done by Negro labor. White labor was used, to be sure, in Texas, but at that time the whole cotton crop of Texas was less than one-twelfth of the country's product.[8] It would probably be a conservative statement to say that at least four-fifths of the cotton was then grown by the Negroes. The only official estimate for any date since that time is that of the Statistician to the Department of Agriculture in 1876.[9] He concluded that about three-fifths of our cotton was raised in that year by Negroes. At the present time, probably not one-half is thus grown. In 1859 Texas produced one-twelfth, in 1897-98 one-fourth,[10] of the cotton of the United States; and, as in that State white labor is usually employed in the cotton fields, the advance of Texas means the advance of white agricultural labor.

Similar changes have been going on in the tobacco crop. In 1859 twenty-eight percent of it was grown in Virginia, and mainly, it seems, by Negro labor. In 1889 less than ten percent of our crop was grown in that State, and the Virginia crop of that year was less than two-fifths of what it had been thirty years before. In 1889 Kentucky produced over forty-five percent of the tobacco of the country, while ten years earlier it produced only thirty-six percent. American tobacco growing evidently is tending to center in Kentucky, and yet it is the only Southern State in which the number of Negroes decreased during the last decade. In over half its counties and in the State as a whole, the Negro population decreased while the white increased between 1880 and 1890.[11] It seems that tobacco growing, like cotton growing, is passing more and more into the hands of the whites. Some light upon this change may be derived from a passage in the last Annual Report of the Secretary of Agriculture:[12] "The tobacco business has become very highly specialized. Each market has its own requirements, each class of users has its own particular style, and each season brings some change of style which must be met by the tobacco grower. There is a great deal of competition in our own country, and very serious competition from abroad. . . . To meet this competition, it is absolutely necessary that our farmers should have at their disposal a thorough knowledge of their own conditions and of the conditions of the soil, climate, methods, and labor conditions of competing districts."

Of the cane sugar crop of the United States in 1889, over ninety-seven percent came from Louisiana, and the increase of yield in the preceding decade was almost confined to that State, where the acreage under cane increased seven percent and the yield forty-two percent.[13] Apparently, the increase of yield in the last ten years, notwithstanding the losses resulting from recent federal legislation, has been quite as rapid. In a paper read in 1898 before the Louisiana Agricultural Society the statement was made[14] that this rapid increase in the production of cane sugar was "due especially to the establishment of large central factories." The machinery in these factories is managed, I am informed, almost entirely by white men.

With regard of the rice crop of the country, in 1879 less than one-fourth of the acreage was in Louisiana, in 1889 over one-half was there.[15] During the last decade, the acreage outside Louisiana decreased forty-two percent, while that within the State more than doubled. In this, as in other staple agricultural industries, there has been a marked tendency towards concentration, and the centre of production has passed away from South Carolina, which in 1849 produced three-fourths of our crop, but in 1889 less than one-fourth. This transfer of the rice growing industry is largely due to the superior efficiency of white labor. A pamphlet distributed at the Louisiana Building during the World's Fair in 1893 and thus given apparently official indorsement, says: Not long since the Carolinas raised the rice of the United States, and the delta of the Mississippi the rice of Louisiana, all done by colored labor. The immigration agent of the Southern Pacific Railroad Company induced the men of the Northwest to come into southwestern Louisiana, bringing their improved farm machinery. They supplanted the hook and sickle then in use by twine-binding harvesters, of which many hundred are now employed in the Louisiana rice fields, and this machinery is handled by white men.[16] Corroborative evidence is found in a recent paper read before the Louisiana Agricultural Society, which states that there are now in the rich fields of Louisiana nearly five thousand selfbinding harvesters with steam threshers by the hundred and that artificial irrigation employing steam pumps has been introduced on a large scale.[17]

From all the evidence obtainable, it seems clear that Southern agriculture is become increasingly diversified and is demanding and receiving a constantly increasing amount of industry, energy, and intelligence—characteristics which the whites more generally possess or more readily develop.

Some evidence upon the lack of industry of Negro farmers in the black belt of Alabama may be derived from a recent bulletin of the United States Department of Agriculture dealing with their food. Eighteen families near Tuskegee, Alabama were selected as typical and studied by officials of the department in cooperation with representatives of the Tuskegee Normal Institute. The agent of the Department reported: "The Negro farmer generally works about seven and a half months during the year. . . . The rest of the time is devoted to visiting, social life, revivals, or other religious exercises and to absolute idleness. Few farmers work on Saturday even during the busy season of cotton picking."[18]

The same study gives evidence of the poor food supply of the Negro farmers. In the diet of the average Negro family, the amount of protein—that is, of the material needed to form blood, muscle, and bone and to make up for the wear and tear of the bodily machine—was from one-third to three-fourths that which has been found in the diet of well-fed American whites and "no larger than has been found in the diet of the very poor factory operatives and laborers in Germany and the laborers and beggars in Italy."[19]

In agricultural pursuits, the competition between whites and blacks can be traced more clearly than elsewhere, because in that field we have fuller information. Still there is some evidence, derived mainly from statements of educated Negroes, that in other occupations also this competition is seriously felt.

Thus Professor Hugh M. Browne of Washington said in a speech five years ago to a Negro audience: "White men are bringing science and art into menial occupations and lifting them beyond our reach. In my boyhood, the household servants were colored, but now in the establishments of the four hundred one finds trained white servants. Then the walls and ceilings were whitewashed each spring by colored men; now they are decorated by skilled white artisans. Then the carpets were beaten by colored men; now this is done by a white man, managing a steam carpet-cleaning works. Then laundry work was done by Negroes; now they are with difficulty able to manage the new labor saving machinery."[20]

Similar testimony comes from another Negro, Mr. Fortune, editor of an influential Negro paper. He said in 1897: "When I left Florida for Washington twenty years ago, every brakeman, every engineer, and almost every man working on the railroad was a black man. Today a black man can hardly get a job at any avocation. This is becuase the fathers did not educate their children along the lines in which they were working, and as a consequence the race is losing its grip on the industries that are the bone and sinew of life."[21] At the same conference, Mr. Fitch, the field missionary of Hampton Normal Institute, reported that he found the old men everywhere working at the trades they learned in slavery, but nowhere did he find young men learning these trades.[22] Similarly, Principal Frissell, in the opening address, said: "There is great danger that the colored people will be pushed out of the occupations that were once theirs, because white tradesmen are coming in to fill their places."[23] This competition between the races is accentuated by the trade-union policy of exclusion, which often denies Negroes the right of membership in labor organizations, and then opposes the employment of non-unionists, the net result of which is to antagonize the entry or continuance of Negroes in the field of skilled labor.[24]

Every improvement in agriculture or industry anywhere tending to lower the price of a staple product is a spur to former producers. They must meet the situation by economies of production or economies of consumption, by improving their own methods or by living on a smaller return. Those who are sanguine of the future of the Negro in the United States usually rest their case upon the evidence of Negro progress since emancipation, measured against some assumed absolute standard. They point to a decreasing illiteracy, to accumulations of property, to a decreasing death rate, etc. But the test which the race has to face is the test of relative efficiency. If they are to hold their own in this country, they must improve as fast as the whites, and the progress of the Southern whites since emerging from the dark shadows of slavery, the war, and reconstruction is one of the marvels of present history.

Partly under the stress of this competition to which the Negroes are being subjected, partly as a natural result of their emancipation, they are gradually drawing apart into social classes. The successful families refuse to associate with those who morally and industrially are stationary or retrogressive. Dr. Du Bois has recently made a valuable report on the members of his race living at a small county seat in the Virginia tobacco district. About 260 Negro families were studied, of which 40 belonged to the higher class, 170 to the middle, and perhaps 50 to the lower. He describes the members of the lower classes "below the line of ordinary respectability, living in loose sexual relationship, responsible for most of the illegitimate children, and furnishing a half-dozen street walkers and numerous gamblers and rowdies. They are not particularly vicious and quarrelsome, but rather shiftless and debauched. Laziness and promiscuous sexual intercourse and their besetting sins."[25] In other words, this class lacks the family virtues and the industrial virtues which have made the white man what he is. It may be styled potentially criminal. A class of such people is found, to be sure, in every civilized country, but in our Southern States the proportion of this potentially criminal class is abnormally and dangerously large. About one-fifth of the Negro families or over one-tenth of the total population in Farmville are assigned by Professor Du Bois to this group. This growing social stratification of the Negroes makes all efforts to judge them as a race rather than by classes, localities, or even individuals, increasingly unjust and irritating to them.

The strenuous and increasing industrial competition between the two races often results in local displacement of colored labor. The Negro cotton grower, unable to live on the decreasing return from his land, gives place to another tenant, white or black, and the former family drifts away. The current of Negroes to the cities is somewhat greater than that of whites and seems to consist of two classes, those who have earned a promotion to city life by their success in the country or small town and those who have failed in country life and flow cityward to live on their neighbors or by their wits. Neighbors and pickings are more numerous in an urban community. This Negro driftwood is likely to feel sore towards the whites. The latter are held responsible for the organization of society, and their fault it is if the Negro can find in it no place for himself. They cared for him in slavery, and either their old masters or their new emancipators are bound to furnish him a chance for a livelihood. He is a voiceless socialist. Hence this driftwood belongs to the potentially criminal class.

A third group of causes leading to a large amount and rapid increase of Negro crime may be embraced under the loose term race friction. All witnesses agree that since emancipation the two races have separated more and more in life and thought. Ex-Governor Northern, in his recent address at Boston, seems to attribute this to the national policy towards the South during the reconstruction period.[26] We may agree with him in part and still believe, as I do, that the industrial competition just sketched was probably inevitable and is another important factor in drawing the races apart. But, whatever be the explanation, the fact is undeniable. Under the slavery system, the main motives in governing the Negroes were personal loyalty and force, and the emphasis upon one or the other varied with the character of the work and of the owner or overseer. As the races have drawn apart; this feeling of personal loyalty has become feeble, and many of the whites have felt that the only alternative mode of governing the increasing number of criminals was force and that the more speedily and surely force could be applied the greater its deterrent influence.

But, as the Negroes have separated from the whites, they have drawn or been crowded together and have come to feel a race unity and race pride and are developing a race public opinion which may prove of great importance in controlling the Negro criminal class. The existence of this Negro public opinion, as distinct from that of the whites, is hardly recognized with sufficient clearness by the dominant race, and to illustrate it the argument must be amplified. This can best be done by the aid of a typical instance, and I have selected for the purpose the series of recent events at Palmetto, Ga., culminating in the death of Sam Hose.[27] (Note: At this point a long digression on the circumstances leading to the lynching of Sam Hose appeared in the original.)

Now it seems clear that the guilt of Sam Hose was established by more convincing evidence than is secured in nine cases out of ten, perhaps in ninety-nine out of one hundred in which a lynching occurs. If this evidence has failed to convince a large proportion of Southern Negroes, including probably nearly all those of criminal tendencies, then in other cases, where the evidence is less conclusive, they must be less convinced. What the facts are is of less importance than what they are believed to be, for belief, not fact, is the motive by which men are swayed.

To make my conclusions upon this subject clearer, I may briefly state certain views with which I cannot agree:

I. I cannot accept a large proportion of the accounts printed in Northern papers, describing the relations of the two races in the South. One of the virtues of civilization imperfectly developed in the Negro race is veracity, and accounts coming from them must be tested carefully before acceptance. Where nothing is known regarding the trustworthiness of the witnesses or the inherent probablility of the statements, the presumption is in favor of the white man's testimony. Hence those newspapers which apparently make the contrary presumption are often misled. One instance which came under my own observation may serve for a hundred. Recently a lynching occurred in Alexandria, Va., within five miles of the national capital. A Washington correspondent of the Boston *Transcript* described the facts and said that the Negro boy was guilty of nothing more than insulting a child. The Springfield *Republican* reprinted the letter, and in editorial comment said that the boy's only crime was his color. I went at once to the mayor of Alexandria and learned from him that at a hearing over which he presided the eight-year-old girl testified that the Negro had been guilty of indecent familiarities upon her by force. Probably any Southern jury, on hearing the child's testimony, would have found the Negro guilty of an attempt to commit rape. Yet repesentative Northern newspapers in reliance upon their sources of information have seriously misrepresented the facts.

2. On the other hand, I cannot admit that all or most of the alienation between the races is due to the grave mistakes of the reconstruction period or to the present policy of Northern papers. Race antagonism appears in other parts of the country and in other countries where this cause does not exist. To ascribe race friction at the South, as certain Southern writers and speakers do, solely or mainly to the past or present policy of the government towards the Southern States or to the tone of Northern papers, and then to say almost in the same breath that race friction and lynching are found in the North, is clearly inconsistent. The friction between the races was probably an inevitable result of emancipation, although hastened and intensified by the blunders of reconstruction.

3.It seems improbable that the policy of enlisting Negroes as federal soldiers has had a decided effect in increasing Negro crime. Certainly, the evidence offered in favor of this claim is by no means sufficient to establish the conclusion.

4. A restricted suffrage in the Southern States will probably not avail materially to improve the conditions. Negro crime is apparently about as frequent and heinous in the District of Columbia, where for a generation the race has had no political privileges, as it is in the States of the far South.

5. Education, in the ordinary sense of that term, will not materially improve the situation. An education which will aid the Negro in securing self-support is of primary importance.

6. No federal legislation, such as that demanded by certain Negroes against lynching or that demanded by certain of both races making large appropriations for deporation of the Negroes, seems likely to be enacted or offers a real and adequate solution of the problem.

Positively, I may sum up my conclusions as follows:—

A large and increasing amount of Negro crime is manifested all over the country. This raises a problem pressing with especial weight upon the States where Negroes are numerous. The causes may be grouped as defective family life, defective industrial equipment and ability in comparison with their competitors, increasing race solidarity among the Negroes, and increasing alienation from the whites.

Southern whites often exaggerate the agency of Northern whites or Northern Negroes in causing the present condition, and thus minimize their own responsibility.

Northern whites often ignore the burden which Southern whites and the better class of Negroes are carrying and the degree to which the federal policy since the war has contributed to increase race friction and Negro crime. Hence they are often ignorant and unjust in their criticisms.

These misunderstandings are the strongest basis for the continuance and possible increase of sectional antagonism between North and South.

Lynching is harmful mainly because it prevents the rise of a public opinion based on a careful sifting of the facts. Where practised under any provocation, however great, by members of one race upon those of another, it fosters the development of separate public opinions one for each race, and hence tends to make cooperation of the two in one government impossible.

There has probably never been a more complete democracy than in the New England towns. Modern governments tend towards a more democratic form, and at the North the belief is very deep seated that the progress of humanity is dependent upon the maintenance and progress of democratic government. Now democratic government is essentially a government by organized legal public opinion. Any attempt to introduce government by disorganized public opinion secures at best the will of only a fraction of the public. Hence, a believer in democracy is bound to be an opponent of lynch law, and the strength of the opposition in the North to lynch law is due, not as is sometimes said to hatred of the South, but rather to a love for democracy.

The greatest problem which modern democracy has to face is perhaps this: Can the democratic forms develop among a homogeneous people with unifying traditions, like the people of England, old and new, be extended to people widely different in race, religion and ethical and social code? Can English forms of government ultimately apply to India and Egypt and South Africa? Can American forms be extended to the two races at the South or in the Philippines? Either the public opinion of one race must dominate, as that of the whites has done in India and the South, or the two races must cooperate so far as to develop a common public opinion. The latter is the only true democracy.

NOTES

1. Eleventh Census, "Crime, Pauperism, and Benevolence," i: 125 and ii: 3.
2. Hampton Negro Conference, No. 2, p. 11.
3. Compare preceding citation from the Eleventh Census with the Tenth Census, xxi: p. 479.
4. The serious difficulties in the way of comparing the criminal tendencies of different classes by inferences drawn from the statistics of prisoners are ably stated by R.P. Falkner, "Crime and the Census" (in *Annals American Academy*, January 1897). I do not believe that his objections vitiate my inferences in the guarded way in which they have been stated. While the statistics of prisoners in one way which he pointed out exaggerate the criminal tendencies of Negroes, yet a comparison between the prisoners and persons of all ages tends to understate the true criminality of a race, a disproportionate number of which are children, and so under the criminal age. These two obstacles to accuracy in quantitative statements of the amount of increase in crime thus tend to neutralize each other.
5. W.E.B. Du Bois, "The Conservation of Races," p. 14 (in American Negro Academy, Occasional Papers, No. 2).
6. Eleventh Census, "Crime, Pauperism, and Benevolence," i: 163.
7. Idem, i: 167.
8. Eleventh Census, Abstract 122-125.
9. Department of Agriculture, Report, 1876, p. 136.
10. Department of Agriculture, Year Book, 1898, p. 683.
11. Eleventh Census, Abstract, p. 40; and Population, i: 412, ff.
12. Department of Agriculture, Year Book, 1898, p. 42, f.
13. Eleventh Census, Abstract, 126-128.
14. State Agricultural Society, Proceedings, Twelfth Session, p. 117 (in Louisiana Commissioner of Agriculture, Biennial Report, 1898).

15. Eleventh Census, Abstract, pp. 131-133.
16. Southwest Louisiana on the Line of the Southern Pacific Company, pp. 45, f.
17. State Agricultural Society, Proceedings, Twelfth Session, p. 39 (in Louisiana Commissioner of Agriculture, Biennial Report, 1898).
18. Department of Agriculture, Office of Experiment Stations, Bulletin 38, "Dietary Studies with Reference to the Food of the Negro in Alabama," p. 18.
19. Idem, p. 68.
20. Reported in *A.M.E. Zion Church Quarterly* for April 1894.
21. *Southern Workman and Hampton School Record,* September 1897, p. 179.
22. Idem, p. 168.
23. Idem, p. 167.
24. As these pages are going to press, the preliminary report of the Third Hampton Conference brings confirmatory evidence on this point. The Committee on Business and Labor reported on the condition of Negro skilled labor in certain large cities. Of Richmond, Va., they say: "Perhaps two thousand are employed in the iron works. This branch of business was at one time controlled almost entirely by colored men, but now they are employed chiefly as common laborers, with only here and there a master mechanic." The general trend of the report is summed up as follows: "The trade unions along the border line of slavery have generally pursued a policy of exclusiveness on account of color and refused to include the colored craftsmen in their scheme of organization. . . . In the North colored men, when competent, are generally received into local unions and treated fairly. In the South they work side by side, when not organized. When organization takes place, the colored workman as a rule is excluded." *Southern Workman,* September 1899, pp. 333, f. Meagre evidence from other sources does not confirm the above statement so far as it applies to the attitude of Northern trade unions.
25. The Negroes of Farmville, Va., p. 37 (in Department of Labor Bulletin, January 1898).
26. W.J. Northern, the Negro at the South, p. 7.
27. My information has been gleaned from a file of the Atlanta *Daily Constitution,* the only Atlanta daily paper of which the current issues are accessible in the Library of Congress, and from correspondents both white and colored, in the North and in the South.

NEGRO CRIME

The Ninth Atlanta Conference

Mr. Wines, the American criminologist, has said: "A modified form of slavery survives wherever prison labor is sold to private persons for their pecuniary profit."[1] The history of crime in the Southern states of America illustrates this. Two systems of controlling human labor which still flourish in the South are the direct children of slavery. These are the crop-lien system and the convict-lease system. The crop-lean system is an arrangement of chattel mortagages, so fixed that the housing, labor, kind of agriculture, and, to some extent, the personal liberty of the free black laborer is put into the hands of the landowner and merchant. It is absentee landlordism and the company-store systems united. The convict-lease system is the slavery in private hands of persons convicted of crimes and misdemeanors in the courts. The object of this section is to sketch the rise and development of the convict-lease system, and the efforts to modify and abolish it.

Before the Civil War, the system of punishment for criminals in the South was practically the same as in the North. Except in a few cities, however, crime was less prevalent than in the North, and the system of slavery naturally modified the situation. The slaves could become criminals in the eyes of the law only in exceptional cases. The punishment and trial of nearly all ordinary misdemeanors and crimes lay in the hands of the masters. Consequently, so far as the state was concerned, there was no crime of any consequence among Negroes. The system of criminal jurisprudence had to do, therefore, with whites almost exclusively, and as is

---

This article was originally published in 1906 by Atlanta University Press, Atlanta, Georgia.
Permission to reprint granted by *Phylon—The Atlanta Review of Race and Culture, 1988.*

usual in a land of scattered population and aristocratic tendencies, the law was lenient in theory and lax in execution.

On the other hand, the private well-ordering and control of slaves called for careful cooperation among masters. The fear of insurrection was ever before the South, and the ominous uprisings of Cato, Gabriel, Vesey, Turner, and Toussaint made this fear an ever-present nightmare. The result was a system of rural police, mounted and on duty chiefly at night, whose work it was to stop the nocturnal wandering and meeting of slaves. It was usually an effective organization, which terrorized the slaves and to which all white men belonged, and were liable to active detailed duty at regular intervals.

Upon this system war and emancipation struck like a thunderbolt. Law and order among the whites, already loosely enforced, became still weaker through the inevitable influence of conflict and social revolution. The freedman was in an especially anomalous situation. The power of the slave police supplemented and depended upon that of the private masters. When the masters' power was broken, the patrol was easily transmuted into a lawless and illegal mob known to history as the Ku Klux Klan. Then came the first and probably the most disastrous of that succession of political expedients by which the South sought to deal with the consequences of emancipation. It will always be a nice question of ethics as to how far a conquered people can be expected to submit to the dictates of a victorious foe. Certainly the world must to a degree sympathize with resistance under such circumstances. The mistake of the South, however, was to adopt a kind of resistance which in the long run weakened her moral fiber, destroyed respect for law and order, and enabled gradually her worst elements to secure an unfortunate ascendency. The South believed in slave labor and was thoroughly convinced that free Negroes would not work steadily or effectively. Elaborate and ingenious apprentice and vagrancy laws were therefore passed, designed to make the freedmen and their children work for their former masters at practically no wages. Justification for these laws was found in the inevitable tendency of many of the ex-slaves to loaf when the fear of the lash was taken away. The new laws, however, went far beyond such justification, totally ignoring that large class of freedmen eager to work and earn property of their own, stopping all competition between employers and confiscating the labor and liberty of children. In fact, the new laws of this period recognized the Emancipation Proclamation and the Thirteenth Amendment simply as abolishing the slave trade.

The interference of Congress in the plans for reconstruction stopped the full carrying out of these schemes, and the Freedmen's Bureau consolidated and sought to develop the various plans for employing and guiding the freedmen already adopted in different places under the protection of the Union Army. This government guardianship established a free wage system of labor by the help of the army, the striving of the best of the blacks, and the cooperation of some of the whites. In the matter of adjusting legal relationships, however, the Bureau failed. It had, to be sure, Bureau courts with one representative of the ex-master, one of the freedmen, and one of the Bureau itself, but they never gained the confidence of the community. As the regular state courts gradually regained power, it was necessary for them to fix by their decisions the new status of the freedmen. It was perhaps as natural as it was unfortunate that amid this chaos the courts sought to do by judicial decisions what the legislatures had formerly sought to do by specific law—namely, reduce the freedom to serfdom. As a result, the small peccadilloes of a careless, untrained class were made the excuse for severe sentences. The courts and jails became filled with the careless and ignorant, with those who sought to emphasize their new found freedom, and too often with innocent victims of oppression. The testimony of a Negro counted for little or nothing in court, while the accusation of white witnesses was usually decisive. The result of this was a sudden large increase in the apparent criminal population of the Southern states—an increase so large that there was no way for the state to house it or watch it, even had the state wished to. And the state did not wish to. Throughout the South, laws were immediately passed authorizing public officials to lease the labor of convicts to the highest bidder. The lessee then took charge of the convicts—worked them as he wished under the nominal control of the state. Thus a new slavery and slave-trade was established.

The abuses of this system have often been dwelt upon. It had the worst aspects of slavery without any of its redeeming features. The innocent, the guilty, and the depraved were herded together, children and adults, men and women, given into complete control of practically irresponsible men, whose sole object was to make the most money possible. The innocent were made bad, the bad worse; women were outraged and children tainted; whipping and torture were in vogue, and the death rate from cruelty, exposure, and overwork rose to large percentages. The actual bosses over such leased prisoners were usually selected from the lowest classes of whites, and the camps were often far from settlements or public roads. The prisoners often had scarcely any clothing; they were fed on a scanty diet of corn bread and fat meat and worked twelve or more hours a day.

After work, each must do his own cooking. There was insufficient shelter; in one Georgia camp as late as 1895, sixty-one men slept in one room, seventeen by nineteen feet, and seven feet high. Sanitary conditions were wretched; there was little or no medical attendance, and almost no care of the sick. Women were mingled indiscriminately with the men, both in working and in sleeping, and dressed often in men's clothes. A young girl at camp Hardmont, Georgia in 1895 was repeatedly outraged by several of her guards and finally died in childbirth while in camp.

Such facts illustrate the system at its worst—as it used to exist in nearly every Southern state and as it still exists in parts of Georgia, Mississippi, Louisiana, and other states. It is difficult to say whether the effect of such a system is worse on the whites or on the Negroes. So far as the whites are concerned, the convict-lease system lowered the respect for courts, increased lawlessness, and put the states into the clutches of penitentiary rings. The courts were brought into politics; judgeships became elective for shorter and shorter terms, and there grew up a public sentiment which would not consent to considering the desert of a criminal apart from his color. If the criminal were white, public opinion refused to permit him to enter the chaingang save in the most extreme cases. The result is that even to-day it is difficult to enforce the criminal laws in the South against whites. On the other hand, so customary had it become to convict any Negro upon a mere accusation, that public opinion was loathe to allow a fair trial to black suspects and was too often tempted to take the law into its own hands. Finally, the state became a dealer in crime, profited by it so as to derive a net annual income from her prisoners. The lessees of the convicts made large profits also. Under such circumstances, it was almost impossible to remove the clutches of this vicious system from the state. Even as late as 1890, the Southern states were the only section of the Union where the income from prisons and reformatories exceeded the expense.[2] Moreover, these figures do not include the county gangs where the lease system is today most prevalent and the net income largest.

The effect of the convict-lease system on the Negroes was deplorable. First, it linked crime and slavery indissolubly in their minds as simply forms of the white man's oppression. Punishment, consequently, lost the most effective of its deterrent effects, and the criminal gained pity instead of disdain. The Negroes lost faith in the integrity of courts and the fairness of juries. Worse than all, the chaingangs became schools of crime which hastened the appearance of the confirmed Negro criminal upon the scene. That some crime and vagrancy should follow emancipation was inevitable. A nation cannot systematically degrade labor without in some degree debauching the laborer. But there can be no doubt but that the indiscriminate method by which Southern courts dealt with the freedmen after the war increased crime and vagabondage to an enormous extent. There are no reliable statistics to which one can safely appeal to measure exactly the growth of crime among the emancipated slaves. About seventy percent of all prisoners in the South are black; this, however, is in part explained by the fact that accused Negroes are still easily convicted and get long sentences, while whites still continue to escape the penalty of many crimes, even among themselves. And yet, allowing for all this, there can be no reasonable doubt that there has arisen in the South since the war a class of black criminals, loafers, and ne'er-do-wells who are a menace to their fellows, both black and white.

The appearance of the real Negro criminal stirred the South deeply. The whites, despite their long use of the criminal court for putting Negroes to work, were used to little more than petty thieving and loafing on their part, and not to crimes of boldness, violence, or cunning. When, after periods of stress or financial depression, as in 1892, such crimes increased in frequency, the wrath of a people unschooled in the modern methods of dealing with crime broke all bounds and reached strange depths of barbaric vengeance and torture. Such acts, instead of drawing the best opinion of these states of the nation toward a consideration of Negro crime and criminals, discouraged and alienated the best classes of Negroes, horrified the civilized world, and made the best white Southerners ashamed.

Nevertheless, in the midst of all this, a leaven of better things had been working, and the bad effects of the epidemic of lynching quickened it. The great difficulty to be overcome in the South was the false theory of work and of punishment of wrong doers, inherited from slavery. The inevitable result of a slave system is for a master class to consider that the slave exists for his benefit alone—that the slave has no rights which the master is bound to respect. Inevitably this idea persisted after emancipation. The black workman existed for the comfort and profit of white people, and the interests of white people were the only ones to be seriously considered. Consequently, for a lessee to work convicts for his profit was a most natural thing. Then too, these convicts were to be punished, and the slave theory of punishment was pain and intimidation. Given these ideas, the convict-lease system was inevitable. But other ideas were also prevalent in the South; there were in slave times plantations where the well-being of the slaves was considered and where punishment meant the correction of the fault rather than brute discomfort. After the chaos of war and reconstruction passed, there came from the better conscience of the South a growing demand for reform in the treatment of crime. The worst horrors of the convict-lease system were attacked persistently in nearly every Southern state. Back in the eighties, George W. Cable, a Southern man, published a strong attack on the system. The following decade, Governor Atkinson of Georgia instituted a searching investigation, which startled the state by its revelation of existing conditions. Still more recently Florida, Arkansas, and other states have had reports and agitation for reform. The result had been marked improvement in conditions during the last decade. This is shown in part by the statistics of 1895; in that year the prisons and reformatories of the far South cost the states $204,483 more than they earned, while before this they had nearly always yielded an income. This is still the smallest expenditure of any section and looks strangely small beside New England's $1,190,564. At the same time, a movement in the right direction is clear. The laws are being framed more and more so as to prevent the placing of convicts altogether in private control. They are not, to be sure, always enforced, Georgia having still several hundreds of convicts so controlled. In nearly all the Gulf states, convict-lease system still has a strong hold, still debauches public sentiment and breeds criminals.

The next step after the lease system was to put the prisoners under regular state inspection, but to lease their labor to contractors, or to employ it in some remunerative labor for the state. It is this stage that the South is slowly reaching today, so far as the criminals are concerned who are dealt with directly by the states. Those whom the state still unfortunately leaves in the hands of county officials are usually leased to irresponsible parties. Without doubt, work, and work worth the doing (i.e., profitable work) is best for the prisoners. Yet there lurks in this system a dangerous temptation. The correct theory is that the work is for the benefit of the criminal—for his correction, if possible. At the same time, his work should not be allowed to come into unfair competition with that of honest laborers, and it should never be an object of traffic for pure financial gain. Whenever the profit derived from the work becomes the object of employing prisoners, then evil must result. In the South today, it is natural that in the slow turning from the totally indefensible private lease system, some of its wrong ideas should persist. Prominent among these persisting ideas is this: that the most successful dealing with criminals is that which costs the state least in actual outlay. This idea still dominates most of the Southern states. Georgia spent $2.38 per capita on her 2,938 prisoners in 1890, while Massachusetts spent $62.96 per capita on her 5,227 prisoners. Moreover, by selling the labor of her prisoners to the highest bidders, Georgia not only got all her money back but made a total clear profit of $6.12 on each prisoner. Massachusetts spent about $100,000 more than was returned to her by prisoners' labor. Now it is extremely difficult under such circumstances to prove to a state that Georgia is making a worse business investment than Massachusetts. It will take another generation to prove to the South that an apparently profitable traffic in crime is very dangerous business for a state, that prevention of crime and the reformation of criminals is the one legitimate object of all dealing with depraved natures, and that apparent profit arising from other methods is in the end worse than dead loss. Bad public schools and profit from crime explain much of the Southern social problem.

Moreover, in the desire to make the labor of criminals pay, little heed is taken of the competition of convict and free laborers, unless the free laborers are white and have a vote. Black laborers are continually displaced in such industries as brickmaking, mining, road building, grading, quarrying, and the like, by convicts hired at $3 or thereabouts a month.

The second mischievous idea that survives from slavery and the convict-lease system is the lack of all intelligent discrimination in dealing with prisoners. The most conspicuous and fatal example of this is the indiscriminate herding of juvenile and adult criminals. It need hardly be said that such methods manufacture criminals more quickly than all other methods can reform them. In 1890, of all the Southern states, only Texas, Tennessee, Kentucky, Maryland, and West Virginia made any state appropriations for juvenile reformatories. In 1895 Delaware was added to these, but Kentucky was missing.

And this in face of the fact that the South had in 1890 over four thousand prisoners under twenty years of age. In some of the Southern states—notably Virginia—there are private associations for juvenile reform, acting in cooperation with the state. These have in some cases recently received state aid. In other states, like Georgia, there is permissive legislation for the establishment of local reformatories. Little has resulted as yet from this legislation, but it is promising.

This section has sought to trace roughly the attitude of the South toward crime. There is in that attitude much to condemn, but also something to praise. The tendencies are today certainly in the right direction, but there is a long battle to be fought with prejudice and inertia before the South will realize that a black criminal is a human being, to be punished firmly but humanely, with the sole object of making him a safe member of society, and that a white criminal at large is a menace and a danger. The greatest difficulty today in the way of reform is this race question. The movement for juvenile reformatories in Georgia would have succeeded some years ago, in all probability, had not the argument been used: it is chiefly for the benefit of Negroes. Until the public opinion of the ruling masses of the South can see that the prevention of crime among Negroes is just as necessary, just as profitable for the whites themselves, as prevention among whites, all true betterment in courts and prisons will be hindered. Above all, we must remember that crime is not normal, that the appearance of crime among Southern Negroes is a symptom of wrong social conditions—of a stress of life greater than a large part of the community can bear. The Negro is not naturally criminal; he is usually patient and law abiding. If slavery, the convict-lease system, the traffic in criminal labor, the lack of juvenile reformatories, together with the unfortunate discrimination and prejudice in other walks of life, have led to that sort of social protest and revolt which we call crime, then we must look for remedy in the sane reform of these wrong social conditions, and not in intimidation, savagery, or the legalized slavery of men.

Causes of Negro Crime

This study is too incomplete to lead us to many definite conclusions. Yet certain causes of crime among Negroes today seem clear. They may be briefly classified as follows:

A. Faults of the Negroes.

1. Abuse of their new freedom and tendency toward idleness and vagrancy.
2. Loose ideas of property, petty pilfering.
3. Unreliability, lying, and deception.
4. Exaggerated ideas of personal rights, irritability, and suspicion.
5. Sexual looseness, weak family life and poor training of children; lack of respect for parents.
6. Lack of proper self-respect; low or extravagant ideals.
7. Poverty, low wages and lack of accumulated property.
8. Lack of thrift and prevalence of the gambling spirit.
9. Waywardness of the "second generation."
10. The use of liquor and drugs.

All these faults are real and important causes of Negro crime. They are not racial traits but due to perfectly evident historic causes. Slavery could not survive as an institution and teach thrift, and its great evil in the

United States was its low sexual morals; emancipation meant for the Negroes poverty and a great stress of life due to sudden change. These and other considerations explain Negro crime. They do not excuse it however, and a great burden of pressing reform from within lies upon the Negro's shoulders. Especially is this true with regard to the atrocious crime of rape. This is not to be sure a crime peculiar to the Negro race. An Englishman tells us that in Jamaica justice has been dealt out impartially, and this has not resulted in impudence on the part of the blacks towards the whites. Indeed, when reasonably treated, they are remarkably courteous—more so than the average Teuton. Attacks by black men on white women are absolutely unknown; a young white woman is safe anywhere, the only terror being from white sailors. There are offenses against black women and children, but not whites. He infers from this that the danger of such attacks on white women, if it exists in the United States, is not really due to race. For his own part, he is sure that the evil, where it exists, is augmented by the state of frenzy with which it is met.[3]

But granting this and making allowance for all exaggeration in attributing this crime to Negroes, there still remain enough well authenticated cases of brutal assault on women by black men in America to make every Negro bow his head in shame. Negroes must recognize their responsibility for their own worst classes and never let resentment against slander allow them even to seem to palliate an awful deed. This crime must at all hazards stop. Lynching is awful, and injustice and caste are hard to bear, but if they are to be successfully attacked, they must cease to have even this terrible justification.

B. Faults of the whites.

1. The attempt to enforce a double standard of justice in the courts, one for Negroes and one for whites.
2. The election of judges for short terms, making them subservient to waves of public opinion in a white electorate.
3. The shirking of jury duty by the best class of whites, leaving the dealing out of justice to the most ignorant and prejudiced.
4. Laws so drawn as to entangle the ignorant, as in the case of laws for labor contracts, and to leave wide discretion as to punishment in the hand of juries and petty officials.
5. Peonage and debt-slavery as methods of securing cheap and steady labor.
6. The tendency to encourage ignorance and subserviency among Negroes instead of intelligence, ambition, and independence.

7. The taking of all rights of political self-defense from the Negro either by direct law or custom or by the white primary system.
8. The punishment of crime as a means of public and private revenue rather than as a means of preventing the making of criminals.
9. The rendering of the chastity of Negro women difficult of defense in law or custom against the aggressions of white men.
10. Enforcing a caste system in such a way as to humiliate Negroes and kill their self-respect.

A Southern man, Professor Andrew Sledd, has perhaps best elucidated the meaning of this latter point: "If we care to investigate, evidences of our brutal estimate of the black man are not far to seek. The hardest to define is perhaps the most impressive—the general tacit attitude and feeling of the average Southern community toward the Negro. He is either nothing more than the beast that perishes, unnoticed and uncared for so long as he goes quietly about his menial toil (as a young man recently said to the writer. 'The farmer regards his nigger in the same light as his mule,' but this puts the matter far too favorably for the Negro); or, if he happen to offend, he is punished as a beast with a curse or a kick and with tortures that even the beast is spared; or if he is thought of at all in a general way, it is with the most absolute loathing and contempt. He is either unnoticed or despised. As for his feelings, he hasn't any. How few—alas how few—words of gentleness and courtesy ever come to the black man's ear! But harsh and imperious words, coarseness, and cursing, how they come upon him, whether with excuse of in the frenzy of unjust and unreasoning passion! And his rights of person, property, and sanctity of home—who ever heard of the rights of a 'nigger'? This is the general sentiment in the air, intangible, but strongly felt; and it is in a large measure this sentiment that creates and perpetuates the Negro problem.

"If the Negro could be made to feel that his fundamental rights and privileges are recognized and respected equally with those of the white man, that he is not discriminated against both publicly and privately simply and solely because of his color, that he is regarded and dealt with as a responsible, if humble, member of society, the most perplexing features of his problem would be at once simplified and would shortly in normal course disappear."[4]

A scientific study of Southern criminal conditions says:

> There is frequently collusion between lawyers and justices. A Negro asks a lawyer how much it will cost her to whip Laura Brown. The

lawyer sees a justice and arranges that the fine be $10. She is cautioned to do no "cutting," only whipping. If her wrath is equal to $10, Laura Brown gets a whipping. The Negro is fined according to contract, but also gets classed among criminals. The justice of peace office is one which few respectable men in the South will accept. The salary is small, and the general rule is no conviction, no fee—for either jury or justice. This is a direct bribe for conviction. There is often small chance for appeal, for a $100 bond is required, and few Negroes are able to secure it. Justices and constables are often in collusion. The constable gives a Negro, called a striker, money to go out and play craps. He informs the constable when and where he will gather men to play. Then the constable swoops down and arrests them. The striker gets a dividend, and the constable and justice also profit by the transaction.[5] . . . (1) Penalties in the South are extreme, and Negroes are serving life sentences for crimes which receive penalties of from one to five years in the North. (2) There are no agencies for preventing crime in the South. There are no parental or vacation schools, no juvenile courts, no societies to aid discharged convicts, no employment bureaus, no cooperative societies, and no municipal lodging houses. There are three reformatories, no manual training schools, few kindergartens, no compulsory education laws, and few Y.M.C.A.s. All of these are recognized as great forces in the prevention of crime. There are no movements or institutions for saving the Negro women, and they largely increase the statistics for female criminals in the United States.[6]

Negro women are thus peculiarly unprotected:

They constitute the domestic class, although they work in all the trades open to them. Necessity compels them to work, and the Negro men do not discourage it. The attitude of white women is not a protection, for many of them are indifferent to their husbands' or brothers' relations with Negroes. This is changing as they get farther away from the precedents of slavery. White men have little respect for the sanctity of family life of Negroes when they would hesitate to enter the Anglo-Saxon's home. Negro women are expected to be immoral and have few inducements to be otherwise. Religion is more often a cause than prevention, for the services are frequently scenes of crime. Physical senses so largely predominate over the intellectual and spiritual perceptions, and but few attempts have been made to develop the latter. The laws against immorality are laxly enforced. Whites within their own circles would

> not countenance acts to which they are indifferent in Negroes. There are small opportunities for Negro women to support themselves through occupations other than menial, which are filled with grave temptation.[7]

And again, once in jail and no attempts at reform are made throughout the Southern States:

> With one exception, there are no educational influences. No trades, are taught, no schools are conducted, and no reading supplied, except at mining camps in Alabama. In factories, sawmills, etc., convicts are given enough instruction to make them productive workers, and that is equivalent to a trade. But the idea is not equipment of individuals so they can support themselves when released.[8]

The surroundings of prisoners suggest slavery and degradation:

> About daylight, convicts start off to the fields, dividing into two gangs when they are busy. The assistant manager takes one gang, and a deputy takes charge of the other. One gang goes to plowing, and the other to hoeing. When they get out into the field, a cordon is formed by the guards, who are armed with winchesters. The manager stands in the midst of the gang or rides horseback, as the case may be, and directs the operations. He, of course, is armed with a revolver and carries the strap for the punishment of the refractory men. This strap is a queer looking affair. It is a piece of leather about 6 inches wide and 2 feet long, attached to a wooden handle. It is customary to give a refractory 'nigger' from one to twenty-five lashes with this strap on his bare back, according to the extent of his offense. The occasions for punishment are comparatively rare, however. It is more often the new men who get a taste of the lash. The lash was adopted by the board some time ago, and it is regarded as the most humane yet put in use. It is impossible to cut the flesh with it, and a liberal use of it does not incapacitate a man for work. The board is also particular about too liberal use of the lash, and sergeants are compelled, among other things, to report at the end of every month the names of convicts lashed, the reason, and the number of lashes.[9]

And finally, instead of efforts to improve workmen and to make them more efficient, one is struck by such demands as this:

> Under the present status, the employing farmer has little or no redress against a breach of agreement on the part of the hands he has engaged to assist in the working and harvesting of his crop. He is at the mercy of the mercenary immigration agent or the machinations of unscrupulous planters in an adjoining county or state. . . . .
>
> The Constitution is of the opinion, however, that outside of the aid of immigration, this bewildering problem can be largely solved in Georgia and other Southern states by the enactment of statutes making a contract between farmer and laborer even more legally binding than under existing laws. . . . .
>
> Making a discretionary term of imprisonment the penalty for such breaches and the consistent enforcement of such a provision for two or three seasons would soon teach this floating, shiftless element to regard their obligations with greater respect and remove one of the very present menaces to the business-like management of our agricultural interests.[10]

There is much difference of opinion on many of the points enumerated above, but it certainly seems clear that absolutely impartial courts; the presence of intelligent Negroes on juries when Negroes are tried; the careful defense of ignorance in law and custom; the absolute doing away with every vestige of involuntary servitude except in prisons under absolute state control, and for the reformation of the prisoner; the encouraging of intelligent, ambitious, and independent black men; the granting of the right to cast an untramelled vote to intelligent and decent Negroes; the unwavering defense of all women who want to be decent against indecent approach; and an effort to increase rather than to kill the self respect of Negroes—it seems certain that such a policy would make quickly and decidedly for the decrease of Negro criminality in the South and in the land.

The arguments against this are often strongly urged; it is said that whites and Negroes differ so in standards of culture that courts must discriminate, that partially forced labor is necessary in the South, that intelligent Negroes become impudent fault finders and disturb a delicate situation, that the South cannot in self-defense permit Negro sufferage; that Negro women are unchaste; and that the Negro must be kept down at all hazards. To all this it can only be said: These arguments have been used against every submerged class since the world began, and history has repeatedly proven them false.

Resolutions

The following resolutions were adopted before the conference adjourned:

The Ninth Atlanta Conference, after a study of crime among Negroes in Georgia, has come to these conclusions:

Amount of Crime. The amount of crime among Negroes in this state is very great. This is a dangerous and threatening phenomenon. It means that large numbers of the freedmen's sons have not yet learned to be law-abiding citizens and steady workers, and until they do so the progress of the race, of the South, and of the nation will be retarded.

Causes of Crime. The causes of this state of affairs seem clear.

First: The mass of the Negroes are in a transient stage between slavery and freedom. Such a period of change involves physical strain, mental bewilderment and moral weakness. Such periods of stress have among all people given rise to crime and a criminal class. Second: Race prejudice, in so far as it narrows the opportunities open to Negroes and teaches them to lose self-respect and ambition by arbitrary caste proscriptions, is a potent cause of carelessness, disorder and crime. Third: Negroes have less legal protection than others against unfair aggression upon their rights, liberty, and prosperity. This is particularly true of Negro women, whose honor and chastity have in this state very little protection against the force and influence of white men, particularly in the country districts and small towns. Fourthly. Laws as to vagrancy, disorder, contracts for work, chattel, mortgages, and crop liens are so drawn as to involve in the coils of the law the ignorant, unfortunate, and careless Negroes and to lead to their degradation and undue punishment, when their real need is inspiration, knowledge, and opportunity. Fifthly. Courts usually administer two distinct sorts of justice: one for whites and one for Negroes, and this custom, together with the fact that judge and court officials are invariably white and elected to office by the influence of white votes alone makes it very difficult for a Negro to secure justice in court when his opponent is white. Sixthly. The methods of punishment of Negro criminals is calculated to breed crime rather than stop it. Lynching spreads among black folk the firmly fixed idea that few accused Negroes are really guilty; the leasing of convicts, even the present system of state control, makes the state traffic in crime for the sake of revenue instead of seeking to reform criminals for the sake of moral regeneration; and finally the punishment of Negro criminals is usually unintelligent. They are punished according to the crime rather than according to their criminal record; little discrimination is made between old and young; male and female; hardened thug and careless mischief maker; and the result is that a single sentence to the chaingang for a trivial misdemeanor usually makes the victim a confirmed criminal for life.

Extent and Cure of Crime. There is no evidence to show that crime is increasing among Negroes in this state. Save in a few of the larger towns, there seems to be a marked decrease since 1896.

The cure for Negro crime lies in moral uplift and inspiration among Negroes. The masses of the race must be made vividly to realize that no man ever has an excuse for laziness, carelessness, and wrong doing. That these are not a cure for oppression but rather invite and encourage further oppression. Negroes then must be taught to stop fighting, gambling, and stealing, which seem to be the usual misdemeanors of the careless, and particularly the law abiding must separate themselves from the dangerous criminal element among us who are responsible for murder, rape, and burglary, and vigorously condemn the crime and the criminal. Four agencies among Negroes may work toward this end: the church, the school, institutions for rescue work, and the juvenile reformatory. The first step in Georgia would seem to be one toward a reformatory for Negro youth.

Appeal to Whites. Finally, this conference appeals to the white people of Georgia for six things: fairer criminal laws; justice in the courts; the abolition of state traffic in crime for public revenue and private gain; more intelligent methods of punishment; the refusal to allow free labor to be displaced by convict labor; and finally a wider recognition of the fact that honest, intelligent, law-abiding black men are safer neighbors than ignorant, underpaid serfs, because it is the latter class that breeds dangerous crime.

NOTES

1. First printed in slightly altered form in the *Missionary Review of the World*, October 1901.
2. Bulletin No. 8, Library of State of New York. All figures in this section are from this source.
3. Sidney Olivier, in the *British Friend*, December 1904.
4. *Atlanta Monthly*, vol. 90, p. 67.
5. Kellor: Experimental Sociology, p. 256.
6. Ibid, p. 34.
7. Ibid, p. 171.
8. Ibid, p. 200.
9. Quoted in Kellor: Experimental Sociology, p. 195.
10. Editorial in the *Atlanta Constitution*, March 30, 1905.

NEGRO CRIMINALITY IN THE SOUTH

Monroe N. Work

Prior to the Civil War, there was not in the South the problem of Negro crime, such as now exists. Although at that time each of the slave states had elaborate and severe laws for dealing with Negro criminals, they were, in proportion to the total number of Negroes, comparatively few. Immediately following emancipation, however, their numbers increased. This was inevitable; for many of the restraints that had been about the slaves were suddenly removed and much of the machinery for state and local government had broken down. As a result, there was confusion and disorder. Many of the slaves left the plantations. There was the beginning of the migration from section to section, from the rural districts to the cities, and from the South to the North. Under all these circumstances, it was not surprising that there should be an increase in Negro crime. The wonder is that there was not more confusion, disorder, and rapine. The great majority of the freedmen did not attempt to be lawless. They exercised the same restraint that they had exercised during the four years that their masters had been away on the field of battle. But to some of the newly enfranchised, freedom meant the license to do what they pleased. It was from this class that the majority of the criminals came.

As an example of the increase in the number of Negro criminals, we will take the state of Georgia. In 1858, there were confined in the Georgia penitentiary 183 prisoners, all of whom were apparently white. Twelve years later, in 1870, there were 393 prisoners in this penitentiary, of whom 59 were white and 334 colored.

According to the United States census, the total number of Negroes

This article was originally published in the *Annals of the American Academy of Political and Social Sciences* Vol. 49: (1913), pp. 74-80.

confined in Southern prisons in 1870 was 6,031; ten years later, the number, 12,973, had more than doubled; twenty years later, the number, 19,224, was three times as great; thirty-four years later, however, that is in 1904, the number of Negroes confined in Southern prisons was 18,550. This would appear to indicate that, so far as prison population is an index, Negro criminality in the South in recent years has not increased. It is probable that there is some decrease, for a study of criminal statistics of cities North and South indicates that between 1890 and 1904 Negro criminality, which up to this time had seemed to be steadily increasing, reached its highest point and began to decrease. It appears that the decrease began about 1894-1895.

The number of prisoners per 100,000 of Negro population also appears to bear out this conclusion. It also shows that there is a much higher rate of crime among Negroes in the North than in the South. This is to a large extent due to the fact that seven-tenths of the Negroes in the North, as against one-tenth in the South, live in cities and are of an age when persons have the greatest tendency to crime.

In the following table (see Table 1) the number of Negro prisoners in Northern and Southern states is compared.

TABLE 1
Comparison of Negro Prisoners in Northern and Southern States

	Negro Prisoners	
Year	Northern States	Southern States
1870	2,025	6,031
1880	3,774	12,973
1890	5,635	19,244
1904	7,527	18,550
	Prisoners Per 100,000 of Negro Population	
1870	372	136
1880	515	221
1890	773	284
1904	765	220

It is significant that the number of lynchings reached its highest point about the same period that Negro crime reached its highest point. From 1882 to 1892, the number of persons lynched annually in the United States increased from 114 to 255. From that time on the number decreased. In 1912, there were 64 lynchings in the United States. The total number of lynchings during the thirty years from 1882 to 1912 were 4,021. Of this number, 1,231 were whites and 2,790 were Negroes. The average per year for Negroes was 93, for whites, 41. From 80 to 90 percent of the lynchings are in the South. Less than one-fourth of the lynchings of Negroes is due to assaults upon women; in 1912 only one-fifth was for this cause. The largest percent of lynchings is for murder or attempted murder. Over 10 percent is for minor offenses.

It is of still greater interest to compare the commitments for rape. In 1904, the commitments for this crime per 100,000 of the total population were: all whites, 0.6; colored, 1.8; Italians, 5.3; Mexicans, 4.8; Austrians, 3.2; Hungarians, 2.0; French, 1.9; Russians, 1.9. Of those committed to prison for major offenses in 1904, the percent committed for rape was for colored, 1.9; all whites, 2.3; foreign white, 2.6; Irish, 1.3; Germans, 1.8; Poles, 2.1; Mexicans, 2.7; Canadians, 3; Russians, 3; French, 3.1; Austrians, 4.2; Italians, 4.4; Hungarians, 4.7. The commitments for assaults upon women are low in the southern states. In the south Atlantic division, the rate per 100,000 of the population in 1904 was 0.5; in the south central division it was 0.7. Some would suppose that the low rate of commitments for rape in the South is due to the fact that the most of the perpetrators of these crimes are summarily lynched, but if, however, all the Negroes who were lynched for rape in the South were included, the rate for colored would be changed less than one-fourth of 1 percent.

The report of the immigration commission in 1911 on *Immigration and Crime* gives the following concerning the percent that rape forms of all offenses by Negroes and whites: of convictions in the New York City court of general sessions for nine months of 1908-1909, Negro, 0.5; foreign white, 1.8; native white, 0.8. Chicago police arrests from 1905-1908—Negro, 0.34; foreign white, 0.35; native white, 0.30; of alien white prisoners, 1908, in the United States, 2.9.

Both North and South the crime rate for Negroes is much higher than it is for whites. In 1904 the commitments per 100,000 in the entire country were for whites, 187; for Negroes, 268. In the southern states, Negro crime compared with white is in the ratio of 3½ to 1. On the other hand, it is interesting to find that the Negro has a relatively lower crime rate than several of the emigrant races who are now coming to this country. The following table (see Table 2) shows the commitments to prison in 1904, per 1,000 of certain nationalities:

TABLE 2
Prison Commitments by Nationality, 1904

Nationality	Number in United States according to census 1900	Prison Commitments in 1904	Commitments per 1,000 of each nationality
Mexicans	103,410	484	4.7
Italians	484,207	2,143	4.4
Austrians	276,249	1,006	3.6
French	104,341	358	3.4
Canadians	1,181,255	3,557	3.0
Russians	424,096	1,222	2.8
Poles	383,510	1,038	2.7
Negroes	8,840,789	23,698	2.7

As a result of emancipation and the increase in Negro crime, great changes were brought about in the prison system of the South. Before the war, the states of the South operated their prisons on state account, and they were generally a burden on the states. After the close of the war, the states found themselves with an increasing prison population and no resources from which to make appropriations for the support of these prisons. Throughout the South, there was great demand for labor. Inside the prisons were thousands of able-bodied Negroes. Offers were made to the states by those needing labor to lease these prisoners, and so it was discovered that what had been an expense could be converted into a means of revenue and furnish a source from which the depleted state treasuries could be replenished. Thus it came about that all the Southern state prisons were, either by the military governments or by the reconstruction governments, put upon lease.

The introduction of the convict lease system into the prisons of the South, thereby enabling the convicts to become a source of revenue, caused each state to have a financial interest in increasing the number of convicts. It was inevitable, therefore, that many abuses should arise. In his report for 1870, less than a year after the Georgia lease had been effected, the principal keeper of the penitentiary complained about the treatment of the convicts by the lessees. An investigation in 1875 of the Texas system revealed a most horrible condition of affairs. From time to time in other states, there were attacks on the systems and legislative investigations. The better conscience of the South demanded reform in the treatment of criminals, for it was found that "the convict lease system had made the condition of the convict infinitely worse than was possible under a system of slavery in which the slave belonged to his master for life." In recent years there has been much improvement in the condition of convicts in the South. Five states, Louisiana, Mississippi, Georgia, Oklahoma, and Texas have abolished the lease, contract, and other hiring systems. All the other Southern states still sell convict labor to some extent, but in each of these, strong movements are on foot to abolish the custom.

After the close of the war and as a part of the reconstruction of the South, there had to be some readjustment of court procedure with reference to Negroes. Hitherto they had been dealt with as slaves or as free persons of color. After the adoption of the war amendments, they came before the courts as full citizens of the United States. From now on, much of the time, in many sections, the major part of the time of the criminal courts has been taken up with trying cases where Negroes were concerned.

Before emancipation, the Negro had noted that wherever the law had been invoked with reference to a Negro that it was generally to punish or to restrain. Thus he came to view the law as something to be feared and evaded but not necessarily to be respected or to be sought as a means of protection. Under freedom, the Negro's experience with the law was much the same as it had been in slavery. He found that the courts were still used as a means of punishment and restraint and that generally they were not the place to seek for protection. Another cause of the Negroes regarding the courts unfavorably was the stringent laws relating to labor contracts. These laws imposed severe penalties upon the laborer who violated his contract and often reduced him to peonage. The result is that at present the attitude of the Negroes toward the law is that many still associate laws with slavery and look upon courts as places where punishment is meted out rather than where justice is dispensed.

This brings us to the question whether the Negroes are fairly tried in the courts. Judge W. H. Thomas, of Montgomery, Ala., after an experience of ten years as a trial judge, in an address before the Southern Sociological Congress at Nashville in 1912, said:

My observation has been that courts try the Negro fairly. I have observed that juries have not hesitated to acquit the Negro when the evidence showed his innocence. Yet, honesty demands that I say that justice too often miscarries in the attempt to enforce the criminal law against the native white man. It is not that the Negro fails to get justice before the courts in the trial of the specific indictment against him, but too often it is that the native white man escapes it. It must be poor consolation to the foreign-born, the Indian, the Negro, and the ignorant generally to learn that the law has punished only the guilty of their class or race, and to see that the guilty of the class, fortunate by reason of wealth, learning, or color, are not so punished for like crime. There must be a full realization of the fact that if punishments of the law are not imposed on all offenders alike, it will breed distrust of administration.

Hon. William H. Sanford, also of Montgomery, Ala., in an address before the same congress on "Fundamental Inequalities of Administration Of Laws," further illuminated this question. He pointed out that the real population of the South is made up of three distinctive communities:

First where the population is composed largely of Negroes, sometimes in the ratio of as many as ten to one. Second, where the population is largely white, usually at a ratio of about two to one. Third, where the population is almost entirely white.

In the first of these, in the administration of the criminal law, the Negro usually gets even and exacts justice, sometimes tempered with mercy. The average white man who serves on the juries in these counties, in his cooler moments and untouched by racial influences, is a believer in fair play and for the most part is the descendant of the men who builded the foundation of our states. But in these communities, a white man rarely, if ever, gets a fair and an impartial trial, and, if indeed he is indicted by a grant jury, his conviction or acquittal is determined more upon his family connections, his business standing, or his local political influence than upon the evidence in the case as applied to the law.

In the second of these communities, the law is more nearly enforced as to both classes, and except in cases where the rights of the one are opposed to those of the other, convictions may be had, and indeed are often had, against the members of both races for offenses of the more serious nature.

> In the third of these communities, the white man usually gets a fair trial and is usually acquitted or convicted according to the evidence under the law, while the Negro, the member of an opposite race, has scant consideration before a jury composed entirely of white men, and is given the severest punishments for the most trivial offenses.

In conclusion, what are some of the principal factors of Negro criminality in the South? The convict lease system has already been indicated as one of these factors. Another factor is the imposing of severe and sometimes unjust sentences for misdemeanors, petty offenses, and for vagrancy. Still another factor is the lack of facilities to properly care for Negro juvenile offenders. Ignorance is, by some, reckoned as one of the chief causes of Negro crime. The majority of the serious offenses, such as homicide and rape, are committed by the ignorant. It appears to be pretty generally agreed that one of the chief causes of Negro crime in the South is strong drink. Attention was called to this fact by the great falling off in crime in those sections of the South where the prohibition law was put into effect. The general testimony is that where prohibition has really prohibited the Negro from securing liquor, the crime rate has decreased; where, however, the prohibition law has not prevented the Negro from securing liquor, there has been no decrease in the crime rate, but, instead, the introduction of a cheaper grade of liquor peddled about in the city and in the country districts, appears to have tended to increase crime.

One of the most significant and hopeful signs for the satisfactory solution of the race problem in the South is the attitude that is being taken towards Negro crime. The Negroes themselves are trying to get at the sources of crime and are making efforts to bring about better conditions. In some sections, they have law and order leagues working in cooperation with the officers of the law. The white people are also giving serious consideration to Negro crime. Its sources, causes, and effects upon the social life of the South are being studied. Movements are on foot for bettering conditions. Under the leadership of the late ex-Governor W. J. Northern, of Georgia, Christian civic leagues, composed of colored and white persons, were organized in that and other states for the purpose of putting down mob violence. The Southern Sociological Congress is taking the lead for the abolition of the convict lease and contract systems and for the adoption, in the South, of modern principles of prison reform.

THE NEGRO AND THE PROBLEM OF LAW OBSERVANCE AND ADMINISTRATION IN THE LIGHT OF SOCIAL RESEARCH

Thorsten Sellin

I have been asked to present to you some data concerning the problem of law observance and administration as it affects the Negro. Since I have already examined this particular question in some detail in the recent volume on "The American Negro," edited by Dr. Donald Young and published by the American Academy of Political and Social Science, and since the memorandum of the research committee has given the gist of several studies made in this limited field with observations or tentative conclusions suggested by them, it would be unprofitable to do more, in the time at my disposal, than to discuss certain general questions facing the student of Negro crime. In doing so, I hope to place in relief certain matters, such as (a) the inadequacy of the data upon which some generalizations concerning the criminality of the Negro have been made; (b) the defects in these generalizations; and (c) some lines along which research may be profitably made in the near future.

The memorandum contains abstracts of studies, which have been made by students engaged in the search for truth. While they may, at times, have been led into errors of interpretation, they have been dominated by the spirit of scientific research. Unfortunately, there have been numerous other writers who have given attention to this problem without being urged by motives of disinterested inquiry. The literature dealing with the

This article was originally published as Chapter 28 in *The Negro in American Civilization*, ed. by Charles S. Johnson (New York: Henry Holt & Co., 1930). Material in the public domain.

The memorandum referred to in this article was one of several reviews of social research prepared for the National Interracial Conference held in 1928, at which Professor Sellin spoke.

social problems of the Negro is filled with statements which in no uncertain terms accuse the Negro of excessive lawlessness. They have charged him with failure to appreciate or utilize the freedom which his emancipation from slavery gave him. They have accused him of filling our prisons with dangerous criminals because his inferior mentality and primitive emotions made it impossible for him to develop the self-control or the conformity to standards of conduct, which life in a civil society demands. Occasionally his criminality had been laid at the door of the unequal struggle for existence under conditions which have encouraged crime. Whether biological or social inferiority had been stressed, the high, one might say the abnormally high, criminality of the Negro has been accepted as an established fact, supported by quantitative data which such writers are in the habit of using without inquiring too seriously into their validity.

The result of these popular assumptions, fostered or spread by persons without qualifications which would entitle them to consideration by a group such as this, has been that up to the present time the attention of the *students* of Negro criminality has been to a large degree focussed on the *amount* of that criminality and its relationship to that of the whites. They have consulted the records of the various agencies of criminal justice and have arrived at the general conclusion, explicit or implicit in various studies digested in the memorandum, that the Negro commits more crimes than the white. This is in harmony, then, with popular belief. I shall try to indicate that, considering the poverty of our source material, such a conclusion requires considerable modification.

Before entering upon the interpretation of data such as those contained in our memorandum, let me for a moment bring to your attention the quality of the source material upon which statistical studies of the amount of Negro crime have been based. If you were to embark upon such a study, you would naturally consult those agencies of criminal justice, from the police to the penal institution, which have come into professional contact with Negro offenders and have thus been in position to secure information about them and their offenses, information which can be expressed in quantitative terms for purposes of tabulation.

Presumably, all police agencies gather data concerning their work. Most of these data, however, never see the light of day. Some of them are published in the form of annual reports, varying in length from a typewritten sheet to booklets of respectable size. The information they contain is designed to satisfy the administrative heads of the community. It is no exaggeration to say that in no case is any effort specifically made to give data of any value to the student of criminology. This situation has led the National Crime Commission in a recent report to make this facetious comment: "For the most part the annual police reports are little less than ridiculous. Information as to the number of horses, bushels of oats for the horses, pairs of puttees bought, days of illness, number of guns, and sometimes the number of arrests, can be had." Even for administrative purposes, these statistics are woefully inadequate. There are, for instance, only a handful of police departments which publish (or, rather, dare to publish) the number of complaints or the number of crimes known to the police, absolutely essential administrative data for estimating the efficiency of a department's work.[1]

To permit him to develop arrest rates for Negroes and whites, the investigator should, of course, like to know the number of all arrests made by the police and the race of those arrested. He should like to know, in addition, the sex, the age, and the charge for Negroes and whites respectively. This would give him some idea of the composition of the two groups and the nature of the criminality charged to each. This is the minimum of useful data.

By contrast, this is what he finds. Out of 75 cities, with a population of more than 100,000 in 1925, only half publish reports which aim at some completeness. Only a quarter give any information about the race of the arrestant and then not always for all complaints. Fewer than half a dozen of these cities are in the South. New York and Chicago, with large Negro populations, give no information in their relatively voluminous reports, regarding the color of all offenders. The New York report never mentions race. The Chicago report gives the color and the sex of those arrested who have been disposed of by the Municipal Court. In addition, it gives the sex and color of those arrested for homicide and of their victims. Philadelphia, although compiling information about color, sex, and age, has not published a report since 1923. A couple of years ago, I asked a high police official of that city why the publication ceased. His answer was indicative of the value placed by many upon criminal statistics, "You see, it was very expensive and, furthermore, we used to have very few demands for it." If the circulation figure of a statistical report is to be the measure of its value, most of our statistical bureaus would have to be scrapped. The official in question apparently had no conception of the fact that police work is the public's business and that the public is entitled to consult the balance sheet, even though it is not a best seller. The observations here made explain in some degree why the memorandum contains such meager information about recent arrest rates in the 75 cities studied by the research committee.

Very few students of Negro crime rates have used judicial statistics. I shall, therefore, spend little time in discussing them. I merely wish to emphasize that what has been said about police statistics is in a great measure true of judicial statistics. They have been compiled for administrative purposes, are not published except by a handful of states, or by a few municipalities, and even when thus made accessible the race of the defendant is only occasionally given.

Penal statistics are, in addition to police statistics, the most important source which has been used for the compilation of comparative crime rates. Theoretically speaking, these are statistics dealing with penal treatment, both non-institutional and institutional—from the suspended sentence to the death penalty on the one hand, to imprisonment on the other. Since data concerning suspended sentences, fines, and probation are usually included in judicial statistics, these data become subject to the criticisms leveled against the latter. As a matter of fact, the investigator has relied mostly upon institutional statistics found in the annual reports of individual penal institutions, the reports of administrative state boards, and the census reports occasionally published by the Federal Census Bureau and constituting our only national criminal statistics. The last of these national reports was published for part of the year 1923, the one immediately before that, in 1910, another, in 1904, etc. In these reports, the student finds two kinds of enumerations, a census of the institutional population taken on a given day and the number of admissions, or commitments, to the institution during a given period. Like the earlier ones discussed, these reports have been compiled for administrative purposes. A great deal of space is given to the economy of the institutions, its labor problem, its staff, its religious work, reports by the teacher, the librarian, the parole officer, etc. As for the prisoner, his race is usually given, but rarely for each offense.

Upon data drawn from the above source, conclusions have been reached that the Negro is responsible for a "larger proportionate share of crime" and that "the Negro has committed more crime than any other racial group" and that "the Negro crime rate as measured by all comparative records is greater than that of the white." These are statements drawn from the memorandum of the research committee. Their inaccuracy will be made apparent in subsequent paragraphs. The data hitherto compiled from the sources discussed above permit only one conclusion, namely, that the Negro appears to be *arrested, convicted,* and *committed to penal institutions* more frequently than the white. Any other conclusion would be based on the assumption that the proportionate number of arrests, convictions, or commitments to the total number of offenses actually committed is the same in both groups. This assumption is untenable, for there are specific factors which seriously distort the arrest, conviction, and commitment rates for Negroes without affecting these rates for whites in a similar manner. No measurement has as yet been devised for the evaluation of these factors. Besides, our inability to refine the crude rates mentioned should counsel prudence in their use.

The greatest of the disturbing factors to which reference has been made is the racial attitude of the dominant white group. Take arrest rates, for instance, employed by half a dozen of the studies abstracted in the memorandum. To what extent do unfavorable racial attitudes so distort the arrest rates as to invalidate any generalization regarding comparative criminality based upon them? It has been suggested that the Negro is arrested more frequently than the white on insignificant charges and that the dragnet, a common device used by the police in their work of crime repression, has been frequently employed in a discriminatory manner. There is considerable truth in these charges. The very high rate of acquittals for Negroes on certain complaints brought into court would seem to support them. The way in which race discrimination affects the arrest rate of the Negro appears from the following illustrations. In a park of a Northern city about a year ago, a young woman was assaulted. Her assailant, a young Negro, escaped. The police immediately determined upon a suitable campaign for the arrest of the criminal. Every Negro who passed that particular spot in the park during the five weeks subsequent to the event was arrested. The campaign ended when the young woman identified her assailant. Whether or not the identification was correct does not concern us here. What is significant for our purposes is that had the assailant been a white man, the method used by the police to apprehend him would hardly have been practical. Furthermore, the Negro arrest rate in the community was seriously raised. The Detroit survey referred to in the memorandum is rich in similar case material.

The police can hardly be blamed for this condition. A policeman is, of course, supposed to enforce the law equitably. On the other hand, he is the product of a group which has fostered in him the racial attitudes which characterize it. Knowing the strong emotional basis for such attitudes, it would be too much for us to expect a policeman to shed them when he dons his uniform. His failure to do so makes the task of the statistical criminologist so difficult that he cannot rely upon arrest rates as indexes of comparative criminality.

Such judicial statistics as have been studied would seem to lend support to the belief that unfavorable racial attitudes are reflected in the conviction rates as well. The Detroit study showed that the race of the defendant influenced the nature of the sentence. It also suggested that the high acquittal rate for Negroes for certain offenses proved the frequency of unwarranted arrests. It would seem perfectly natural that the treatment of the Negro at the hands of white prosecutors, juries, and judges would be conditioned by popular feeling toward his race. The degree of this influence cannot at the present time be measured, one reason why judicial statistics are of little or no value as indexes of comparative criminality.

The same is true, with even greater force, of institutional penal statistics. Here the culminating effects of race discrimination are most clearly observed. As has already been mentioned, imprisonment is but one of several forms of penal treatment. There is evidence for the claim that the Negro is not granted a suspended sentence or probation so frequently as the white. Since he is as a rule in the lowest economic class, his inability to pay a fine opens still another road to prison. Unfavorable discrimination by our courts and the poverty of the Negro offender thus combine to increase the number of commitments to prison. As an index of comparative criminality, as it is used in some of the studies abstracted in the memorandum, institutional penal statistics are therefore of absolutely no value.

The rates which have been used as crime indexes are deficient for other reasons than those discussed. Criminal statistics would be of no value for the purpose we are considering at the moment if we had no general population statistics; in fact, the degree to which the former can be made useful depends on the quality of the latter. Once upon a time we used to see birth rates computed on a total population basis; we now prefer to compute them on the basis of the number of women of childbearing age. In practice, we have not yet reached that stage in criminal statistics, as can be seen from an examination of the memorandum. Even when the student is conscious of the need for refining his rates, he is frequently unable to do so, due to the absence of population statistics.

Criminality, like the capacity for bearing children, is not evenly distributed over the entire population. There are no criminals at all among the infants, very few among children and the very old and relatively few among women. The majority of all criminals who reach our agencies of justice are young men. The proportion of men, particularly young men, in a given population group will consequently bear a direct relationship to the number of crimes committed by that group. Can we accuse a group of being more criminal than another because it has higher proportion of adult males? With no greater justice than we can accuse of a low birth rate a group which has a small proportion of women of child-bearing age. In other words, we cannot estimate, for comparative purposes, the criminality of different groups unless we know at least the most elementary facts about the composition of these groups with regard to size and age and sex distribution.

The importance of these observations with reference to Negro crime need not be emphasized. Some of the most valuable studies of such crime have been made since the great war and the beginning of the northward migration of the Negro. The effect of this migration on the composition of the Negro population in the North, where most of these recent studies have been made, can be seen from an examination of the diagrams of age and sex distribution in Chicago, for instance, as given in the memorandum on population. That arrest, conviction, and commitment rates from such communities need to be refined before they are used as a point of departure for theories on racial factors in crime is obvious. Failure to do so has led some investigators to completely erroneous conclusions, as can be seen from even a cursory examination of the comparative figures for rape, quoted in the memorandum.

No matter then how much we perfect the record systems of our agencies of justice and the tabulations made from them, the ultimate usefulness of these statistics as indexes of comparative criminality will depend upon the extent to which we can develop our general population statistics.

I hope that I have made clear the difficulties which face the student who wants to determine whether or not the Negro commits more crime than the white. First, he has to take his raw material from sources which are inadequate and not always accurate. Then, in interpreting his tables, he must take into account disturbing factors for which he possesses no measurement, such as race discrimination. Finally, he arrives at a crude rate, which he finds it practically impossible to refine for lack of necessary population data. These facts suggest the greatest discretion in the interpretation of criminal statistics. Until we have gathered more data and subjected them to a much more searching analysis, it would be foolhardy indeed to draw any other conclusion than the following: There is reason to believe that the Negro as a group comes more frequently into contact with criminal justice than does the white, but whether or not this means that he is more criminal than the white, it is impossible to say with any degree of certainty.

It is unfortunate that the belief in the Negro's excessive criminality has made students of Negro crime expend so much energy in attempts to verify the charge. Attention has thus been diverted from much more fundamental matters, such as the causes of crime and the relationship of the Negro to our agencies of justice. We all realize that if crime is to be prevented we must know what causes it. I am not unmindful of the fact that many of the writers in, or out of, the memorandum have enumerated causes of Negro criminality, but such statements have been based more upon the "common sense" of the observer than upon conclusions derived from intensive scientific study of the Negro offender or the conditions which made him. Criminologists have been asserting for a considerable time that such studies are essential for the intelligent development of programs of prevention. It may be argued that since the mechanisms of human behavior are the same regardless of race, such studies need not take their clinical material specifically from the Negro group. This argument is not without merit, but considering the fact that the social status of the Negro in our country provides him with a sufficiently different environmental setting, the constant accumulation of case material concerning him would form an exceedingly valuable basis for specific preventive policies.

It would be unjustified to claim that statistical studies of the type given in the memorandum lack all value. I have merely criticized the assumption, expicit or implicit, in some of them that it is possible today to determine the relative criminality of the white and the Negro groups. These studies clearly demonstrate the very high proportion of Negroes among those arrested, convicted, and sent to prison for offenses against the criminal laws. Furthermore, they suggest interesting departures for future research. In closing, may I suggest in a very general way the problems which demand attention of the student in this field.

a. There is an imperative need for facts concerning the treatment of the Negro at the hands of the police, the courts, and the penal institutions. Due to the unreliability or absence of statistical data for large areas, such studies should be confined to small selected type-areas, such as rural counties, villages, urban areas of different sizes, etc., both in the North and in the South. Social survey methods should be utilized or developed as the need arises.

b. By all methods known to modern criminology, the Negro offender should be studied, particularly the delinquent and the pre-delinquent, in order to acquire more definite knowledge regarding the causes of crime among Negroes and thus permit the formulation of preventive programs.

Here are rich fields awaiting the explorer who can traverse the high mountain ranges of our ignorance.

Questions For Discussion

Does the larger recorded Negro crime rate point to a racial lack of emotional stability?

To what extent are crime figures a measure of Negro crime?

To what extent is unfamiliarity with city life a factor in the Negro crime rate?

Is there a growing tendency toward the administration of justice, or does there seem to be an actual lessening of crime among Negroes?

Is it not true that a great many convictions of Negroes in the South are due to a need for road building or some other service rather than law enforcement?

Is the Negro crime rate as much a question of race as economic status?

Is there evidence to support the statement that there is better law observance by Negroes where they have a hand in its administration, through police force, judiciary, etc.?

How can the traditional concern of Christian churches in visiting the prisons be transformed into fuller cooperation with social agencies and scientific research in the modern approach to crime?

In what particular ways is it possible for social agencies to reduce Negro crime?

What can be done to secure justice for the Negro at the hands of the courts?

Is it not possible to select one state in which to promote a constructive program of the administration of criminal offenses?

Is it right to demand that a law or certain laws be obeyed and at the same time the lawmaker makes no provision for literary training of those whom they demand should keep the law?

Does the excess of recorded Negro crime with the evidence of greater willingness to suspect, arrest and convict Negroes and give them longer sentences, suggest that less severity is required for Negroes or that more severity is required for whites?

How far is the defect in treatment of Negro offenders dependent upon more enlightened treatment of all offenders?

What can be done to get the states to draft Negroes for jury service when members of their race are being tried?

NOTE

1. Since this was written, the splendid work of the Committee on Uniform Crime Records of the International Association of Chiefs of Police has resulted in the publication of a manual of police statistics, which undoubtedly will be widely used by the police. The International Association has already pledged itself to the annual reporting of data to a central bureau, which will, it is hoped, be established in Washington in connection with the Department of Justice. Some of the conditions referred to in my paper may thus be remedied, in a measure, in the near future.

INEQUALITY OF JUSTICE

Gunnar Myrdal

The American tradition of electing, rather than appointing, minor public officials has its most serious features in regard to the judiciary branch of the government.[1] Judges, prosecuting attorneys, minor court officials, sheriffs, the chiefs of police, and in smaller communities sometimes the entire police force, are either elected for limited terms or are dependent for their offices upon political representatives of this uncertain tenure. In some places, they can even be recalled during their terms of office, though this is comparatively rare.[2]

The immediate dependence of court and police officials upon popular election—that is, upon local public opinion and political machines—instead of upon appointment strictly according to merit and the uncertainty of tenure implied in this system naturally decreases the attractiveness of these important positions to many of the best persons who would otherwise be available. Professional standards are thus kept lower than those which could be attained under another system. The courts do not get the cream of the legal profession. The social prestige of judges in local courts is not as supreme as could be wished. Corruption and undue political influences are not absent even from the courtrooms. These facts themselves have the circular effect of keeping the best men from judicial positions.

But apart from such general effects, the fact that the administration of justice is dependent upon the local voters is likely to imply discrimination against an unpopular minority group, particularly when this group is disfranchised as Negroes are in the South. The elected judge knows that

---

sooner or later he must come back to the polls and that a decision running counter to local opinion may cost him his position. He may be conscious of it or not, but this control of his future career must tend to increase his difficulties in keeping aloof local prejudices and emotions. Of course, the judge's attitudes are also formed by conditions prevalent in his local community, but he has a degree of acquaintance with the law and with public and legal opinion outside his community. This would tend to emancipate him from local opinion, were it not for his direct dependence on it.[3]

The dependence of the judge on local prejudices strikes at the very root of orderly government. It results in the danger of breaking down the law in its primary function of protecting the minority against the majority, the individual against society, indeed democracy itself against the danger of its nullifying in practice the settled principles of law and impartiality of justice. This danger is higher in the problem regions where there is acute race friction and in rural areas where the population is small and provincial and where personal contacts are direct. Under the same influences as the judges are the public prosecutors, the sheriffs, the chiefs of police, and their subordinates. The American jury system, while it has many merits, is likely to strengthen this dependence of justice upon local popular opinion. If, as in the South, Negroes are kept out of jury service, the democratic safeguard of the jury system is easily turned into a means of minority subjugation.

The popular election of the officers of law and the jury system are expressions of the extreme democracy in the American handling of justice. It might, in spite of the dangers suggested, work excellently in a reasonably homogeneous, highly educated, and public spirited community. It might also work fairly well anywhere for cases involving only parties belonging to a homogeneous majority group which controls the court. It causes, however, the gravest peril of injustice in all cases where the rights of persons belonging to a disfranchised group are involved, particularly if this group is discriminated against all around and by tradition held as a lower caste upon whose rights it has become customary to infringe. *The extreme democracy in the American system of justice turns out, thus, to be the greatest menace to legal democracy when it is based on restricted political participation and an ingrained tradition of caste suppression.* Such conditions occur in the South with respect to Negroes.

If there is a deficiency of legal protection for Negroes, white people will be tempted to deal unfairly with them in everyday affairs. They will be tempted to use irregular methods to safeguard what they feel to be their interests against Negroes. They will be inclined to use intimidation and even violence against Negroes if they can count on going unpunished. When such patterns become established, the law itself and its processes are brought into contempt, and a general feeling of uncertainty, arbitrariness, and inequality will spread. Not only Negroes but other persons of weak social status will be the object of discrimination. "When an exception to the rule of justice is allowed the structure of the legal machinery is damaged, and may and does permit exceptions in cases which do not involve Negroes," observes Charles Johnson.[4] In the South there have been frequent occasions when the legal rights of poor white persons have been disregarded and even when general lawlessness prevailed. When the frequency of lawbreaking thus increases, it becomes necessary to apply stronger penalties than is necessary in an equitable system of justice. In all spheres of public life, it will of course be found that legislation is relatively ineffective, and so the sociologists will be inclined to formulate a general societal law of "the futility of trying to suppress folkways by stateways." Lawlessness has then received the badge of scientific normalcy.

The Negroes, on their side, are hurt in their trust that the law is impartial, that the court and the police are their protection, and, indeed, that they belong to an orderly society which has set up this machinery for common security and welfare. They will not feel confidence in and loyalty toward a legal order which is entirely out of their control and which they sense to be inequitable and merely part of the system of caste suppression. Solidarity then develops easily in the Nergro group, a solidarity against the law and the police. The arrested Negro often acquires the prestige of a victim, a martyr, or a hero, even when he is simply a criminal. It becomes part of race pride in the protective Negro community not to give up a fellow Negro who is hunted by the police. Negroes who collaborate with the police become looked upon as stool pigeons.

No one visiting Negro communities in the South can avoid observing the prevalence of these views. The situation is dynamic for several reasons. One is the growing urbanization and the increasing segregation of the Negro people. The old-time paternalistic and personal relationship between individuals of the two groups is on the decrease. Another factor is the improvement of Negro education which is continually making Negroes more aware of their anomalous status in the American legal order. A third factor, the importance of which is increasing in pace with the literacy of the Negro people, is the persistent hammering of the Negro press which, to a large extent, is devoted to giving publicity to the injustices and injuries suffered by Negroes. A fourth factor is unemployment, especially of young Negroes, with resulting insecurity and dissatisfaction.

Because of these changes, as Du Bois tells us, "... the Negro is coming *more and more* to look upon law and justice, not as protecting safeguards, but as sources of humiliation and oppression."[5] He expresses a common attitude among Southern Negores when he continues: "The laws are made by men who have absolutely no motive for treating the black people with courtesy or consideration: ... the accused law-breaker is tried, not by his peers, but too often by men who would rather punish ten innocent Negroes than let one guilty one escape." To the present observer, the situation looks far from peaceful and quiet, as white people in the South have tried to convince him. It has rather the appearance of a fateful race between, on the one hand, the above-mentioned tendencies which increase Negro mistrust, unrest, and asociality, and, on the other, the equally apparent tendency for the white group increasingly to be prepared to give the Negro personal security and equality before the law.

The literature is replete with statements that point to the Negro's restlessness and the need of giving him legal justice.[6] The representatives of the tradition of lawlessness do not write books even if they still, in many places, dominate practice.[7] We shall have to try to understand them in their historical setting from their actual behavior.

Having accepted the American creed as our value premise in this study, we must also accept a corollary of this creed for the purposes of this part, namely, that *Negroes are entitled to justice equally with all other people.* This principle has constitutional sanction and is held supreme in the legislation of all states in the Union. In this part we do not discuss inequalities *in law* or the results of the inequitable administration of the laws: all these material inequalities in legal status of the American Negro are dealt with in other parts of our inquiry. The subject of the discussion here is only the actual handling of justice, the manner in which inequalities in the enforcement of the laws against whites and Negroes are entering into the judicial procedures, and also such lacks in personal security of Negroes concomitant with those inequalities.

RELATIVE EQUALITY IN THE NORTH

There are defiencies in the working of the machinery of the law in the North too. American justice is everywhere expensive and depends too much upon the skill of the attorney. The poor man has difficulty in securing his rights. Judges and police officers are not free from prejudices against people of lower economic and cultural levels. Experienced white and Negro lawyers have told the author that in criminal cases where only Negroes are involved there is sometimes a disposition on the part of the prosecutors, judges and juries to treat offenses with relative lightness. In matters involving offenses by Negroes against whites, Negroes will often find the presumptions of the courts against them, and there is a tendency to sentence them to a higher penalty than if they had committed the same offense against Negroes. Instances have been related to me in which Negro witnesses have been made the butt of jests and horseplay. I have, however, received the general impression that such differential treatment of witnesses is rather the exception than the rule, and that it will practically never happen to a Negro plaintiff or deffendant who is assisted by good counsel.[8]

A more serious matter is the treatment of Negroes by the police. In most Northern communities, Negroes are more likely than whites to be arrested under any suspicious circumstances. They are more likely to be accorded discourteous or brutal treatment at the hands of the police than are whites. The rate of killing of Negroes by the police is high in many Northern cities, particularly in Detroit.[9] Negroes have a seriously high criminality record,[10] and the average white policeman is inclined to increase it even more in his imagination. The Negroes are, however, not the only sufferers, even if they as usual reap more than their fair share. Complaints about indiscriminate arrests and police brutality are raised also by other economically disadvantaged and culturally submerged groups in the Northern cities. The attitudes of the police will sometimes be found among the most important items considered in local Negro politics in the North. Usually there is much less complaint about not getting a fair trial before the courts.

Another form of discrimination in the North against Negroes is in the market for houses and apartments; whites try to keep Negroes out of white neighborhoods by restrictive covenants. The legality of these covenants is open to dispute, but in so far as the local courts uphold them, the discrimination is in the legal principle, not in the individual cases brought to court.[11] In some Northern cities—as, for instance, Detroit—I have heard complaints that the police will sometimes try to restrict Negroes to the Negro districts, particularly at night. There have been bombings against Negroes who tried to invade white territory and even race riots, particularly in the wake of the sudden migration of great masses of rural Negroes from the South during and immediately after the First World War.[12] The police have not always been strictly impartial during such incidents.[13] But the courts have usually not shielded the white transgressors afterwards in the way which has become a pattern in the South.

Vigilantism occasionally occurs in the North. The Western frontier formerly saw much of it, but manifestations of it are rare now. During the 1920s, the Ku Klux Klan operated in Indiana, Illinois, Michigan, and other Northern states almost as much as it did in the South. Immigrant sections of a few Northern cities occasionally witness such activities (e.g., the Black Hand society in Italian areas and the Tong wars in Chinese sections). Occasionally vigilantism of the Southern type will still occur in the North:

> On the night of August 11, 1939, seven Negro migratory workers including one woman were routed out of their sleep in an isolated one-room shack on a farm near Cranbury, New Jersey, by a mob of white men with handkerchief masks and guns. All seven were stripped naked, their hands tied and they were told to start across a field. The five single men escaped into the bushes, shots fired after them going over their heads. Jake and Frances Preston, the married couple, were threatened with mutilation and rape, were beaten with a robber hose, had white enamel poured over them and were told to "head South."
>
> Many believed prominent local citizens had instigated the attack. Local workers were aroused; migrants threatened to leave. Local farmers feared the loss of their laborers. The Workers Defense League offered a $100 reward for information leading to the arrest and conviction of the assailants. After two weeks the state police made ten arrests, one a minor. At first freed on $250 bail the nine self-confessed adult assailants were later given suspended sentences of three to five years. But intimidation of Negroes persisted. So civil suits were then instituted and on May 10, 1940, the Federal District Court of Newark awarded the Preston's damages of $2,000 each, and the other five $1000 each.[14]

In many Northern cities, Negroes relate that they find it difficult to get the courts to punish violations of the civil rights laws; for example when Negroes are not permitted in certain restaurants and hotels. In such cases, it is often difficult to obtain proofs which substantiate the charges, but this does not explain satisfactorily why those laws have yet so largely remained paper decrees. In the over-all balance, however, infringements of Negro rights that are supposed to be prevented by the civil rights laws are of comparatively little importance.

There are, in many Northern places, Negro judges, Negro court officers, and Negro policemen. Commonly, there are Negroes on the jury lists. The large majority of all Negro lawyers find it to their advantage to practice in the North.[15] They generally plead cases before the courts and are not, like most of their Southern colleagues, restricted to trying to settle things outside of court. They occasionally have white people among their clientele. Negro lawyers in the North do not generally complain of being treated differently in court from their white colleagues or of meeting prejudice from the juries.[16]

Since, on the whole, Negroes do not meet much more discrimination from officers of the law than do white persons of the same economic and cultural level, *there is in the North no special problem of getting justice for Negroes, outside the general one of improving the working of the machinery of the law for the equal protection of the rights of poor and uneducated people.* The further reservation should be added that Negroes in Border cities—for instance, in Washington and St. Louis—meet relatively more prejudice both from the police and from the courts,[17] and the same thing holds for a city like Detroit which has a large population of white immigrants from the South.[18] In a comparable way, the Upper South is considerably more like the North in this respect than is the Lower South.

Part of the explanation of why the Negro gets more legal justice in the North is the fact that Negroes can vote in the North and, consequently, have a share in the ultimate control of the legal system. Nevertheless, the importance of political participation as a cause of equality before the law should not be exaggerated. The lack of discrimination in both respects has a common cause in a general inclination of white people in the North to regard Negroes as full citizens in their formal relations with public authority, even if not in economic competition or social intercourse. This is one point where the ordinary Northerner is unfailingly faithful to the American Creed. He wants justice to be impartial, regardless of race, creed or color.

The North is further removed from the memories of slavery, and its equalitarian philosophy became more rigorously formulated in the prolonged conflict with the South during and after the Civil War. Also, Northern Negroes are concentrated in big cities, where human relations are formalized and where Negroes are a small minority of the total population. The legal machinery in those cities might sometimes be tainted by the corruption of the city administration, but its size alone tends to objectify its operations and prevent its being influenced by the narrowest type of local prejudice. Other reasons would seem to be that Northern Negroes are better educated and have a higher economic status on the average, that Northern Negroes can be and are more inclined to stand up for their rights, and that most organizations fighting for the Negro have their headquarters in the North. Whatever the reasons, it seems to be a fact that *there is a sharp division between North and South in the granting of legal justice to Negroes.* In the North, for the most part, Negroes enjoy equitable justice.

CRIME[19]

Negro crime has periodically been the subject of serious debate in the United States, and, at least since 1890, has often been the object of statistical measurement. Just as the past year has seen an epidemic of reports in New York newspapers of assault and robbery by Negroes, so other periods have seen actual or alleged crime waves among Negroes in other areas. At all times, the stereotyped notion has prevailed that Negroes have a criminal tendency, which manifests itself in acts ranging all the way from petty thievery by household servants to razor-slashing homicide.

The statistical studies of Negro crime have not been consistent in their findings, and each has evoked much criticism in scientific circles. The census of 1890 contained a criticism of its own crime statistics:

> The increase in the number of prisoners during the last 40 years has been more apparent than real, owing to the very imperfect enumeration of the prison population prior to 1880. Whatever it has been, it is not what it might be supposed to be, if we had no other means of judging of it than by the figures contained in the census volumes.[20]

Since that time, there have been many pertinent criticisms of Negro crime statistics.[21] Johnson and Kiser express the attitude of all honest students of Negro crime toward the statistics:

> The statistical data upon which we are forced to base our knowledge of Negro crime measure only the extent and the nature of the Negro's contact with the law and is of value for that purpose. However, our information relates to apparent crime only and not to the actual amount of crime committed by any one group or by the population in general. There is no consistent and measurable relation between apparent and real criminality and, as a result, it is not possible to estimate

> from available criminal data the amount and proportion of Negro crime or the extent to which it is increasing or decreasing.[22]

This attitude, as well as the conflict of conclusions, is not difficult to understand when one realizes the nature of the statistics on Negro crimes and the character of the legal process which defines a given act as a crime. Crime statistics are generally inadequate, despite a tremendous improvement within the last decade, and Negro crime statistics are further complicated by discrimination in the application of the law and by certain unique traditions. It may be stated categorically that there are no statistics on crimes *per se*: there are only statistics on crimes known to the police, on arrests, on convictions, on prisoners. Honest studies based on different sets of statistics will give different findings. Crime is not uniformly defined from state to state and from time to time. Statistics on one area at one time will show different conclusions from statistics on another area at another time. Finally, the conclusions of a given study are largely determined by the factors one takes into account in analyzing the statistics.

It is necessary to consider all the weaknesses of the statistics on Negro crime because these statistics have been used to buttress stereotypes of Negro criminality and to justify discriminatory practices. Even capable and honest scientists like Walter Willcox have used the available statistics to prove Negro criminality.[23] But Willcox did this in 1899; competent scientists are no longer so uncritical of their data. Incompetent popularizers, however, continue to misuse the statistics. In this situation, it becomes more important to criticize the statistics than it is to present them. To such a criticism, we shall now proceed.

Statistics on Negro crime have not only all the weaknesses of crime statistics generally—such as incomplete and inaccurate reporting, variations between states as to definitions and classification of crimes, changes in policy—but also special weaknesses due to the caste situation and to certain characteristics of the Negro population. One of the basic weaknesses arises out of the fact that those who come in contact with the law are generally only a selected sample of those who commit crimes. Breaking the law is more widespread in America than the crime statistics indicate, and probably everyone in the country has broken some law at some time. But only a small proportion of the population is arrested, convicted, and sent to prison. Some major crimes (such as violation of the Sherman Anti-Trust Act and avoidance of certain tax payments) are even respectable and are committed in the ordinary course of conducting a business;[24] others (such as fraud and racketeering) are not respectable but are committed frequently and often go unpunished. It happens that Negroes are seldom in a position to commit these white collar crimes; they commit the crimes which much more frequently result in apprehension and punishment. This is a chief source of error when attempting to compare statistics on Negro and white crimes.

In the South, inequality of justice seems to be the most important factor in making the statistics on Negro crime and white crime not comparable. As we saw in Part VI, in any crime which remotely affects a white man, Negroes are more likely to be arrested than are whites, more likely to be indicted after arrest, more likely to be convicted in court and punished.[25] Negroes will be arrested on the slightest suspicion, or on no suspicion at all, merely to provide witnesses or to work during a labor shortage in violation of anti-peonage laws. The popular belief that all Negroes are inherently criminal operates to increase arrests, and the Negro's lack of political power prevents a white policeman from worrying about how many Negro arrests he makes. Some white criminals have made use of these prejudices to divert suspicion away from themselves onto Negroes: for example, there are many documented cases of white robbers blackening their faces when committing crimes.[26] In the Southern court, a Negro will seldom be treated seriously, and his testimony against a white man will be ignored, if he is permitted to express it at all. When sentenced he is usually given a heavier punishment and probation or suspended sentence is seldom allowed him.[27] In some Southern communities, there are no special institutions for Negro juvenile delinquents or for Negro criminals who are insane or feeble-minded. Such persons are likely to be committed to the regular jails or prisons, whereas similar white cases are put in a separate institution and so do not swell the prison population.

Some of the "crimes" in the South may *possibly* be committed only by Negroes: only Negroes are arrested for violations of the segregation laws, and sometimes they are even arrested for violation of the extra-legal racial etiquette (the formal charge is disturbing the peace, insolence to an officer, violation of municipal ordinances, and so on). The beating of Negroes by whites in the South is seldom regarded as a crime, but should a Negro lay hands on a white man, he is almost certain to be apprehended and punished severely. As Frazer points out: "In the South, the white man is certainly a greater menace to the Negro's home than the latter is to his."[28] Similarly, when white lawyers, installment collectors, insurance agents, plantation owners, and others, cheat Negroes, they are never regarded as criminals.[29] But stealing by Negroes from whites—beyond that petty stealing which is part of the patriarchal tradition from slavery—is almost always punished as a crime.

In one respect, Southern discrimination against Negroes operates to reduce the Negro's crime record. If a Negro commits a crime against another Negro and no white man is involved and if the crime is not a serious one, white policemen will let the criminal off with a warning or a beating, and the court will let him off with a warning or a relatively light sentence. In a way, this over-leniency stimulates greater crimes since it reduces risks and makes law enforcement so arbitrary. Life becomes cheap and property dear in the Negro neighborhood—a situation conducive to crime.

These things occur in the North, too, although in much smaller degree. In the North it is not so much discrimination which distorts the Negro's criminal record, as it is certain characteristics of the Negro population. In the first place, unorganized crime is much more prevalent in the South than in the North, both among whites and among Negroes, and when the Negro migrates North, he brings his high crime rate along with him. Specific cultural practices brought from the South also affect the Negro's crime record in the North. A member of New York's grand jury told the author that part of the high Negro juvenile delinquency and crime rate was due to the Negro practice of fighting with knives instead of with fists, as whites do. "The fights start in the same way among both groups, but the law defines the Negro's manner of fighting as a crime, and the white's manner of fighting as not a crime."[30]

A third impersonal cause of distortion of the Negro's crime record is his poverty. He cannot bribe the policeman to let him off for a petty offense; he cannot have a competent lawyer to defend him in court, and when faced with the alternatives of fine or prison by way of punishment, he is forced to choose prison. The Negro's ignorance acts in a similar fashion. He does not know his legal rights, and he does not know how to present his case; thus even an unprejudiced policeman or judge may unwittingly discriminate against him. Also associated with the Negro lower class status in distorting his crime record is his lack of influential connections: he does not know the important people who can help him out of petty legal troubles. In the North, the fact that an unusually large proportion of Negroes are in the age group of 15-40, which is the age group to which most criminals belong, operates to make the Negro crime rate based on total population figures deceptively high. Negro concentration in the cities in the North, where the crime rate is generally higher than in rural areas, acts in the same manner. The Negro crime rate is further inflated by

TABLE 1
Prisoners Received from Courts by State and Federal Prisons and Reformatories by Sex, Race and Nativity: 1939

	Number Received from Courts			Rates per 100,000 Population		
Race and Nativity	Total	Male	Female	Total	Male	Female
White	47,971	45,796	2,175	42.3	77.0	3.7
Native	45,280	43,257	2,023	42.4	80.9	3.8
Foreign-born	2,691	2,539	152	23.6	42.2	2.8
Negro	17,324	16,135	1,189	134.7	257.4	18.0
Other Races	729	698	31	123.8	202.9	12.7

Sources: U.S. Bureau of the Census, Prisoners in State and Federal Prisons and Reformatories: 1939 (1941), p. 11; and Sixteenth Census of the United States: 1940, Population, Preliminary Release, Series P-10, No. 6. The population bases are as of 1940.

greater recidivism: a given number of Negro criminals are sent to jail more often than are the same number of white criminals.[31] The longer prison sentence meted out to Negroes raises the number of Negroes in prison at any one time beyond what it would be if crime statistics reflected only the total number of criminals.

In general, our attitude toward crime statistics must be that they do not provide a fair index of Negro crime. Even if they did, a higher crime rate would not mean that the Negro was more addicted to crime, either in his heredity or in his culture, for the Negro population has certain external characteristics (such as concentration in the South and in the young adult ages) which give it a spuriously high crime rate. With this attitude in mind, we may examine some of the statistics. The most nearly complete, and the most reliable, set of statistics on crime for the nation are the recent annual reports of the United States Bureau of the Census, *Prisoners in State and Federal Prisons and Reformatories.* We shall use the set for 1939, the most recent set available at the time of writing. These statistics have two important weaknesses (in addition to those just reviewed). First, they do not include criminals in local jails, but only those in state and federal prisons and reformatories. For this reason, they do not include

TABLE 2
Male Felony Prisoners Received from Courts by State and Federal Prisons and Reformatories, by Geographic Areas and by Race and Nativity: 1939

	Number		Rate per 100,000 Population	
Race and Nativity	Southern States	Northern and Western States	Southern States	Northern and Western States
Total	19,430	28,894	46.6	32.1
Native White	10,659	22,759	34.3	30.0
Foreign-born White	132	1,435	21.1	13.3
Negro	8,548	4,402	86.3	148.7
All Other Races	91	298	88.6	61.3

Sources: U.S. Bureau of the Census, Prisoners in State and Federal Prisons and Reformatories: 1939 (1941), p. 28; and Sixteenth Census of the United States: 1940. Population, Preliminary Release, Series P-10, No. 1. Population bases are as of 1940. Southern states include, according to this census publication: Delaware, Maryland, District of Columbia, Virginia, West Virginia, North Carolina, South Carolina, Florida, Kentucky, Tennessee, Mississippi, Arkansas, Louisiana, Oklahoma and Texas. Georgia and Alabama did not report. All Northern states reported.

most of the petty crimes, and to get a relatively complete picture of types of offense we shall have to turn to other sources. Second, prisoners are a very selected group of criminals: they have been apprehended, arrested, indicted, convicted and committed. Criminologists generally hold that the further the index from the crime, the poorer it is as a measure of crime. This may be true for white prisoners, but it is not nearly so true for Negro prisoners. So many Negroes are arrested on the vaguest suspicion that those who are actually sent to prison may more likely be a representative group of criminals than those who are only arrested.

Table 1 shows that there are about three times as many Negro males in prisons and reformatories as there are native white males, in proportion to the sizes of their respective populations, and that the rate for Negro women is more than four times as great as that for native white women.

Foreign-born whites have rates much lower than native whites and members of races other than white and Negro (that is, Indians, Chinese, Filipinos, and others) have rates almost as high as do Negroes. Table 2 reveals that the difference between Negroes and whites is much larger in the North than in the South. In the South the number of Negro male felony prisoners is only between two and two-and-a-half times as great (in proportion to population) as the number of native white male felony prisoners. In the North, however, the Negro rate is almost five times as large as the white rate. This would seem to be due mainly to the fact that Northern Negroes are concentrated in cities, where social disorganization is greater and law enforcement is more efficient. We shall return to the problem of causes of crime after considering the types of offenses which are most characteristic of Negroes.

NOTES

1. This tradition was referred to in Chapter 20, Section 2, as a main reason why the vote, or the lack of the vote, is of such paramount importance for the Negro people.
2. "In many a small town and city [of the South], the mayor and councilmen offer for election with a complete list of police and other public officers." Arthur Raper, "Race and Class Pressures," unpublished manuscript prepared for this study (1940), p. 14.
3. A shift from election to appointment of court and policy officials would also be expected to increase efficiency, reduce corruption, and raise the level of the persons appointed. This would tend to occur if appointments were made under the civil service system and generally even if the higher appointments were made directly by the governor of the state.
4. Willis D. Weatherford and Charles S. Johnson, *Race Relations* (1934), p. 61.
5. W.E.B. DuBois, *The Souls of Black Folk* (1903), p. 176.
6. As early as 1904, Murphy recognized the "morbid and exaggerated solidarity" among Negroes against the white agencies of justice as the "blind moving of the instinct of self-protection." (Edgar Gardner Murphy, *Problems of the Present South* (1909; first edition, 1904), p. 174. Weatherford observes how the reaction breaks down "... one of the most powerful deterrents of crime; namely, the loss of status among those who are of the same class as the possible criminal." (Weatherford and Johnson, *op. cit.*, p. 430) The Negro spokesmen generally do not deny the charges against their people of being inclined to shield criminals of their own race. But they unanimously point to the defects in the working of justice as the explanation: "The Negro feels that he cannot expect justice from Southern courts where white and black are involved. In his mind accusation is equivalent to condemnation. . . . The very spirit in which, he feels, the law is administered makes it difficult for the colored citizen to exercise cheerful co-operation and acquiescence." (Kelly Miller, *Race Adjustment* [1908], p. 79)

Robert R. Moton, a most conservative Negro educator and leader, writes in the same vein:

> In the light of these facts [the attitudes and activities against the Negro in the First World War] it ought not be difficult to understand why the reproach is so often hurled at the Negro that he does not cooperate with officers of the law in ap-

prehending criminals and those accused of crime. To the Negro the law where these practices obtain appears not as an instrument of justice, but as an instrument of persecution; government is simply white society organized to keep the Negro down; and the officers of the law are its agents authorized to wreak upon the helpless offender the contempt, the indignation, and the vengeance that outraged law and order feels when stimulated by prejudice. There is no such hue and cry over crime when the victim is a Negro and the perpetrator either white or black as when the victim is white and the suspect is black or supposed to be black. (*What the Negro Thinks* (1929), pp. 154-155.

and:

The Negro knows, perhaps better than he knows any else, that his chances of securing justice in the courts in those sections of the country where discrimination is in other things legal and common are so slim that in most instances he has nothing to gain by resorting to the courts even for litigation with members of his own race; while it is accepted by most as a foregone conclusion that no court anywhere will render a judgment against a white man in favour of a Negro plaintiff. A Negro defendant may occassionally get a favourable judgment as against a white plaintiff, but the reverse is a far more frequent possibility, so much so that a Negro very rarely brings suit against a white man for any cause in those states where relations between the two races are more or less strained. It is figured that to do so will involve a man in fruitless litigation, with the original loss augmented by the cost of the action. In spite of all the injustices and abuses from which Negroes suffer, one seldom hears of a court action brought by Negroes against any white person in our Southern states." (Moton, *op. cit.*, pp. 141-142.)

A recent investigator of a Southern community, Hortense Powdermaker, testifies concerning the attitudes among the Negroes:

. . . many of the Negroes have long since concluded that their best course is to keep clear of legal complications wherever possible. To go to court for any cause would be to solicit more trouble than the matter at issue might be worth. Since no Negro can expect to find justice by due process of law, it is better in the long run to suffer one's loss—or to adjust it oneself. From this angle, the 'lawlessness' sometimes ascribed to the Negro may be viewed as being rather his private and individual 'law enforcement' *faute de mieux*. The feeling against going to court has in it an element of race-solidarity. Some Negroes will criticize one of the race who takes legal action against another Negro. Such criticism is part of a definite countercurrent against the still prevalent tendency to take one's troubles to a white man. *After Freedom* (1939), p. 126.

On this point, the Southern white liberals—who, in this region, have to defend the principle of legality, since conservatism there is married to the tradition of illegality—agree without reservation with the Negro leaders. Baker reported this more than thirty years ago. One of the Southern liberals told him frankly: "We complain that the Negroes will not help to bring the criminals of their race to justice. One reason for this is that the Negro has too little confidence in our courts. We must give him that, above all things." (Ray Stannard Baker, *Following the Color Line* (1908), p. 49. The statement was made by a Mr. Hopkins, leader of the Civil League of Atlanta, composed of the foremost white citizens of that city.)

Woofter eloquently expresses the view of Southern liberalism today when he says:

In the successful adjustment of the legal relationships of the two races democracy is vitally involved. The right to a fair trial by an impartial jury of peers is one of the bed-rocks upon which freedom rests, and if it cannot be preserved when the courts serve races, then democracy itself rests on quicksand. The problem of legal justice is, therefore, fully as important to the white race as to the Negro race. Any tendency to weaken the feeling that the court system is entirely impartial, unaffected by passion or prejudice, and meticulously just, or any tendency to strengthen the feeling that the court can be biased or made the instrument of a particular class, is a tendency which may wreck society. (T.J. Woofter, Jr., *The Basis of Racial Adjustment* (1925), p. 125.

7. One reason for this is that these persons are usually aware that their practice is inconsistent with their best ideals. Another reason is that such a disproportionately large part of the intellectuals of the region are liberals. (See Chapter 31, Section 5.)

8. For example, Robert A. Warner describes the situation in New Haven, Connecticut in these terms:

Only occasionally are justice betrayed and the colored people robbed of the protection of the law, when the judges of the city court suspect acts of violence in which Negroes are involved are simple assualts. One such case was appealed to Criminal Superior Court successfully. A white man, drunk, was surprised in the act of stealing the car of a reputable Negro couple. When they chased and overtook him, he slashed the woman so severely that a blood transfusion was necessary to save her life. The city court disposed of the case with a cursory $25 fine and costs for breach of the peace, and suspended judgments or penalties for the motor vehicle violations involved. The higher court gave the miscreant a deserved year in jail." *(New Haven Negroes* [1940], p. 224.)

9. See Chapter 27, Section 5.

10. See Chapter 44, Section 2.

11. See Chapter 29, Section 4.

12. The classic case study on this subject is the survey undertaken by The Chicago Commission on Race Relations. (*The Negro in Chicago* [1922].)

13. In Detroit a federal housing project, the Sojourner Truth Homes, was the scene of a riot between whites and Negroes. The project was designed for Negro defense workers. On the day set for occupancy, February 28, whites who lived nearby picketed the project. Moving vans containing the furniture of prospective Negro tenants were stopped. When one van tried to pass the line, the white men climbed all over the truck; a stone was thrown, hitting a Negro driver. Then mounted police charged in. *Life* magazine reports: "Cops charged down on Negro sympathizers of excluded tenants. Police devoted most attention to Negroes, made no effort to open picket lines for vans. Said one inspector: 'It would be suicide if we used our sticks on any of them [the whites].'" (*Life* [March 16, 1942], pp. 40-41.)

14. Henry Hill Collins, Jr., *America's Own Refugees* (1941), p. 156. See also, David W. Anthony, "The Cranbury Terror Case.," *The Crisis* (October, 1939), pp. 295-296.

15. Of 1,247 Negro lawyers, judges, and justices reported in the United States in 1930, only 436 were from the whole South, where over three-fourths of the Negro population were concentrated. (U.S. Bureau of the Census, *Negroes in the United States: 1920-1932,* pp. 9 and 293.)

16. Statements in this paragraph are the conclusions the present author has reached after having interviewed a great number of white and Negro lawyers in Northern cities.

17. E. Franklin Frazier, *Negro Youth at the Crossways* (1940), pp. 34-35 and 169.

18. Detroit also seems to have a larger number of Southern-born policemen than most other Northern cities. In the recent clashes there between the police and the Negroes, many of the police were whites from Kentucky and Tennessee.

19. In preparing this section, we have relied most heavily on an unpublished manuscript prepared for this study: Guy B. Johnson and Louise K. Kiser, "The Negro and Crime" (1940). A part of this study was incorporated in an article by Guy B. Johnson, "The Negro and Crime," *The Annals of the American Academy of Political and Social Science* (September, 1941), pp. 93-104.

20. U.S. Bureau of the Census, *Eleventh Census of the United States: 1890*, "Crime, Pauperism, and Benevolence," Vol. I, p. 126.
21. See Guy B. Johnson and Louise K. Kiser, "The Negro and Crime," unpublished manuscript prepared for this study (1940), pp. 65 and 291 ff.
22. *Ibid.*, p. 95. A similar criticism of Negro crime statistics is given by one of the nation's leading students of crime:

> Conclusions have been reached that the Negro is responsible for a 'larger proportionate share of crime'; and that 'the Negro crime rate as measured by all comparative records is greater than that of the white.' ... The data hitherto compiled from the sources discussed, permit only one conclusion, namely, that the Negro appears to be arrested, convicted and committed to penal institutions more frequently than the white. Any other conclusion would be based on the assumption that commitments to the total number of offenses actually committed is the same in both groups. This assumption is untenable, for there are specific factors which seriously distort the arrest, conviction and commitment rates for Negroes without affecting these rates for whites in a similar manner. No measurement has as yet been devised for the evaluation of these factors." (Thorsten Sellin, "The Negro and the Problem of Law and Observance and Administration in the Light of Social Research," in Charles S. Johnson, *The Negro in American Civilization* [1930], p. 447.)

23. "Negro Criminality," *Journal of Social Science* (December, 1899), pp. 78-98.
24.. Edwin H. Sutherland, "White-Collar Criminality," *American Sociological Review* (February, 1940), pp. 1-12.
25. Quantitative evidence for this and the following paragraphs may be found not only in Part VI of this book, but also in Johnson and Kiser, *op. cit.*, 65-192.
26. Johnson and Kiser, *op. cit.*,p. 347. There are other ways in which white criminals divert suspicion from themselves to Negroes; see *ibid.*, pp. 345-348.
27. After making a special analysis of some statistics on homicides in the South collected for this study by George K. Brown, A.J. Jaffe concludes: "It appears statistically significant that a Negro who murders a white man receives a much stiffer penalty than if he murders a Negro. On the other hand, a white man can murder another white man with about the same (or perhaps even more) impunity as one Negro can murder another. Also a white can murder a Negro with relative freedom from punishment." (Unpublished memorandum prepared for this study [August 19, 1940]). Brown's data are in Appendix B of Johnson and Kiser, *op. cit.*, Johnson and Kiser also present some data which further corroborate this point; see *ibid.*, pp.358-362 and Appendix D. Independently, Powdermaker has presented some similar data for Mississippi (*op cit.*, pp. 395-396).

> With respect to parole and probation, the U.S. Bureau of the Census reported: "It is quite apparent ... that Negroes remain in the institutions to the expiration of their sentence in much greater proportions than do whites." (*Prisoners in State and Federal Prisons and Reformatories: 1939* [1941]m p.. 43.) With respect to length of prison term, it reported: "... among the State prisoners, the Negroes generally served longer periods of time than did the whites.... It is quite apparent that whites served less time than Negroes in the Southern States, for murder, manslaughter, burglary, forgery, rape and other sex offenses. The whites serve a little longer for aggravated assault, and for larceny ... [and] for auto theft." (*Ibid.*, p. 70).

The Detroit survey reported similar findings:

> The Detroit survey disclosed that of the number of whites convicted of felonies 13.5 per cent were given the alternative of a fine or a prison sentence while only 7.1 per cent of the Negro felons were so favored. Over 12 per cent of the white

defendants were placed on probation as compared with 7.2 per cent Negroes. Similar disproportions were revealed in the number of suspended sentences. The Detroit Survey is typical of situations throughout our state jurisdictions." (Nathaniel Cantor, "Crime and the Negro," *The Journal of Negro History* [January, 1931], p. 63.)

28. E. Franklin Frazier, "The Pathology of Race Prejudice," *The Forum* (June, 1927), p. 860.

29. Johnson and Kiser, *op. cit.*, 411-412.

30. Interview (November 18, 1942).

31. Johnson and Kiser, *op. cit.*, pp. 258-263.

THE RELATION OF CRIMINAL ACTIVITY TO BLACK YOUTH EMPLOYMENT

Richard B. Freeman

This article reports on a study which attempts to estimate the extent to which current and previous criminal activity reduces the employment of inner city black male youths from high poverty neighborhoods. The study finds a significant trade-off between employment and crime, with crime associated with a 10 to 12 percent reduction in employment of these youths. The policy implication is that increased criminal deterrence, as well as other programs, has a role to play in efforts to resolve the employment crisis for disadvantaged youths.

To what extent is youth crime associated with joblessness? If youth crime were reduced as a result of, say, a successful deterrence program, what is the likely consequence for the employment of persons in a high-unemployment high-crime population?

Economic studies of crime and the labor market, which focus on the impact of unemployment and other measures of market opportunities on criminal behavior, do not readily provide answers to these questions. By making crime the dependent variable they neglect potentially important causal links from crime to employment, such as the effect of past criminal behavior on future employment prospects. Moreover, because crime and employment are far from dichotomous alternatives (some employed persons commit crimes; most unemployed persons do not commit crimes), it is necessary to study separately the crime-to-employment link to evaluate what a change in criminal behavior would do to employment.

In this article I provide such an analysis. I reverse the direction of standard labor market-crime analyses by studying the impact of crime on employment, focusing on out-of-school black males aged 16-24 from the

1979-80 National Bureau of Economic Research (NBER) Survey of Inner City Youths in the worst poverty tracts in Chicago, Boston, and Philadelphia. The principal conclusion reached is that for these youths crime is associated with substantially less employment, implying that criminal deterrence programs can play a role, along with other programs, in increasing their employment.

HOW CRIME AFFECTS EMPLOYMENT

There are six distinct ways in which criminal activity and the incentive to commit crime can reduce employment in legitimate activities.

First, in the framework of standard labor supply models, when crime is more rewarding than legitimate work, it may substitute for employment. While crime often requires little time and may complement rather than substitute for employment (white collar crimes, in particular, take place at the work place), the direction and magnitude of this effect is uncertain, dependent on the technology of crime and work.

Second, there is likely to be an income effect from successful crime, with persons who earn a lot choosing leisure over work: Make a fortune robbing Fort Knox and you are less likely to show up for work tomorrow.

Third, there is an "incapacitative effect" because unsuccessful crime that lands someone in jail removes him from the labor force. While for most demographic groups reductions in employment due to jail time is small, for black youths the effect is far from negligible. Criminal justice figures suggest that approximately 187,500 black men aged 18-29 were in prison in the early 1980s—roughly 5% of the population in that age bracket.[1] Census of Population data tell a similar story, showing 5% of young black men "institutionalized" in 1980.[2]

Fourth, upon release from jail, an ex-offender is likely to have trouble getting a job. Employers generally shun persons with criminal records. Moreover, persons are more likely to learn criminal than legitimate work skills in jail.

Fifth, criminal activity that injures the criminal or victims may also reduce employment possibilities. In its most extreme form, criminal activity kills people, and homicide rates are extraordinarily high for black youths: in 1979, there were 126.9 deaths by homicide per hundred thousand black males 25-29 compared to 14.8 deaths by homicide per hundred thousand white males 25-29.[3] These figures and those for adjacent age groupings imply that nearly 1% of black youths die of homicide in their twenties, and thus are removed from the potential work force. By age 40 the percentage roughly doubles.[4]

Finally, to the extent that crime is concentrated in an area, the costs of doing business or working there will be high, reducing business activity, demand for labor, and employment. The fact that inner city poverty areas tend to be high-crime areas thus lowers employment prospects.

In sum, the concentration of the crime literature on the effect of unemployment (and deterrence) on crime notwithstanding,[5] there is an important feedback from crime to employment that deserves study.

THE TRADE-OFF IN THE INNER-CITY MINORITY YOUTH SURVEY

In 1979-80 as part of its project on minority youth employment the NBER commissioned Mathematica Policy Research to survey some 2400 inner city youths from the worst poverty tracts in Boston, Chicago, and Philadelphia—a set of youths with lower employment and school-going than found among black youths in general or among white youths.[6] Because of concern with the relation between crime and employment, one module of the survey dealt with self-reported criminal behavior and the youths' perceptions of opportunities for crime. In an important set of papers Viscusi has analyzed the determinants of criminal behavior in these data, finding a significant role for economic factors,[7] which suggests that the module can be fruitfully used to evaluate the crime-employment trade-off.

Does the survey show a substantial inverse relation between criminal activity and employment? The cross-tabulations of the number of out-of-school youths who reported working the survey week with various measures of criminal activity and perceptions of criminal opportunity shown in table 1 indicates that it does. Relatively fewer youths who admitted committing crimes were working than other youths: the rate of employment was 30% for those who committed crimes the previous month (33% for those committing crimes the previous year) compared to 46% for those who did not commit a crime. Moreover, youths who had relatively high crime earnings had exceptionally low proportions employed, as did those who spent time in jail or who were on probation. Finally, the data on perceptions of crime show lower employment among youths who see the environment as offering a significant "chance to make money illegally" and among youths who view their neighborhoods as particularly dangerous.

Because criminal behavior in the NBER Survey is self-reported, it is

TABLE 1
The Relation Between Criminal Behavior and Perception of Crime and Employment for Out of School Inner City Black Youths, 1979-80

Self-Reported Criminal Behavior: (number of respondents in parenthesis)		Proportion with Jobs Last Week
Commited Crime, last month	yes (273)	30
	no (1153)	46
Committed Crime, last year	yes (330)	33
	no (1096)	46
Earnings from Crime, last year	>$1000 (85)	20
	<$1000 (229)	38
Self-Reported Incarceration/Probation:		
Time in Jail in last year	yes (52)	17
	no (1374)	44
On Probation during last year	yes (124)	23
	no (1302)	45
Perception of Criminal Opportunities:		
How often respondent perceived a chance to make money illegally	daily (337)	36
	weekly (327)	44
	few (211)	46
	none (547)	45
Perception of Crime in Neighborhood:		
Respondent viewed crime and violence as serious problem in neighborhood	true (234)	40
	somewhat (229)	43
	false (146)	49

Source: Tabulated from NBER Inner City Survey

---

subject to reporting bias. Comparisons of self-reported crime with independent police records show, in fact, that underreporting is substantial among black youths,[8] with crime *understated* by 2 to 4 fold.[9] Assuming, as seems reasonable, that the youths who committed but failed to report crimes have lower employment rates than youths who did not commit crimes, the underreporting will significantly bias *downwards* the measured tradeoff between crime and employment. Assume, conservatively, an underreporting factor of 2, and assume further that youths who commit but do not report crimes had the same employment probability as youths who admitted committing crime. Then the true rate of employment for youths who did not commit crimes in table 1 would be 51% rather than 46%, increasing the tradeoff by five percentage points. If the underreporting rate were as large as 4 the gap would be understated by 10 points.[10] As the employment of youths who committed but did not report crimes may lie somewhere between that of youths who did not commit crimes and that of youths who reported crimes, these calculations probably overstate the impact of the self-reporting bias. However, they make clear that the true relation between crime and employment is likely to be larger than shown in the table.

Does the existence of a sizeable tradeoff between crime and employment hold up under econometric probing? To answer this question I have estimated the impact of measures of criminal behavior and perceptions of criminal opportunity on employment using multivariate regressions. While the statistical properties of my dependent variable (1 = employed in week; 0 = not employed) suggest that logit or probit functional forms would be preferable, I report linear probability results to simplify exposition. As the mean of the employment variable is around one-half, the linear form does not cause any serious problem.

The results of this analysis, summarized in table 2, show that the crime-employment trade-off is significant in the presence of diverse control variables, including city of residence, age, years of schooling, grades in school, residence in a housing project, and so forth. When crime in the past year is the only crime variable it reduces employment by 10 points (equation 1); with the inclusion of other behavior that may be crime-related (use of alcohol, marijuana and other drugs) its effect falls to 7 points. For reasons of self-reporting bias noted above, these estimates probably understate the impact of current crime on employment by perhaps five (or more) points. As for ex-offenders, those who spent time in jail in the past year had employment rates that were 13 points lower than other youths.

With respect to other variables, education had a significant positive effect on employment, as did attendance at church, while age tended to reduce employment. Measures of drinking, drugs, and marijuana (pot) usage, on the other hand, had no effect on employment. The effect of

TABLE 2
Regression Estimates of the Effect of Criminal Activity on Employment*

Dependent Variable: Work in Survey Week = 1(mean = .43)

	Equation 1		Equation 2	
constant	-.004		.028	
crime in year	-.099	(.029)	-.074	(.032)
years of schooling	.053	(.01)	.052	(.01)
grades in A-B range	.079	(.039)	.082	(.039)
grades in C range	.049	(.035)	.051	(.035)
age	-.013	(.006)	-.014	(.006)
mother worked when youth aged 14	.064	(.025)	.063	(.025)
resident in public housing (1=yes)	-.125	(.027)	-.126	(.027)
attends church (1=yes)	.07	(.025)	.066	(.025)
health status (1= impairs work)	-.128	(.059)	-.131	(.059)
married (1=yes)	.09	(.044)	.094	(.045)
household size	-.001	(.005)	-.001	(.005)
jail (1=time in jail in past year)	---		-.131	(.072)
probation (1=on probation in past yr)	---		-.041	(.049)
liquor (1=any use)	---		.016	(.029)
pot (1=any use)	---		-.014	(.028)
drugs (1=any use)	---		-.043	(.060)
Boston (1=resident)	.213	(.031)	.215	(.031)
Chicago (1=resident)	-.025	(.030)	-.024	(.030)

* Numbers in parenthesis are standard errors.

--- variable not included in the regression equation.

these variables on employment differs sharply from Viscusi's estimates of their impact on crime (he found that education was only weakly inversely related to crime, and that drinking, drugs, and pot were highly correlated with crime), supporting our claim that crime equations with employment as an explanatory factor and employment equations with crime as an explanatory variable are not mirror images.[11]

INTERPRETATION

Given the preceding estimates of the routes by which criminal activity is associated with lower employment, how substantial is the overall crime-employment tradeoff for inner city youths from poverty neighborhoods?

In part, the answer to these questions depend upon how much crime inner city youths commit and thus on the underreporting issue discussed earlier. If we take the self-reported figures in the NBER sample as valid, 20% of the out-of-school youths committed crimes; multiplying this figure by our minimal estimate of the impact of crime on employment (.07) yields a reduction in employment of 1.4 percentage points. More realistically, given the underreporting of crime, 40% of the youths might be expected to have committed crimes, and the effect of crime might be 12 points (.07 plus .05 for underreporting), yielding a likely employment effect of 4.8 percentage points.

What about the effects of time in jail, having a criminal record, and death by homicide? As we have already seen, 5% of black youths are institutionalized in a given year, reducing potential employment by 5 points. The effect of having a criminal record on employment depends on the fraction of the population with such records. If, because of turnover of the jail population, 15-20% of black youths have such a record by the time they are in their late-twenties,[12] the 13 point effect of jail on employment found in table 2 implies a further reduction in employment of some 2.0 to 2.6 percentage points. Finally, the homicide rate among inner city black youths can be expected to further reduce possible employment by one percentage point.

Adding together all of these effects (1.4 to 4.8 points from the impact of crime on current employment; 5 points for incapacitation in jail, 2 to 2.6 points for the ex-offender effect, 1 point for death by homicide) suggest that crime may be associated with a 9 to 13 percent reduction in the potential employment of black youths. In this summing up I use the words "potential employment" and "associated" rather than "employment" and "caused" because the estimates are not based on experimental data, and because differences among individuals need not translate into effects for an entire group. Moreover, for potential employment to become actual employment, jobs have to be available. Given these provisos, however, the figures indicate that inner-city black youth joblessness is intertwined with criminal behavior and thus suggest that increased criminal deterrence in inner cities has a role to play in any effort to resolve the black youth employment crisis.

NOTES

The author would like to acknowledge the assistance of Alida Castillo.

1. My estimate is obtained by taking the number of blacks in jail or prison in 1981-82 and multiplying it by the approximate proportion in the age group less than 30. The number in jail in 1982 was 78,385; the number in prison in 1981 was 168,129, according to U.S. Department of Justice (1984), tables 6.17 and 6.24. On the basis of figures on age of sentenced inmates from U.S. Department of Justice, *Profile of State Prison Inmates: Sociodemographic Findings from the 1974 Survey of Inmates of State Correctional Institutions*, (Washington, D.C.: Department of Justice, 1980), table 35, I estimate that 75% of black inmates were less than 30 years of age. Data on arrests by age from U.S. Department of Justice, *Sourcebook of Criminal Justice Statistics-1983*, (Washington, D.C.: Bureau of Justice Statistics, 1984), table 4.4 show a comparable proportion. I divide the number by the population of black men ages 18 to 29 from U.S. Department of Commerce, Bureau of the Census, *Statistical Abstract of the U.S.-1986* (Washington, D.C.: U.S. Government Printing Office, 1986), table 28: 2,998,000.

2. The specific figures are from the U.S. Bureau of the Census, *Census of the Population-1980*, U.S. Summary (PC80-D1-A) (Washington, D.C.: U.S. Government Printing Office, 1983), table 266. While not all institutionalized persons are in jail or prison, the vast majority are.

3. U.S. Department of Health, Education, and Welfare, *Vital Statistics of the United States, 1977*, volume B.

4. Estimated by assuming a rate of 100 per hundred thousand per year and cumulating for 10 years for youths and for 20 years to reach age 40.

5. See Richard Freeman, "Crime and Unemployment" in *Crime and Public Policy*, James Q. Wilson (Ed.) (San Francisco: ICS Press, 1983), pp. 89-106.

6. Freeman, Richard and Harry Holzer, *The Black Youth Joblessness Crisis* (Chicago: University of Chicago Press, 1984). Chapter 1 describes the survey and summarizes results of the study.

7. W. Kip. Viscusi, "Market Incentives for Criminal Behavior," chapter 8 in Freeman and Holzer, pp. 301-346, and W. Kip Viscusi "The Risks and Rewards of Criminal Activity: A Comprehensive Test of Criminal Deterrence" *Journal of Labor Economics* Vol. 4, No. 3, part 1 (July 1986) 317-340.

8. M.H. Hindelang, T. Hirsch, and J. Wies, *Measuring Delinquency* (Beverly Hills, Calif.: Sage, 1981).

9. See the two papers by Viscusi cited above for a detailed discussion of underreporting in the National Bureau survey.

10. Specifically, I estimate the "true" employment rate for youths who do not commit crimes by solving the equation: the observed rate for those who report no crime is the sum of the rate for those who committed but did not report crimes weighted by the

estimated proportion underreporting crime and the "true" rate for those who did not commit crimes weighted by proportion who truly did not commit crimes.

11. Viscusi in "Market Incentives" also finds a significant employment-crime trade-off in his analysis, so that whichever direction one looks in this data, one finds a crime-employment trade-off. Note, however, that Viscusi analyzes all youths, including those in school, while our sample is limited to out of school youths.

12. Approximately one-third of inmates in state prisons have no past sentence, implying a significantly larger group with criminal records than in jail at a point in time. See U.S. Department of Justice, *Profile of State Prison Inmates: Sociodemographic Findings from the 1974 Survey of Inmates of State Correctional Institutions*, Washington, 1974, table 32.

A SIMULTANEOUS PROBIT MODEL OF CRIME AND EMPLOYMENT FOR BLACK AND WHITE TEENAGE MALES

David H. Good and Maureen A. Pirog-Good

This study examines the relationships between the employability and criminality of white and black male teenagers. A disequilibrium model of employment and crime is formulated and estimated as a simultaneous probit equation system. Our results show that black teenagers who are employed engage in fewer criminal activities. Thus, it appears that blacks view employment and crime as alternative income-generating activities. On the other hand, the criminal behavior of white male teenagers is unaffected by their employment status. The evidence that we provide indicates that whites tend to use employment as a cover for crime or to moonlight in crime. The differences in the behaviors of whites and blacks can be explained, in part, by different legitimate opportunity structures for whites and blacks. One of the more important policy implications is that job opportunities targeted to high risk, black teenage populations will have the additional beneficial effect of reducing crime rates.

Racial differences in the labor experiences of white and black teenagers have been well documented. For example, the rate of unemployment among black youths exceeds fifty percent, more than double that of white youths. Moreover, black youth unemployment has been rising relative to white teenage unemployment rates.[1] Among teenagers sixteen and seventeen years of age, the lower labor market participation rates of blacks are primarily explained by a greater inability to find work, rather than job loss.[2] Two additional observations noted in the labor economics literature suggest structural differences in the employment relationships of white and black youths. First, white youths find employment at earlier ages than blacks.[3] Second, the inability of blacks to find work is only loosely related to the geographical proximity of places of employment.[4]

Racial disparities are also reported in the frequency of arrests of white and black teenagers. In 1983, arrests of black teenagers accounted for 54.7 and 28.6 percent of all violent and property offenses committed by juveniles, respectively. The impact of this observation becomes clear when one notes that only 14.9 percent of the U.S. population 14 to 17 years of age is black.[5] Additionally, the incarceration rate of black male teenagers is nearly seven times that of white teenagers.[6]

Although prolific, research on discrimination in arrests and judicial processing is inconclusive.[7] This literature lacks formal models of judicial processing, often ignores serious sample selection biases, and frequently employs arbitrary scales to combine qualitatively different court dispositions.[8] Two hypotheses have been forwarded in the literature to account for the higher arrest, prosecution, and incarceration rates of blacks: greater involvement of blacks in crime and criminal justice system selection biases. Regardless of the hypothesis one chooses to adopt, there is sufficient evidence to indicate that race is potentially interactive with official measures of criminal involvement.

This article focuses on the interrelationships between employment and crime. The limited empirical literature is critiqued in the following section. In the third section we describe our disequilibrium model of crime and employment. The methodological approach and estimation techniques are described in section four. The third and fourth sections follow the work of Good, Pirog-Good and Sickles,[9] which extends the earlier work on the economic model of crime by Becker.[10] The data are discussed, and results of simultaneous probit models for white and black teenage males are then given. The estimation of separate models for both races acknowledges the potentially interactive effect of race. In conclusion, we present our implications for policy formation.

PREVIOUS LITERATURE

Ultimately, policy-relevant research should be able to establish a *causal* relationship between employment and crime. Previous studies fall short of this objective either because of data limitations or because critical, albeit technical, econometric requirements are not satisfied. Considering first the data problems, most of the early research on employment and crime[11] inappropriately utilizes aggregate data to draw inferences about individual level behavior.[12] The recent and more methodologically sophisticated studies which use aggregate data[13] also leave questions of causality unresolved. Even if these aggregate data studies had achieved a consensus on the direction of the relationships of unemployment and crime rates, it would be impossible to determine whether crimes were committed by individuals who were employed, unemployed, or out of the labor force.

Several recent studies have used data on individuals, thus making a much more compelling case regarding causality. Even so, these studies have yet to demonstrate a consistent set of relationships between employment and crime.[14] This is due, in part, to the use of employment and crime data averaged over lengthy periods of time. This data reduction process eliminates the ability to determine whether offenses were committed while employed, unemployed, or out of the labor force. Again, the problem of aggregation tends to cloud issues of causality.

Moving now to consider the second problem, the satisfaction of critical, econometric requirements, we suggest that few individual level studies have adequately dealt with the interrelationships between crime and employment. Several authors who have utilized individual level data have estimated reduced form models.[15] While technically correct, these models do not provide estimates of the coefficients of the greatest interest, specifically the direct effects of employment on crime and crime on employment. More complex simultaneous equation systems require detailed data, estimation procedures which are technically difficult to implement, and a theoretical motivation for identification restrictions. As for the identification restrictions, the estimation of a simultaneous equation system requires one to identify at least one variable which affects crime but not employment and at least one more variable which affects employment but not crime. The identification restrictions selected determine, in large part, the estimated effects of the policy-relevant variables, employment and crime, on one another. Consequently, one must make a reasonable argument to justify the choice of these restrictions if the conclusions of the analysis are to have any credibility. The economic model of crime, phrased in general terms, provides no criteria for the selection of these variables. Prior to the theoretical extension of the economic model of crime provided by Good, Pirog-Good and Sickles,[16] exclusion restrictions were determined on a purely *ad hoc* basis.

Given the variety of circumstances in which researchers have attempted to establish causality, each with their own different set of problems, it is not surprising that the literature as a whole leads to widely varying and inconclusive policy implications. Analyses of adults, limited to ex-prisoners and ex-convicts, report mixed findings on the deterrent effect of employment and crime.[17] For juveniles, it appears that employment has a deterrent effect on crime and that more extensive criminal records reduce the probability of employment. That is to say, whether or not one is currently participating in criminal activities does not directly effect employability, rather it is one's cumulative record of delinquency that reduces the likelihood of employment.[18]

Also considering the difficulties of estimating employment and crime relationships with individual level data, it is understandable that only minimal attention has been given to the effects of race on these relationships. This remains so despite the fact that the economics, criminology, and sociology literatures frequently provide racial comparisons of labor market experiences and patterns of delinquency. Some limited, preliminary evidence indicates that racial differences in the employment and crime choices of youths are substantial.[19] This is not surprising, given that race influences the age at which legitimate opportunities become available,[20] the durations of employment and unemployment,[21] and the probabilities of arrest and conviction.[22]

THE THEORETICAL MODEL

Following Becker and Erlich,[23] we employ an economic model of crime where the joint employment/criminal/other activity decision is the result of individual expected utility maximization. Our work differs from the traditional approach in two major respects. The first difference is that our observability of employment and criminal activity is very limited. From a modeling perspective, corner solutions to the youth's maximization problem will be quite common. Further, criminal activity is subject to even more severe censoring since we observe only that an arrest has occurred over a given period of time rather than the actual hours spent in criminal activity. Both types of data limitations are the subject of the next section.

Our second major departure from the traditional approach taken in time allocation problems is a consequence of employing the economic model. Simple utility maximization leaves us with reduced form models to estimate. The traditional economic model does not motivate the exclusion restrictions necessary to identify a simultaneous system. A solution to this problem comes with the realization that merely wanting a job is no guarantee that such employment will be realized. As in our previous work,[24] our theoretical model (the subject of this section) employs a disequilibrium approach to modeling individual behavior.

In the typical model of crime, time is allocated to legal (employment,

H_{et}), illegal (criminal activity, H_{ct}) and other activities (including leisure, H_{ot}) at time period t. Along with several taste parameters, these three variables are components in an individual's utility function. The first order conditions are used to derive individual demand functions for the three activities. These are reduced form equations. In general, because the sum of three equations must always add up to the fixed time constraint, a variable which enters one equation must enter into at least one other equation. Motivating exclusion restrictions in this framework is bound to be a highly dubious venture.

We motivate our exclusion restrictions outside of the context of this traditional approach by allowing *ex ante* and *ex post* time allocations to differ. Let the *ex ante* time allocations to employment, crime, and other activities at the beginning of each time period be H^*_{et}, H^*_{ct}, and H^*_{ot} and the *ex post* levels to be H_{et}, H_{ct}, and H_{ot}. Assume, for the moment that a youth may plan to spend 10 hours in employment during a given week. However, if there is an excess supply of labor the youth may not have the opportunity to spend any time working. As a result of the deviation from his plan, part of the difference between H^*_{et} and H_{et}, may be spent in crime and so that:

$$H_{ct} = H^*_{ct} + p(H^*_{et} - H_{et}). \tag{1}$$

Hence, the *ex post* time allocation to employment now determines the *ex post* time allocation to crime. Moreover, if one's *ex ante* time allocation to employment exceeds the *ex post* realization, the individual may become disillusioned by the spell of unemployment or underemployment. In this case, p may exceed one as the disillusioned individual might reallocate leisure time and spend more than the difference, $H^*_{et} - H_{et}$, in crime. Negative values of p are clearly at odds with our notion of crime and employment activites as substitutes. Instead, it suggests complementarity. Moonlighting, is an example of one of many alternative theories consistent with this situation.

The same possibility exists for *ex ante* and *ex post* time allocations to criminal activities and thus:

$$H_{et} = H^*_{et} - s(H^*_{ct} - H_{ct}). \tag{2}$$

From equation (2), we see that the actual amount of time spent in employment is determined in part by the amount of time spent in crime. Thus feedbacks can occur between crime and employment, and variables which proxy the terms ($H_{et}^* - H_{et}$) and ($H_{ct}^* - H_{ct}$) provide identifying exclusion restrictions since, logically, these terms appear in only one equation. Arguments concerning what variables provide appropriate proxies for these terms follow.

First, search time in the legal labor market clearly should affect both employability and criminality since total time spent in the legal and illegal labor markets is constrained. However, the lack of success of search in the legal labor market should have an independent effect on employability as it acts as a wedge between desired and observed hours of work. We proxy this variable by the number of weeks since one's job rejection (TSLJR). Thus, we assume that the effect of TSLJR on criminality operates indirectly through employability.

Second, prior research on gangs has indicated that members may be pressured into participating in some crimes and sanctioned for others deemed inappropriate by gang leaders.[25] Given unanticipated pressure from gang members, a youth may participate in more or fewer criminal activities than planned at the beginning of the period and thus gang variables should affect criminality directly, and affect employability indirectly through changes in criminality. The two variables used to proxy gang affiliation in this study are whether or not the youth was referred to a delinquency prevention program because of a gang affiliation (RGANG) and the average number of conspirators in all previous arrest incidents (HELPERS). Also, if a variable affects the actual but not the subjective probability of apprehension, it would provide another exclusion restriction in the employment equation. During our study period, law enforcement activities were substantially stepped up. With imperfect information, the juveniles in our sample would be unlikely to immediately incorporate the effects of the special police enforcement, SPE, into their subject probabilities of apprehension. Thus, the gang affiliation variables and the special police enforcement dummy provide us with a set of exclusion restrictions which identify the employment equation. Because we are more concerned with the identification of the employment equation parameters than with efficiency losses resulting from possible redundancy, all three variables are included as identification restrictions.

THE METHODOLOGICAL APPROACH AND ESTIMATION TECHNIQUE

The model developed in the last section shows how the hours spent in criminal activity may be simultaneously related to the hours spent in employment. Unfortunately, we have no information on the number of hours worked (H_{et}) or spent in crime (H_{ct}), by the youth. Rather, we know only if the youths were employed and if they had a police contact. Consequently, we use a simultaneous probit model in our analysis to reflect this censoring of the data.[26] The latent variable interpretation we give to the endogenous variables is still completely consistent with the economic theory of crime discussed previously. Whether youth i incurs a police contact during time period t, C_{it}, is modeled as an indicator of the latent variable C_{it}^*; the propensity to be delinquent. Whether youth i was employed at time t, E_{it}, is modeled as the indicator of the youth's employability, E_{it}^*; which is the outcome of both supply and demand factors.

The simultaneous model is specified as

$$\begin{aligned} C_{it}^* &= \gamma_1 E_{it}^* + \underset{\sim}{\beta}_1 \underset{\sim}{X}_{1it} + e_{1it} \\ E_{it}^* &= \gamma_2 C_{it}^* + \underset{\sim}{\beta}_2 \underset{\sim}{X}_{2it} + e_{2it} \end{aligned} \qquad (3)$$

where the vectors $\underset{\sim}{X}_{1it}$ and $\underset{\sim}{X}_{2it}$ contain historical police contact and labor market variables, seasonal dummies, demographic and unemployment rate variables. A more detailed description of the components of $\underset{\sim}{X}_{1it}$ and $\underset{\sim}{X}_{2it}$ can be found in Table 1.[27]

This use of a simultaneous probit model is not without a price as we no longer can interpret the coefficient of employment on crime as the effect of an additional hour worked on the number of hours spent in illegal activity. Instead, we concentrate our attention on the significance of the relationship. The coefficients of the endogeneous variables still have the interpretation of the change in one's employability or criminality given a one standard deviation change in criminality or employability, respectively (i.e., very similar to the interpretation of a standardized regression coefficient).

We first obtained maximum likelihood estimates of the reduced form system. These were used to construct starting values for the structural equation system. The log likelihood function was maximized using the Davidon-Fletcher-Powell algorithm. Because our interest is in discussing the structural parameters, only these estimates are presented in Table 2.

THE DATA

The data for this analysis are based on 135 white and 87 black inner-city males who participated in a three year delinquency prevention demon-

TABLE 1
Variable Definitions

EMPTT:	A dummy variable equal to 1 if the individual was employed in the current 30 day interval. This is the indicator of EMPLOYABILITY.
PCECT:	A dummy variable equal to 1 if the individual had a police contact for an economically motivated crime in the current 30 day interval. This is the indicator of CRIMINALITY.
HELPERS:	The average number of conspirators in all previous police contacts.
SPE:	A dummy equal to 1 after a police crackdown on juvenile delinquents.
RGANG:	A dummy equal to 1 if referred to the crime prevention program because of gang affiliations.
TSLJR:	The number of weeks since one's last job rejection.
TPCE:	Total number of prior police contacts for economically motivated crimes.
TSLEPC:	The number of weeks since one's last police contact for an economically motivated crime.
RPOLICE:	A dummy equal to 1 if referred to the crime prevention program because of a police contact.
RJOB:	A dummy equal to 1 if referred to the crime prevention program because of job problems.
URATE:	The general, monthly unemployment rate of the Philadelphia SMSA.
AGE:	Age measured in years.
RSCHOOL:	A dummy equal to 1 if referred to the crime prevention program because of school problems.
RDRUG:	A dummy equal to 1 if referred to the crime prevention program because of drug problems.
RINCORR:	A dummy equal to 1 if referred to the crime prevention program because of incorrigibility.
SPRING:	A dummy equal to 1 if Spring.
SUMMER:	A dummy equal to 1 if Summer.
FALL:	A dummy equal to 1 if Fall.

TABLE 2
Results

	White Males		Black Males	
	Employability	Criminality	Employability	Criminality
EMPTT		- .01 (- .06)		- .46 (-2.45)
PCECT	.80 (18.36)		- .93 (-19.63)	
HELPERS		.05 (1.20)		.02 (1.62)
SPE		.39 (3.42)		- .05 (- .99)
RGANG		.27 (1.35)		.57 (1.48)
TSLJR	- .0025 (- 2.37)		- .0013 (- 2.22)	
TPCE	- .043 (- .91)	.050 (.82)	.036 (1.46)	.037 (1.58)
TSLEPC	.0015 (4.80)	- .0018 (- 5.13)	- .0015 (6.52)	- .0016 (-7.40)
RPOLICE	- .32 (- 1.64)	.20 (.73)	- .23 (- 1.59)	- .17 (-1.08)
RJOB	.11 (.43)	- .20 (- .60)	.20 (.04)	.15 (.33)
URATE	- .02 (- .21)	.06 (.50)	- .17 (- 1.80)	- .20 (-2.01)
AGE	.19 (4.31)	.04 (.63)	.06 (1.39)	- .00 (- .00)
RSCHOOL	- .20 (- 1.26)	.44 (1.98)	- .26 (- 1.76)	- .20 (-1.29)

TABLE 2 cont.

	White Males		Black Males	
	Employability	Criminality	Employability	Criminality
RDRUG	1.68 (4.54)	- 2.15 (- 4.05)	- .53 (- .97)	- .65 (-1.05)
RINCORR	.42 (1.88)	- .43 (- 1.35)	.35 (2.03)	.39 (2.15)
SPRING	.18 (.74)	- .17 (- .54)	- .36 (- 1.84)	- .43 (2.08)
SUMMER	- .02 (- .07)	.38 (1.39)	.43 (2.06)	.12 (.59)
FALL	- .16 (- .77)	.25 (.89)	.45 (2.61)	.39 (2.14)
Constant	- 1.65 (- 1.51)	- 3.11 (- 2.55)	- 1.22 (- 1.08)	.12 (.10)

*The numbers in parentheses are Z scores.

stration project funded by the Law Enforcement Assistance Agency. The 222 males used in this study comprise the entire population of male participants in this program. The demonstration project, located in Philadelphia, was monitored from January, 1975 to November, 1978. Arrest records, job search and employment histories, demographic and limited homelife variables are available for each youth.

The police records, collected at the end of the study, are cumulative from birth. These records permit us to calculate the dummy variable, PCECT, whether or not a police contact for an economically motivated crime occurred in the given 30 day period. This information is used for the dependent variable, employability. Additionally, we use the police records to calculate the number of prior police contacts for economically motivated crimes, TPEC, and the number of weeks since one's last police contact for an economically motivated crime, TSLEPC. Finally, these data were used to obtain a measure of gang affiliation, the average number of conspirators in all preceding arrests, HELPERS.

The employment and job search data cover the period of program participation and were sufficiently detailed to allow us to construct two variables. First, we determined if a youth was or was not employed during the 30 day time period, EMPTT. This provided the necessary information for the dependent variable, employability. Second, we obtain a measure of unsuccessful job search, the number of weeks since one's last job rejection, TSLJR. The smaller the value of this variable, the more recently an individual applied for work but did not obtain the position. Thus, TSLJR captures an unfulfilled desire to work.

Program records provided the birthdates of the youths from which ages of participants were calculated. Program records were also utilized to determine if the youth was referred to the program as a result of employment problems, (RJOB), police contacts, (RPOLICE), known gang affiliation, (RGANG), school difficulties, (RSCHOOL), drug addiction, (RDRUG), and/or incorrigibility (RINCORR). These variables not only measure the existence of different forms of behavioral deviance but are also used to control for the possibility that some types of individuals were treated differentially within the program, thus making some subgroups of program participants alter their behavior as a result of program participation. This possibility has been explored extensively in the three year evaluation of this project. Utilizing two control groups and a variety of outcome measures including self-esteem, arrest records, self-reported delinquency, offense severity, penetration into the juvenile justice system, and program satisfaction, no beneficial or deleterious program effects could be reported. The monthly unemployment rate for the Philadelphia SMSA and seasonal dummies were also included in all equations.

To avoid the ambiguity of interpretation resulting from the aggregation of data over time, these data are disaggregrated into 30 day observations. This disaggregation allows us to capture the cotemporaneous as well as historical relationships between employment and crime. The disaggregation resulted in 1,453 observations for white males and 1,283 for black males.

It must be noted that the higher likelihood of employment and lower likelihood of arrest for whites reported in national statistics are also present in this sample. Whites and blacks were employed in 27.1 and 17.4 percent of the monthly observations, respectively. In addition, blacks possess offense records which are more than twice as extensive as whites. The average number of police contacts for economically motivated crimes is 1.6 for blacks and .6 for whites.

DISCUSSION

Employability

The employability results for white and black males are given in Table 2. Turning first to the effects of criminal involvement on employability, we find that current criminality is a significant predictor of current employability for both white and black males. In addition, the magnitude of this effect is large for males of both races. However, the opposite signs of these coefficients reflect fundamentally different effects of current criminal involvement on the likelihood of employment for whites and blacks. Months in which black males are more criminally inclined are months in which their employability declines. This implies that black youths are either less likely to seek and/or accept work when they are more heavily involved in crime or are simply less likely to receive job offers. In stark contrast, white youths who are more criminally involved in a given month have higher probabilities of having procured employment.

The results for white males found in this study parallel those found by Phillips and Votey.[28] There are several plausible interpretations of the positive coefficient of CRIMINALITY. First, in conjunction with the evaluation of the demonstration project, we noticed a tendency on the part of judges to give more lenient sentences, provided that the youths could demonstrate that they had reformed. One of the more common methods of demonstrating reformation was by obtaining employment. If white youths have more social resources available to help procure employment under such adverse conditions, then the coefficient of CRIMINALITY in the EMPLOYABILITY equation would be positive. That is, employment would be obtained in the same 30 day interval as the police contact but after the police contact had occurred. An alternative explanation of the fact that white youths are likely to be employed when they are most criminally active is that employment is used as a cover for crime. Thus, white youths may reduce their perceived risks of apprehension by participating in crime more frequently when they are employed.

It is important to note that it is the *current* criminal involvement of white and black males that affects their *current* employability. The total number of prior police contacts for economically motivated crimes (TPCE) is insignificant in determining the criminality of white and black males. Hence, extensive police records do not reduce the likelihood of employment for white or black teenage males. This may be due, in large part, to the fact that juvenile records are confidential. Thus, unless a youth honestly reports his prior convictions on job applications, employers will be unaware of their prior criminal involvement.

The length of time since one's last police contact for an economically motivated crime (TSLEPC) is a significant determinant of the employability of both white and black males. However, the direction of the effect is quite different for whites and blacks. Our initial expectation was that more recent arrests would have a more deleterious effect on employability than arrests which occurred in the more distant past. While this is true for whites, the opposite appears to be true for blacks. Still, for both whites and blacks, the total effect of TSLEPC on employability (as manifested in the reduced form equations) is of the expected sign.

The overall pattern of our results suggests that for blacks, it is current participation in crime rather than past criminal involvement which more significantly impedes one's success in the legitimate labor market. Conversely, for whites, past criminal involvement significantly impedes success in the legal labor market. Further, for whites, current criminality suggests increased employability. This result is consistent with the notions of moonlighting or using employment as a cover for crime.

We focus next on the number of weeks since one's last job rejection (TSLJR), our measure of the unfulfilled desire to work. Recall that in our model, more recent job rejections imply that the current unfulfilled desire to work is large. This variable is negative and significant for both whites and blacks. The negative coefficient implies that those who have recently and unsuccessfully sought work have lower employability. This may well imply that within this high risk, delinquency-prone population of male teenagers, the discouraged worker effect is strong. After one or more job rejections, the youths quickly become disillusioned, drop out of the labor market, and therefore, reduce the probability of procuring employment. Moreover, it should be noted that the magnitude of this effect is three times greater for whites when compared to blacks.

With regards to age, a one year increase in age significantly improves the employability of white males. In contrast, the effect of age on the employability of blacks is insignificant. This is not surprising and is consistent with previous findings that job opportunities open up at age sixteen for white teenagers but are not nearly as available to black teenagers until age nineteen.[29] Given that youths age 18 and over are not included in our study, we would not expect to see a significant effect on the employability of blacks.

We turn now to the effects of seasonality and the unemployment rate on the employability of the youths. While not directly controllable by policy makers, these variables serve to indicate when both subgroups of the population are most likely to be employed. Looking first at seasonality, we find no significant effects for whites but large and significant effects for blacks. In comparison to the Winter months, black youths are more likely to be employed during the Summer and Fall and are less likely to be employed during the Spring. This may be the result of the greater participation of blacks in federally-funded summer job programs. Regarding the unemployment rate, we find that the effects of changes in this variable have small and insignificant effects on the employability of whites. By comparison, changes in the rate of unemployment have large, significant effects for blacks. Increases in the general unemployment rate create large decreases in the probability of employment for black, male teenagers. This is consistent with the very large swings in unemployment rates experienced by minority teenagers.

We conclude by discussing the effects of the various reasons for program referral on the employability of the youths. Recall that reasons for referring clients to this demonstration project included police contacts (RPOLICE), employment difficulties (RJOB), school problems (RSCHOOL), drug addiction (RDRUG) and incorrigibility (RICORR). Males of both races with family problems had higher levels of employability. Whites, but not blacks, with drug addictions were more likely to obtain employment. Blacks, but not whites, with behavior problems in school were less likely to be employed. These effects may be attributed to the differential treatment of these youths by program operators when it comes to assisting youths to find jobs.

Criminality

The criminality results for white and black teenage males are also given in Table 2. Our first and most important result for policy makers is that employment has a strong deterrent effect on crime for blacks but not whites. While employability is negatively related to the criminality of whites, the magnitude of the effect is close to zero and insignificant. Hence providing jobs to white, teenage males will not directly affect their criminal behavior. Blacks, however, appear to treat employment and crimes committed for economic gain as substitutes. Thus, providing black teenagers with jobs has the beneficial effect of reducing their criminality. The signs and significance of CRIMINALITY and EMPLOYABILITY imply a vicious circle for blacks in which lower employability increases their criminality which further lowers their employability, and so on. On the other hand, providing a job increases the employability of blacks which subsequently lowers their criminality, having the effect of further enhancing their employability.

Turning next to the effects of past criminal involvement on current criminality we find that the total number of prior arrests for economically motivated crimes (TPCE) does not significantly predict future occurrences of such crimes. It is the timing of past offenses (TSLEPC) rather than their absolute number that predicts current criminal behavior. The more recent an arrest, the greater the current criminal involvement of both whites and blacks. Moreover, the size of this effect is the same for teenage males of both races. This is consistent with the observation of Good, Pirog-Good and Sickles[30] that youths who remain crime-free for three years do not commit further offenses.

Special police enforcement (SPE) is a significant predictor of criminality for whites but not blacks. The large, positive coefficient of SPE indicates that this police crackdown on delinquency substantially increased the probability of arrests for white male teenagers. The fact that white teenagers alone were more likely to be arrested after the police crackdown strongly suggests that the increased enforcement took place largely in white neighborhoods. Thus, in some respects, SPE can be viewed as a measure of selective police productivity.

The seasons do not influence the criminality of white youths. In comparison to the Winter months the criminal behavior of black youths is lower in the Spring and greater in the Fall. While the coefficients of SUMMER for whites and blacks are positive, they are insignificant. This finding stands in contrast to the popular belief that offensivity increases over the Summer months when temperatures are high and school is out.

The rate of unemployment has a significant effect on the criminal involvement of blacks but not whites. When the rate of unemployment increases in this sample, blacks commit fewer economically-motivated crimes. Cantor and Land[31] have addressed the relationship between unemployment rates and criminal behavior. They posit that changes in unemployment rates have two opposing effects, an effect on criminal motivations and an effect on criminal opportunities. The latter effect, the one which appears to dominate for blacks implies that increases in unemployment reduce the victim proneness of potential crime targets. Thus, Cantor and Land view the unemployment rate as an index of *total system activity*, lower unemployment levels corresponding to lower rates of circulation of property and people, providing fewer criminal targets.

Different reasons for program referral are significant for whites and blacks. Whites referred to this program for school attendance and/or behavioral problems in school (RSCHOOL) are more likely to commit crimes for economic gain. Surprisingly, white youths referred to the program for the reason of drug abuse (RDRUG) are less likely to commit economically-motivated crimes when compared to youths who were not referred to the program because of drug involvement. Finally, black male teens who entered this program because of family problems (RFAMILY) were more likely to commit economically-motivated crimes.

POLICY IMPLICATIONS

The reciprocity of unemployment and crime for blacks in conjunction with the rest of our results has several policy relevant implications. First, providing black teenagers with jobs benefits the most disadvantaged demographic group in the labor market. Second, money spent on jobs for black teens will lower the offensivity of these youths. Hence, third, some and perhaps all of the dollars spent on the provision of jobs will be saved in lower costs incurred by the juvenile justice system and society at large. Thus, it would be unfortunate to see beneficial youth employment programs even further reduced as a result of pressures to eliminate budget deficits.

Let us further elaborate on the notion of providing jobs to teenagers. Our results indicate that if crime reduction is an important objective of these programs, they should be targeted specifically to black teenagers. Employment does not reduce the criminal behavior of whites. In fact, white male teenagers are slightly more criminally involved when employed, suggesting that they view employment as a cover for crime and/or moonlight in crime. While targeting jobs for black teenagers may not be politically popular and may be subject to charges of reverse discrimination, such targeting will direct social resources in a way which most benefits society.

Our results do not discriminate between different types of jobs or job programs. In fact, our sample included a fairly representative mix of jobs in both the public sector and private sector, and jobs obtained both with and without the assistance of the youth center.

Our results should not, however, be interpreted as supporting programs which enhance employability through job training, improved work habits, remedial education, etc. These types of programs are likely to have mixed effects on the participants. While they *may* increase the employability of youths, they also increase the expectations and aspirations of those youths. If these increased expectations are realized through explicit employment then these individuals should be less likely to commit offenses. On the other hand, if the increased expectations are not met, our results suggest that this increased departure between desired and actual employment will lead to increased criminality for blacks. That is, the real worth of these programs is limited by the extent that real jobs are available at the end of training.

Finally, if one is to target job programs to high-risk, delinquency-prone black teenagers, then our results suggest that the public employment program be counter-cyclically funded. A counter-cyclically-funded job program would partially offset the dramatic decrease in the probability of employment for black youths which occurs in recessionary periods. This is particularly pertinent as this is translated into increased criminal behavior.

NOTES

The authors would like to thank Llad Phillips and Jack Votey for helpful suggestions on an earlier draft.

1. U.S. Bureau of Labor Statistics, *Handbook of Labor Statistics* (Bulletin 2217, U.S. Government Printing Office, Washington, D.C., 1985).
2. See Kim B. Clark and Lawrence Summers, "The Dynamics of Youth Unemployment" in *The Youth Labor Market Problem: Its Nature, Causes, and Consequences,* Richard B. Freeman and David Wise, editors, (Chicago: University of Chicago Press, 1986). Also Peter Jackson and Edward Montgomery. "Layoffs, Discharges and Youth Unemployment," in *The Black Youth Employment Crisis,* Richard B. Freeman and Harry J. Holzer, editors. (Chicago: The University of Chicago Press, 1986).
3. Mercer L. Sullivan, *New York Affairs* (NYU Urban Research Center, N.Y., New York, 1983); Michelle Sviridoff and James L. Thompson, "Links Between Employment and Crime: A Qualitative Study of Rikers Island Releases," *Crime and Delinquency* 29 (April 1983), pp. 195-212.
4. David T. Ellwood, "The Spatial Mismatch Hypotheses: Are There Teenage Jobs Missing in the Ghetto?" in *The Black Youth Employment Crisis,* Richard B. Freeman and Harry J. Holzer, editors. (Chicago: The University of Chicago Press, 1986).
5. Timothy J. Flanagan and Edmund F. McGarrell, *Sourcebook of Criminal Justice Statistics* (U.S. Government Printing Office, Washington, D.C., 1985), pp. 484.
6. Alfred Blumstein, "The Impact of Changes in Sentencing Policy on Prison Populations," in *Research on Sentencing,* Alfred Blumstein ed. (Washington, D.C.: National Academy Press, 1983), pp. 460-489.
7. Dall Dannefer and R.D. Schutt, "Race and Juvenile Processing in Court and Police Agencies," *American Journal of Sociology* Vol. 87, No. 5 (1982), pp. 1113-32; G. Kleck, "Racial Discrimination in Criminal Sentencing: A Critical Evaluation of the Evidence with Additional Evidence on the Death Penalty." *American Sociological Review* 46 (December 1981), pp. 783-805; M. Farnworth and P.M. Horan, "Separate Justice: An Analysis of Race Differences in Court Processes," *Social Science Research* 9 (1980), pp. 381-99; M.J. Hindelang, "Race and Involvement in Common Law Personal Crimes," *American Sociological Review* 43 (1978), pp. 93-109.

8. S. Kepper, D. Nagin and L. Tierney, *Research on Sentencing* (National Academy Press, Washington, D.C., 1983); John Hagan and Marjorie S. Zatz, "Crime, Time and Punishment: An Exploration of Selection Bias in Sentencing Research," *Journal of Quantitative Criminology* Vol. 1, No. 1, (1985), pp. 103-26.

9. David H. Good and Maureen A. Pirog-Good, "Employment, Crime and Race," *Contemporary Policy Issues* Vol. 5, (July 1987), pp. 91-104. David H. Good, Maureen A. Pirog-Good and Robin C. Sickles, "An Analysis of Youth Crime and Employment Patterns, 1986," *Journal of Quantitative Criminology* 2 (September 1986), pp. 219-236.

10. Gary Becker, "Crime and Punishment: An Economic Approach," *Journal of Political Economy* 76 (March-April 1968), pp. 169-217.

11. D. Bogen, "Juvenile Delinquency and Economic Trends, 1944," *American Sociological Review* 9 (April 1944), pp. 178-84; Llad Phillips, Donald Maxwell and Harold Votey, "Crime, Youth and the Labor Market," *Journal of Political Economy* 80 (June 1972), pp. 491-504; Daniel Glaser and Kent Rice, "Crime, Age, and Unemployment," *American Sociological Review* 24 (October 1959), pp. 679-86; Belton Fleisher, *The Economics of Delinquency* (Chicago: Quadrangle Books, 1966); Belton Fleisher, "The Effect of Income on Delinquency," *American Economic Review* 56 (March 1966), pp. 118-37; Larry D. Singell, "An Examination of the Empirical Relationship Between Unemployment and Juvenile Delinquency," *The American Journal of Economics and Sociology* 26 (October 1967), pp. 377-86; John C. Weicher, "The Effect of Income on Delinquency: Comment," *American Economic Review* Vol. 61, No. 1 (1970), pp. 249-56.

12. Peter Schmidt and Anne Witte, *An Economic Analysis of Crime and Justice* (New York: Academic Press, Inc., 1984); Richard B. Freeman, "Crime and Unemployment," in *Crime and Public Policy*, James Q. Wilson, ed., (California: ICS Press, San Francisco, California, 1983), pp. 89-106.

13. David Cantor and Kenneth C. Land, "Unemployment and Crime Rates in the Post-World War II United States: A Theoretical and Empirical Analysis," *American Sociological Review* 50 (June 1985), pp. 317-32; Michael Massourakis, Farahmond Rezvani and Todashi Yamada, "Occupation, Race, Unemployment and Crime in a Dynamic System," National Bureau of Economic Research Working Paper No. 1256, 1984, 17 pp.

14. R.L. Christenson and Terence P. Thornberry, "Unemployment and Criminal Involvement: An Investigation of Reciprocal Causal Structures," *American Sociological Review* 49 (June 1984), pp. 398-411; Schmidt, op. cit.; Samuel L. Myers, "Race Differences in Post-Prison Employment," *Social Science Quarterly* 64 (September 1983) pp. 655-69; Anne Witte, "Estimating the Economic Model of Crime with Individual Level Data," *Quarterly Journal of Economics* 94 (February 1980), pp. 57-84.

15. Maureen A. Pirog-Good, "Modeling Employment and Crime Relationships," *Social Science Quarterly* 67 (December 1986), pp. 767-784; Samuel L. Myers, "Employment and Crime: An Issue of Race?," *The Urban League Review* 6, (Fall 1981), pp. 9-24; Witte, op. cit.

16. Good, et al., op. cit.

17. Witte, op. cit.; Sviridoff, et al., op. cit.; Harold Holtzman, "The Serious Habitual Property Offender as 'Moonlighter': An Empirical Study of Labor Force Participation Among Robbers and Burglars," *Journal of Criminal Law and Criminology* 73 (1983), pp. 1774-92; Myers, 1983, op. cit.

18. Good, et al., op. cit.; Christenson and Thornberry, op. cit.

19. Pirog-Good, op. cit.

20. Mercer L. Sullivan, *New York Affairs* (New York: NYU Urban Research Center, N.Y., New York, 1983).

21. Peter Jackson and Edward Montogomery, "Layoffs, Discharges and Youth Un-

employment," *The Youth Labor Market Problem: In Its Nature, Causes, and Consequences*, (Chicago: University of Chicago Press, 1986).

22. Flanagan, et al., op. cit.

23. Becker, op. cit.; Isaac Ehrlich, "Participation in Illegitimate Activities: A Theoretical and Empirical Investigation," *Journal of Political Economy* 81 (May-June 1973), pp. 521-65.

24. Good and Pirog-Good, 1987, op. cit.; Good, et al., 1986, op. cit.

25. Sullivan, op. cit.

26. T. Amemiya, "The Estimation of Simultaneous Equation Generalized Probit Models," *Econometrica* 46 (1978), pp. 193-205; J. Heckman, "Dummy Endogenous Variables in a Simultaneous Equation System," *Econometrica* 46 (1978), pp. 931-959.

27. For more detailed information on econometrics of this model, see Good, et al., 1986, op. cit.

28. See, Llad Philips and Harold J. Votey, "Rational Choice Models of Crime by Youth" in this volume.

29. Sullivan, op. cit.

30. Good, et al., op. cit.

31. David Cantor and Kenneth C. Land, "Unemployment and Crime Rates in the Post-World War II United States: A Theoretical and Empirical Analysis," *American Sociological Review* 50 (June 1985), pp. 317-32.

RATIONAL CHOICE MODELS OF CRIMES BY YOUTH

Llad Phillips and Harold L. Votey, Jr.

This article presents research findings from three analyses of criminal activity among youth. The data set used in all three is the National Longitudinal Survey of Young Americans, a data set that is particularly appropriate for this type of analysis. The work examined the relationship between criminal behavior and family and moral influences; the impact of legitimate labor market activity on participation in crime; and the effect of school enrollment on criminal activity. The findings confirm the hypothesis that black and white differences in criminal participation partially reflect differences in economic opportunity.

OBJECTIVES AND APPROACH

The three sections of this article represent an effort by the authors to make use of a highly detailed data set to broaden understanding of why youth are involved in crime. The work represents an exercise in applying choice theory to the evaluation of behavior by youth. The three analyses, collectively, constitute testing of the general hypothesis that crimes for income are a consequence of a rational choice process that considers the alternatives available to youth, i.e., the constraints to their choice set, their previous experience, and individual characteristics that may reflect constraints that are not directly measurable or tastes that lead to variations in the way individuals value their alternatives.

Precursors to this research include an early Phillips, Votey, and Maxwell study that used aggregate data,[1] testing the hypothesis that crimes for income could be explained by the lack of legitimate labor market opportunities, and our more recent work that provides the impetus for a renewed look at the same hypothesis after a dynamic study of the impact of prior contacts by the police on individual young offenders and their choice to continue to be involved with crime or to desist from further crime participation.[2] Both studies had dissaggregated the analysis to focus separately on blacks and whites. Both found great similarity in behavior between blacks and whites, but significant differences in degree. The latter study, using individual data, finds highly significant results regarding the deterrent effect of early police interventions and of the effect of alternative income sources on involvement in crime. However, the proportion of explained variance is less than we would desire.

This set of three studies begins with two kinds of efforts, conducted in parallel, to improve on the explanations provided by the earlier research. One is to seek broader explanations for observed criminal behavior, while keeping the analysis within the context of individual choice. The influences of one's upbringing, as reflected by data on family characteristics, are taken into account. A beginning is made in examining patterns by age in this context. The basic hypothesis tested is that family and moral influences condition a young person's choices with respect to participation in crimes. Following extensive investigation of an exploratory nature to discover appropriate measures of family and moral influence on the choice process, the hypothesis that moral compliance affects the decision to be involved in crime is tested in a framework that takes account of both deterrence measures and the effects of alternative income sources that had previously been found to influence the choice.

The second effort is to strengthen the theoretical basis both for the relations to be tested and the econometric techniques used in testing, by resorting to the literature and investigative techniques of labor economics. We had been concerned for a considerable period of time about the simultaneity of relationships at the aggregate level in regard to choice and crime control. Earlier work had focused on the interaction between control forces and the choice to commit crime. This article is a first cut at taking into account, at the individual level, the joint decision to participate in crime and in the legitimate labor market. Attention is also given to the role of school enrollment and educational attainment in the choice to work. Econometric modeling is carefully worked out in a sequential process that moves from simple to more complex formulations, using alternative estimation techniques to guarantee the soundness of the results in establishing the thresholds at which youth choose to be involved in legitimate work.

The results of the first two sections of this work were originally presented as separate papers at the Western Economic Association International Meetings in July 1986, held in San Francisco, the first by Harold Votey, the second by Llad Phillips.

In the third section, findings of the first two sections are taken into account in an attempt to bring together into a single framework a broadened approach to estimation and hypothesis testing. The modeling advances from the techniques of the second section, modeling an expanded choice process that does not require legitimate work and crime to be mutually exclusive activities. School enrollment continues to play an important role, along with work experience and the availability of work. The role of family influences and moral compliance is formally integrated into the labor market choice model at this stage. Particular attention is given to appropriate econometric methods to guarantee the integrity of the results. That research was presented by Harold Votey at the American Economic Association Annual Meetings, December 1986, at New Orleans. Llad Phillips served as a discussant of the other papers of the session.

Our three analyses begin with the presumption that race, *per se* is not a variable that explains crime. Rather, crime is presumed to be explained by individual characteristics and environmental conditions, some of which may be due to a wide variety of factors that affect tastes and constrain choices. In estimating within such a framework this presumption can, in fact, be tested as a hypothesis. This is done, for example, in a two-stage process using predetermined variables that depend on race in the first stages of the analysis and then by incorporating race (black or white) as a variable at the last stage of the analysis to reveal whether the model has explained crime without the crutch of resorting to race as a variable.

We believe that another point can be made about the approach that is being followed in our continuing research, including that which has preceded the studies presented here and work that is continuing. It relates to the often repeated quote attributed to James Duesenberry that economics is all about how people make choices, while sociology is about how people don't have any choices to make. The reason people don't have any choices to make is presumably because of the constraints they face. We would argue that, if econometric studies are properly designed and conducted, the presumed criticism of work by economists is not a valid one. Properly specified estimates effectively take the constraints individuals face into account, thus incorporating what both sociologists and economists have to say about involvement in crime into the estimation process. This is the direction, at least, that we are attempting to pursue.

The data for these three analyses is from the National Longitudinal

Survey of Young Americans (NLS). These data follow 12,686 individuals over the years 1979 through 1984. The data are balanced evenly by sex but represent an oversampling of individuals who might be expected to face a more limited range of economic opportunities. As a consequence, in a carefully detailed manner, poorer whites, blacks, and Hispanics are over-represented. Blacks comprise roughly 25 percent of the population. The individuals were between the ages of 14 and 21 in 1979.

A broad range of questions is covered in the interviews, involving family background and characteristics, marital status, educational experience, civilian work and military experience, attitudes in different environments, expectations, and tastes in regard to the individuals' current situations. In one year, 1980, a very detailed list of questions was asked regarding participation in crime, and involvement with the police and courts, including detailed retrospective information regarding any contacts with the authorities. Questions were repeated in such a manner as to check for inconsistencies.

These data are ideal for the study we have been conducting because they do not simply represent a choice-based sample of individuals involved with crime, but a sample that includes true innocents, experimenters with crime, and persons with fairly lengthy records who persist in crime, as well as those who appear to have experimented with crime but now desist. Thus, the entire range of possible outcomes among participation in leisure, education, work, and crime is represented among this group of youth who are in the process is preparing for and making career decisions.

If there is a bias in our approach with respect to this volume, it is in the determination that the purpose of our research has not been to investigate differences between whites and blacks but rather to explain why youth are involved in crime. The bias may be that we believe that much of the behavior we are evaluating can be explained by economic and social forces. This is not to argue that blacks and whites face the same level of impacts from these forces, but rather that if all of these forces are taken into account properly, then black/white differences with respect to criminality should disappear. This position, of course, yields a set of hypotheses, and our research is a continuing attempt to conduct tests regarding them.

I. THE SELF SORTING PROCESS OF CHOOSING A CRIMINAL VERSUS A LEGAL CAREER: AN ECONOMIC ANALYSIS

Introduction

This section of the article relies on a decision theory framework to analyze the process of choice between criminal and legitimate earning activities. It assumes that individuals differ in their experience among legal and illegal alternatives, they differ in their degree of need for income, they come from different backgrounds, and they reside in differing environments. We presume that these individuals attempt to achieve the most desirable of alternatives available to them, but they may suffer from inadequate information about their range of choices. Relatively little market information is available for much of their decisionmaking, thus relative values of options will be subjective and may differ among individuals for identical opportunities. We model this process and test the resulting formulations on the extensive and unusually complete NLS data set that was designed to provide much of the appropriate information.

The resulting empirical evidence makes intuitive sense and tends to bring together divergent views of how young people respond to opportunities to be involved with crime and to face control efforts by the authorities.

Background

There has been an ongoing debate among economists, sociologists and criminologists regarding the causes of crime including whether deterrence is an effective force for its control. Almost all of these efforts have been to establish the "economic model" (in which economic factors such as lack of economic opportunities and potential costs imposed on criminals are major factors influencing crime levels) or, alternatively, to satisfy the hypothesis that some model excluding these effects is a superior predictor of crime. Those who object to the economic model argue (1) that individuals faced with opportunities to commit crime respond to influences other than economic ones, perhaps ones that relate to moral convictions, (2) that deterrence must fail as a concept simply because surveys have shown that individuals have little knowledge of true probabilities of apprehension, and/or that the true extent of sanctions they can expect if they are apprehended as criminals are not well known, or (3) simply that crime is not rational behavior and models presuming rationality cannot be expected to predict crime satisfactorily.

The research reported here suggests that there may be a way to reconcile some of these concerns, while accepting the notion that there is a logical decision process determining crime that is essentially consistent with the early views of the utilitarians from whom modern decision theory, as used by economists, has descended and from which the classical criminological theory has been derived.

The problem is one of beginning with an internally consistent theory and then contriving to find reasonable ways to test its implications. As with much theorizing about criminal behavior, the variables one might want to observe are not easily obtained, but there are ways to overcome some of the worst difficulties.

Decision Making Under Uncertainty

The argument begins with the very straightforward assumption that individuals are optimizers when they are able to be, that is they are rational and will pick the best among their alternatives to the extent that "best" can be determined. Individuals face uncertainties and have vague and imperfect notions of true probabilities. Nonetheless, they do their best to pick the best expected outcomes. In the jargon of economics, we say the individual will maximize his expected utility.

When we attempt to apply such an objective to criminal behavior, in theory, the choice among crime and legitimate activities is clear. The individual will choose the activity or combination of activities with the greater expected utility. Were we to examine a distribution of essentially identical individuals facing differing environments and opportunities that affect utility levels, we would expect all those would be crime free for whom

$$\text{EU(Legal Activity)} > \text{EU(Crime)}. \tag{1}$$

There would be a threshold at which behavior would convert from legal to illegal or some portion of it would be illegal.

We can postulate, from the utility functions, what the precise level of the threshold would look like

$$\frac{\text{EU(Legal Activity)}}{\text{EU(Crime)}} = \frac{B(x_1 \ldots x_n)}{C(y_1 \ldots y_n)} \tag{2}$$

expressed in marginal terms, in which, in theory, there are quantifiable marginal benefits B(x) and costs C(y) associated with the choice. The difficulty in moving from such a reasonable beginning to anything operationally useful in validating such a conceptual process is that marginal benefits and costs are highly subjective, perhaps unmeasurable. Nonetheless, it is useful to consider what some of the relevant influences might be.

The economic model of crime suggests that benefits of crime will be the return or take, relative to the value of legitimate income possibilities. Costs would be legitimate income foregone plus expected costs of apprehension. The expectation of any of these will depend on how an individual obtains his notions of the likelihood that, should he commit a crime, he will be apprehended. This is likely to be strongly related to his knowledge of his or his peers' previous experience with authorities. Costs of apprehension would be the product of the subjective probabilities of apprehension times the perceived value of all the costs associated with it: loss of freedom, loss of legitimate income, the chance of disgracing one's self, family, or friends. Expected foregone income would be affected by the expectation that legitimate work is available. The individual may have the notion of some survival constraint, i.e., some level of income needed to live, below which desperate measures might be resorted to. All of these are highly subjective factors that the rational individual will consider, imperfectly perhaps, before choosing to commit some act that has serious long-range implications for his future. Both economists' notions of costs and benefits and sociologists' notions of moral constraints are incorporated into this loosely specified model, as are the effects of apprehensions, depending on subjective notions of the individual. The question is not whether these elements are legitimate in an economic model. In theory, each of these elements has some psychic value. The issue is what the relative weights are—and whether there is any practical way to find out.

In theoretical analyses it is common to assume that tastes are given and consumers are identical, hence the relevant variables in consumption are all price variables. This is not to say economists are unwilling to believe populations of individuals are not homogeneous with respect to tastes. Rather, for many kinds of decisions, e.g., those regarding commodities in well-established markets, such concerns have been revealed to be relatively unimportant in determining market behavior, and hence can be ignored.

What we believe is needed to understand choices that may involve crime is that the choice is more complex than one in which the homogeneity assumption is good enough. We can argue that every person has his price, in order to preserve the analytical or decision theory framework. In fact, we must do so in order to regard the process as a rational one. If one abandons the notion of rationality, a meaningful predictive theory about criminal behavior becomes impossibly elusive.

If we accept this approach, we are not in conflict with notions of many sociologists and criminologists who believe individuals make choices based on analytical decisions. Many differences among disciplines border on being semantic rather than substantive. People do have thresholds beyond which certain behaviors become acceptable. That economists regard this threshold as being represented by some shadow price is an analytical convenience that fits in well with their theory. If one is a statistician, the need is to be able to quantify the point at which the threshold is reached.

To formally integrate such thoughts into a model of behavior based on maximization of expected utility, the concept of indirect utility functions becomes useful. We can believe individuals consume commodities or a stream of services from acquired commodities, but we can consider all those influences on satisfaction from those streams of services. We can continue to handle uncertainty in terms of the probabilities of events taking place that yield these streams of "services." With a non-homogeneous population of "consumers," however, those services may not yield identical responses across consumers. If, however, we can distinguish among classes of consumers, normal concepts of utility maximization remain valid with shifts of utility associated with shifts among groups of consumers with different characteristics. In effect, what is required is for the arguments in the utility function to be indexed by the characteristics that represent unique differences among the consuming population.

Since all of the relevant factors, even those that are easily measurable, depend for their influence, on how each individual values them, we can think of the choice to commit crime as one of determining a threshold that is based on perceptions associated with an extensive array of individual characteristics (x_i) or information (y_i) that relates to subjective utility, i.e.,

$$EU = u(x_{ij}, y_{ik}), \quad (3)$$

where i = 1, . . n individuals
j = 1, . . m characteristics
k = 1, . . r information measures

The expected utility of legal employment can then be represented by a kind of indirect utility function that relates to some subset of the x_{ij} and y_{ik}, and the same will be true of the expected utility of crime. Each individual is likely to have his own threshold at which he will undertake illegal activity. It may depend primarily on moral considerations. It may depend only on purely economic factors such as income or the lack of it, and it may involve perceived costs of apprehension. Most likely, all of these will play a role, but not the same role for everyone.

We can speculate on what influences the subjective valuations that control individual behavior. This might be translated into a probability model by which an individual selected at random will indulge in crime.

```
P(Crime) = f(legitimate income, family influences, peer
             influences, subjective probability of arrest,
             expected punishment if caught,...).
```

This is a step in the right direction, but hardly implementable as yet. The test of what really matters depends on having some notion of what to expect and of what measures one might use to find out.

An important concern, if results are to be socially useful, should be to separate casual or experimental behavior from major decisions. Any individual who is making a career decision will try a number of activities regarding which he may not be too serious or too committed to continue. For example, he may be involved in short-term jobs to learn about related opportunities or short-term jobs may be only for the purpose of tagging along with a friend or filling time. Every short term experience need not have weighty long-term implications. Similarly, an individual may experiment with theft or shoplifting. He may have no intention of doing so for more than a lark—or he may be curious about how easy it is and whether it really is worth the effort. What we really want to know is what influences most individuals to avoid crime for most of their lives and for smaller numbers to become committed to it for as long.

Related Current Research

It can be observed that individuals do sort themselves into what Blumstein, et al. have called "innocents, desisters, and persisters."[3] Their analysis suggests that the sorting process takes place at an early age—perhaps 10 to 12 years of age. More recent work of our own suggests that the sorting process continues through adolescence into young adulthood.[4] Over this life cycle, the population of innocents suffers some attrition, but relatively little. A group of desisters emerges who end up crime-free, while the persister population grows and remains in force over much of the life cycle. The Blumstein et al. analysis suggests that the individual's environment and experience with the law are major influences. Ours suggests that the turning point, i.e., the switch from experimentation to crime or to desister depends, in part, on exposure to the law and economic opportunities.

Both the work by Blumstein, et al. and by ourselves suggest that which subset the individual sorts himself into depends upon an extensive set of individual characteristics that relate to attitudes, experience, and the environment in which he lives. Our objective is to make use of that knowledge to test a model in which moral attitudes toward illegal behavior affect the subjective benefit/cost calculus of the individual who weighs alternatives in the process of a career decision.

In our model of behavior, the individual is perceived as establishing whether or not he is willing to even experiment with crime, based on the intensity of moral convictions. That is, we will first be examining our sample population to characterize the innocents as to how they differ from those who experiment with crime. Those who are indifferent between experimenting with crime and remaining innocents are then examined to determine the factors that influence the choice between becoming desisters and persisters. We will be checking to see whether those factors that tend to influence individuals into remaining innocents still play some role in reversing the possible path toward persistent criminal behavior.

Modeling the Decision Process

There is a certain logic in viewing the outcome as deriving from a multi-stage decision process, but a compelling one in our case has simply to do with the nature of the statistical problem. While it might be most satisfying to consider the entire population with a single statistical procedure to determine which factors influence sorting into which outcomes, there is a difficulty with investigating the impact of specific deterrence.

Before considering the ways one might investigate a hypothesis of specific deterrence it needs to be made clear that general deterrence is not a matter we can investigate with the data at our disposal. To do so would require knowing how the perceived probability of apprehension varies among the individuals in our sample and, perhaps to take into account other relevant information, e.g., how the objective probability of apprehension varies among the various communities from which our sample is derived. The latter information is simply not available to us nor do we have any information for persons never in contact with the law as an index of their subjective probabilities of apprehension.

What we do have is retrospective information from those stopped by the police for other than minor traffic violations but not charged. We have this information for the "previous twelve months" and "ever." From this, we can calculate the number of stops by the police prior to the year for which we have detailed self-reported offense information. Our hypothesis is that an individual's subjective probability of apprehension is a function of his previous experience with the police that can be proxied by the number of prior contacts. Furthermore, we hypothesize that there is a learning process such that one or two contacts will be inclined to cause some who experiment with crime to revert to the class of desisters, having learned the unpleasantness associated with being apprehended by the police. These behavioral assumptions are consistent with earlier work on drunken driving with Swedish data by Shapiro and Votey,[5] as well as the more recent work by ourselves.[6]

Having detailed, retrospective, information on previous contacts with police allows us to determine how those who have had such contacts will behave as a consequence. It is inappropriate, however, to compare these data with a general model to determine the effect of stops by police on the entire sample including innocents. Since innocents, by definition, have had no involvement with crime or stops by police, examining the relationship between police stops for the approximately 20 percent of the population that have some, and crime for all of the population will be bound to show a positive relationship between offenses and stops by the police. For this reason, it makes sense to investigate the hypothesis of a learning effect on a population limited to those who might have reason to respond to the effect.

The population we have at our disposal can be partitioned readily into four rather than three subsets. There is a group who neither committed a crime for income or goods in 1979 nor have ever been stopped by the police for previous offenses. These we have categorized as the "innocents" of the Blumstein, et al. analysis. Additionally, we have a group who have admitted to some crime but have never been apprehended by the authorities. We refer to these as experimenters. We do not know whether they will go on to a career of crime or will reach a decision, with or without police contact, to desist from further crime. Then there is the population of "desisters." These individuals report no offenses in 1979 but acknowledge previous contact with the police. Finally, there is a population of "persisters," who were involved with crime in 1979 and who admit to some or even many prior contacts with the police. It is this group who most clearly seem to have made a choice of criminal careers, in contrast to the "desisters" who may have learned from unpleasant contact with the

TABLE 1
Cross Tabulation of Crimes for Income and Prior Stops by the Police

ECRIM(1979)	NEVER STOPPED	PRIORST = TSTPEVER - TSTPLYR 0	1	2	3+	TOTALS
"Innocents" 0	5972	0	0	0	0	5972
"Desisters" 0	0	304	230	117	148	797
"Experimenters" 1	3328	0	0	0	0	3328
"Persisters" 1	0	475	301	175	327	1278
TOTALS	9300	779	531	292	473	11,375

(Cases in which interviews were incomplete regarding these questions [431] or respondents refused to answer [263] and non-interviews in 1980 [545] have been excluded.)

law, and the "innocents," for whom crime has not seemed to be an acceptable option.

The distribution among these categories for our sample is displayed in Table 1. A surprisingly large number of individuals have been involved in one or more criminal acts. The sum of experimenters, desisters, and persisters comes to 5,403 out of a sample population of 11,375 who responded to all of the questions regarding offenses and stops by the police. The difference between this latter sum and the 12,686 individuals in the original survey year includes 545 who were not interviewed in 1980, the first year crime was discussed, another 431 who were not asked relevant crime questions, and 263 who refused to respond to one or more questions about crime. If we regard the relevant sample population as the 12,141 who were contacted in 1980 about involvement in crime, it seems likely that the truest figure for participation exceeds the 5,403 who admit to it.

Conducting a preliminary analysis of prior stops by the police and offenses reveals a turning point in the data relating to experience with the police. This was demonstrated by regression analysis relating the number of prior stops and the frequency of thefts. The analysis was conducted using four dummy variables for the incidence of prior stops of 0, 1, 2, and 3 + in a standardized form. The population in this case, was limited to "desisters" and "persisters," individuals who have had one or more stops by the police "ever" or only in the year prior to the interview; in which case they would not be tabulated as "prior" stops. It was seen that the frequency of thefts among this group declines from zero stops to one or two prior stops by the police, but rises dramatically, almost doubling on the average, for persons with more than two prior contacts with the police. These results were highly significant (t's > 12.0) and explained 33 percent of the variance.

Those who have had zero prior stops (PS0) but at least one in the immediate past year will become divided between persisting and desisting in the subsequent year. In fact, we have shown that a Markov analysis of the sorting process yields an outcome to that effect that is consistent with the lifetime and most recent history of stops and theft from this sample data.[7] This relationship tends to be obscured in an estimation process that includes all thefts and all those who don't indulge in theft along with a variety of measures of individual characteristics. Consequently, we used a stepwise analytical strategy in order to deal with the likelihood that the individuals in our sample were far from homogeneous in terms of their historical behavior.

The first stage has been to determine among the entire population whether there are factors, as represented by individual characteristics, that determine the threshold between involvement in crime for an economic return and no involvement. Involvement in crime implies committing a theft; shoplifting, or any other offense that leads to a proportion of income generated from illegal activities being greater than zero and/or being stopped by the police in a prior year, presumably because of evidence of participation in some offense. Note that, by including persons admitting to stops but not offenses for economic gain, we may be including some who have offended for other reasons, since there is no way to separate stops associated with particular offense types. Nonetheless, we felt that ours was the better way to measure innocents, although it creates some ambiguity about the types of offenses involved. The objective is to be able to separate true "innocents" from the rest of the population in order to identify factors that contribute to the self-sorting process. Since males tend to predominate among offenders, it may be useful to divide this population between males and females to determine whether differences in behavior by sex can be attributed to measurable differences in characteristics. Similarly, it is reasonable to further divide the population by race to determine the extent to which apparent differences by race could be attributed to differences in factors common to both races. There would be no point in attempting to examine effects of deterrence variables with our data because, as noted previously, we have no measures that would reflect forces for general deterrence. In this article we limit ourselves to the aggregates among the four basic groups in the sample population: innocents, experimenters, desisters, and persisters.

The next stage of the analysis was to determine the extent to which factors that distinguish between innocents and non-innocents relate to distinctions among experimenters, desisters, and persisters. One possibility is that those who are never involved in crime are different from all others who may be at different points in their careers regarding involvement in crime. The alternative hypothesis is that among those who become involved in crime there are identifiable distinctions that eventually lead to a more or less permanent state of desisting or persisting in crime. In such a process, we speculate that desisters may possess some characteristics of innocents, since, after brief exposures to the law, they revert to crime free behavior, whereas persisters differ substantially, becoming criminal and remaining so. In such a world, experimenters would be at a transition stage, thus far unaffected by exposure to apprehension, and perhaps as a consequence, not turned into either desister or persister.

Analyzing the sub-populations helps to reveal the extent to which these speculations are borne out. If that vision is approximately true, we might expect that forces that appear to sort between crime and no crime, or innocents and everyone else, might help to differentiate among innocents, experimenters, and desisters because experimenters include some future persisters. Those forces might be expected to have similar effects in distinguishing between desisters and persisters to those between innocents and all others, if a reason for desisting is largely a consequence of previous conditioning by family, peers, and social institutions rather than simply because of exposure to the law. This speculation implies that tastes for crime versus legal activities differ because of environment and previous conditioning so that the perceived "price" variables associated with costs of apprehension differ.

The Empirical Evidence

The estimation process has been designed to attempt to learn whether the population must be treated as heterogeneous with respect to factors influencing criminal behavior. The first objective has been to identify factors that influence the decision to commit a crime for economic gain or not. To that end, an extensive list of variables was considered as indices of economic well-being as well as family, environmental, and social influences that contribute to moral compliance with the law.

Preliminary analysis with an extensive list of variables led to the estimation of two sets of principal components that captured most of the variance in three variables associated with religion and eight revealing family attitudes. This was after a similar analysis with some fifteen variables, not including family attitudes, revealed that the religious variables plus a limited set of other family variables appeared to best represent the effects of the more extended set. The initial testing procedure was to use the principal components as explanatory variables for the incidence of theft as a test of their power to explain crime. While it is clear that additional work is warranted to isolate indices of relevant influences, it seemed evident that the income variables, family attitude variables, religious variables, and a limited set representing family characteristics adequately represented the effects of some thirty-five variables that characterize individual differences in economic opportunities, family situation, attitudes, and environment. The results of the principal component analyses for religious influences and family attitudes are detailed in Table 2.

To summarize results in Table 2, the NLS Survey provided eight measures of family attitudes to which the respondent indicated strong disagreement, disagreement, agreement, or strong agreement, using a scale from one to four. The statements to which the respondent revealed his attitude are under DEFINITIONS. Principal component analysis was used to create from these indices four orthogonal variables that captured 70.76 percent of the variance of the eight attitudinal variables. These principal components are entitled FAM1 through FAM4. The influence (weighting) of the eight variables in the reduced set are presented under "Loadings." Thus, FAM1 is strongly positively influenced by the statements "Women's place is in the home," "A wife has no time for employment," "A working wife leads to juvenile delinquency," "Traditional husband-wife relationships are best," and "A wife is happier in a traditional role." In contrast FAM4 essentially represents the position, "Both parents need not work to make ends meet." A similar analysis was conducted with the religious variables, leading to the calculation of the two principal components REL1 and REL2.

There is some immediate evidence of the heterogeneity of the overall population associated with the degree of involvement in crime that is revealed by perusal of summary statistics of the variables used in subsequent regression analyses by population subset. These are displayed in Table 3. We note, for example, that among the religion variables the values associated with more intense involvement with crime change signs and radically differ in magnitude across the table from the index values

TABLE 2
Principal Component Definitions/Loadings

Variable	FAM1	FAM2	FAM3	FAM4
WOMPH	.751	-.080	-.181	-.019
WNTWK	.745	-.019	-.019	-.016
WWFMU	-.052	.988	.035	-.100
WWDEL	.635	.053	.020	.150
B2PWK	-.024	.101	.063	-.981
TRBST	.752	.010	-.164	.006
MSHRW	-.179	.036	.971	-.066
WHTDR	.715	-.079	-.100	-.048
%Var. Explained	32.94	12.55	12.73	12.54 / 70.76

Principal Component/Loadings

Variable	REL1	REL2
ORIGREL	.758	.500
PRESREL	.843	.111
GOCHRCH	.629	-.751
%Var. Explained	56.02	27.55 / 83.57

DEFINITIONS:

Family Attitude Variables	Definition/Attitude
WOMPH	"Women's place is in the home"
WNTWK	"A wife has no time for employment"
WWFMU	"A working wife feels more useful"
WWDEL	"A working wife leads to juvenile delinquency"
B2PWK	"Both parents need to work to make ends meet"
TRBST	"Traditional husband-wife relationships are best"
MSHRW	"The man should share in household chores"
WHTDR	"A wife is happier in traditional role"

Religious Variables	
ORIGREL	Respondent was raised in a religion
PRESREL	Respondent presently has a religion
GOCHRCH	Frequency of attendance at church

for innocents. Note for example that the index value for the first religion variable (REL1) goes from .098 for innocents to becoming increasingly negative as we move toward persisting in crime (−.195). The case with the family attitude variables is similar. Area of residence (RES), while it turns out to be a significant influence on criminal behavior, differs very

TABLE 3
Summary Statistics (Mean/Std. dev.) of Variables

Variable	INNOCENTS	EXPERIMENTERS	DESISTERS	PERSISTERS	PRO-3*
N	5972	3328	797	1278	1037
REL1	.098	-.042	-.070	-.196	-.154
	(.935)	(1.03)	(1.01)	(1.11)	(1.11)
REL2	-.086	.023	.133	.175	.136
	(.985)	(1.00)	(.970)	(1.02)	(1.02)
FAM1	-.052	-.045	.074	.121	.118
	(1.03)	(.952)	(.946)	(.958)	(.963)
FAM2	-.036	.036	.029	.067	.063
	(1.02)	(.988)	(.954)	(.937)	(.938)
FAM3	.043	.010	-.050	-.146	-.140
	(.992)	(.984)	(.959)	(1.01)	(1.01)
FAM4	.007	-.005	-.019	.023	.031
	(.995)	(1.015)	(.982)	(.983)	(.979)
RES	1.29	1.25	1.24	1.21	1.21
	(.569)	(.533)	(.529)	(.486)	(.490)
EINC	2767	2806	3676	2968	2709
	(4067)	(4092)	(4613)	(4022)	(3870)
SINC	1724	1059	945	813	788
	(4300)	(321)	(2637)	(2806)	(2910)
AGE	18.9	18.6	19.2	18.6	18.5
	(2.31)	(2.28)	(2.28)	(2.21)	(2.20)
SEX	.396	.509	.734	.783	.762
	(.489)	(.500)	(.442)	(.412)	(.426)
THEFT	0	.962	0	1.69	1.51
	---	(1.51)	---	(2.29)	(2.06)
SHOPLFT	0	1.23	0	1.55	1.50
	---	(1.340)	---	(1.57)	(1.52)
ILINC	1.00	1.54	1.00	1.83	1.77
	---	(.936)	---	(1.08)	(1.04)
PRIORST	0	0	2.55	3.04	.877
		---	(7.32)	(7.12)	(.972)

Definitions of Variables:

REL1, REL2, FAM1,...FAM4 defined in Table 2 and in text; RES:Area of residence, 1-urban, 2=rural non farm, 3=rural town; EINC: Respondent's earned income - all sources; SINC: respondent's supplemental income - all sources, family, welfare, etc.; AGE: Chronological age (years); SEX: Male=1, Female=0; THEFT: Number of thefts in previous 12 months; SHOPLFT: Number of incidents of shoplifting in previous 12 months; ILINC: fraction of income illegally earned 0,-,6 (almost all); PRIORST: number of stops by the police, but not being charged, prior to the past 12 months.

*PRO-3 are PERSISTERS with zero to three prior stops.

little in mean value among the subsets. Participants in crime tend to have lower supplemental incomes (SINC) on the average than innocents and higher earned incomes (EINC). However, the group with the highest mean earned income and highest variance are the desisters who have gotten out of crime. Desisters also tend to be older, on the average, than persisters or anyone else, for that matter. Not surprisingly, using an index of 0, 1, SEX reveals the population of more intensive participation in crime to be more male, a not surprising result.

In view of these results, it make sense to view the population subsets of innocents, experimenters, desisters, and persisters as distinctly differing population subsets. The nature of the variables included in this list would seem to justify the expectation that tastes among these subsets differ and consequently that subjective "prices" associated with legal versus illegal gains and costs can be expected to differ as well. The subsequent regression analysis reveals the extent to which these expectations are borne out.

The results of estimating a linear probability model in which the dependent variable takes on the value zero, or one for the commission of one or more economic crimes, or admitting to some positive proportion of income earned from illegal activities, is displayed in the first three columns of Table 4. In the first column are results including the entire population of the sample who have responded to the relevant set of questions (N = 10,546). These results suggest that moral guidance is important, i.e., having a religion and going to church (REL1 and REL2) moderates the probability of the commission of one or more offenses. Having some form of supplemental income (SINC) also is a strongly significant factor in not committing an offense. Individuals from a rural environment (RES) are less likely to be involved with crime than urban residents. There could, obviously, be a number of reasons why this is so that these results cannot reveal. Finally, three of the family attitude variables are revealed to be strongly related to the probability of committing an offense for economic gain. Coming from a family in which the key attitude favors sharing household responsibilities and tasks (FAM3) is strongly negatively related to crime. Surprisingly, coming from a traditional, male-dominated household (FAM1) is positively related to the probability of involvement in crime. Coming from a household in which the prevailing attitude is that a working wife feels more useful (FAM2) is also positively related to the probability of committing one or more offenses. Having income from a job, military service, or self-employment is not significantly related to the probability of committing a crime.

Among these population subsets that exclude persisters (col. 2) and both persisters and desisters (col. 3), the results are essentially the same, with the exceptions that attitudes favoring neither the traditionally male-dominated family nor the sharing family attitude appear to relate to the probability of an offense.

TABLE 4
Estimation Results: Effects of Dependent Variables on Committing a Crime or Not (Columns 1-5) or on Fraction of Income Earned Illegally (Columns 6, 7)

DATA SET:	ALL	NON PERSISTERS	INNOCENTS EXPERI-MENTERS	DESISTERS PERSISTERS	DESISTERS PERSISTERS PRIORS 0-3	PERSISTERS	PERSISTERS PRIORS 0-3
Variable	1	2	3	4	5	6	7
REL1	-.078*	-.055*	-.066*	-.051*	-.060*	-.057**	-.072*
	(8.07)	(5.37)	(6.19)	(2.24)	(2.42)	(1.90)	(2.21)
REL2	.061*	.037*	.049*	.047*	.062*	.048	.070*
	(6.28)	(3.57)	(4.55)	(2.07)	(2.48)	(1.62)	(2.13)
FAM1	.027*	.003	.011	.034	.045**	.046	.051
	(2.76)	(0.25)	(1.01)	(1.45)	(1.76)	(1.54)	(1.54)
FAM2	.033*	.029*	.032*	.032	.028	.040	.032
	(3.40)	(2.77)	(3.03)	(1.44)	(1.14)	(1.38)	(1.02)
FAM3	-.027*	-.008	-.013	-.101*	-.098*	-.124*	-.119*
	(2.79)	(0.74)	(1.20)	(4.45)	(3.92)	(4.27)	(3.70)
FAM4	.003	-.001	-.002	-.044*	-.041**	-.055**	-.058**
	(0.36)	(0.14)	(0.17)	(1.98)	(1.68)	(1.92)	(1.84)
RES	-.046*	-.032*	-.037*	-.042**	-.045**	-.036	-.035
	(4.79)	(3.13)	(3.47)	(1.87)	(1.83)	(1.25)	(1.11)
EINC	-.003	-.006	.006	-.047**	.003	-.046	.020
	(0.34)	(0.58)	(0.58)	(1.69)	(0.09)	(1.29)	(0.50)
SINC	-.088*	-.073*	-.086*	-.018	-.022	-.030	-.030
	(9.37)	(7.30)	(8.27)	(0.76)	(0.83)	(0.98)	(0.87)
AGE				-.112*	-.144*	-.105*	-.155*
				(3.91)	(4.57)	(2.85)	(3.84)
SEX				.046**	.032	.044	.028
				(1.87)	(1.17)	(1.41)	(0.79)
PS0				-.115*	-.057	-.117*	-.028
				(3.88)	(1.18)	(3.19)	(0.47)
PS1				-.086*	-.026	-.073*	.008
				(2.99)	(0.57)	(2.05)	(0.14)
PS2				-.031	.024	-.018	.055
				(1.19)	(0.59)	(0.55)	(1.10)
R^2	.014	.006	.010	.047	.043	.052	.049
F	22.57	9.01	12.42	7.82	6.08	5.63	4.50
	7,10538	7,9361	7,8624	14,1917	14,1588	14,1162	14,947
N	10546	9369	8632	1932	1603	1177	962

* Significant at the 1% level (1-tailed test)
**Significant at the 5% level (1-tailed test)

PRIORS 0-3 indicates that the sample in question is limited to individuals with no more than 3 prior stops.

When the sample is limited to individuals with a greater involvement with crime *and* the criminal justice system: persisters and desisters (N = 1932), there are some important differences. It should be noted that, if one wishes to learn about factors influencing the extent of involvement in crime among persisters, the estimation must be modified since the crime variables take on the value of one for all persisters (and zero for desisters). Consequently, the dependent variable used in the results with persisters only is the proportion of income earned from crime, from zero to almost all (95%).

If one considers col. 4, it can be seen that, having been brought up in a religion (REL1) remains highly significant, as does going to church (REL2). It should be noted that, if the influence of a variable is unchanged, relative to its variance except for sample size, in going from the sample size of persisters and desisters (1,932) to ALL (10,546) that t-values should increase by 5.53. In fact, if it increases less than this, it suggests that religious factors are more rather than less important in terms of significance among persons *more* involved with crime. Differences from those less involved with crime are that now supplemental income (SINC) is no longer significant, whereas earned income becomes so at the 5% level of significance (1-tailed test). Additionally, the fourth family attitude variable, which is associated with the attitude that the wife's income is not needed is now strongly and negatively associated with crimes for income.

Additionally, with this sub-population, it is possible to evaluate the learning effect associated with prior stops by police. From running the regression as shown, again separately excluding the dummy variable for zero prior stops (PS0) and including prior stops greater than two (not shown), the results of the earlier analysis are confirmed. One or two prior stops tends to discourage crime; only one stop does so significantly, however. Note also that "zero" stops discourages crime, but in the case of zero prior stops, this means one or more stops in the current year, since the key to deleting observations is for the individual to never have been stopped by police.

These results appear to reveal a kind of paradox. If we use as our index the variance in crime participation explained (based on the adjusted coefficient of determination), those persons who are or have been most involved with crime (DESISTERS and PERSISTERS) appear to be most influenced by personal calculations. That is, adding the effects of the expectation of apprehension appears to influence the decision more for them than the remaining variables do for the population as a whole. The adjusted coefficient of determination is still low but nearly five times as great as for the overall population (ALL) or the less criminal subsets. Surprisingly, however, the variables associated with moral compliance appear to impact this group as much or more strongly than they do the general population of youth, particularly, if the difference in significance is only due to sample size. That is, a positive attitude toward family sharing is a highly significant moderating factor to crime as are having a religion and actively following it.

One might think that the influences of religion and family are having a stronger impact on those who are turned from crime, the desisters, than on persisters. To test that hypothesis, the same relationship is run on persisters only. Comparisons from Table 4 indicate that while persisters have not given up crime, the influence of religion and the family tends to moderate criminal activity. Furthermore, when these factors are included in the estimated relationship for persisters, both income variables become insignificant, whereas the experience of prior stops by the police retains its significance.

If we proceed to Table 5, we see that both earned income and supplemental income are highly significantly related to fewer crimes being committed, when these variables and the effects of prior stops are considered in isolation. Table 5 shows the case for all desisters and persisters, and for persisters only in the case in which prior stops greater than three have been eliminated from the sample. The implication would seem to be that what the income variables are measuring may be the stabilizing effects associated with religion and family that increase the likelihood that a person will seek and obtain legitimate income and tend to desist from crime.

To further test this latter hypothesis, these estimates of desisters and persisters, and persisters alone, are estimated restricting the population to individuals at the turning point of zero to three prior stops by the police. Relevant results are in Table 4, columns 5 and 7, and Table 5, column 2. For this group, prior stops in this limited range lose their significance, as we might expect. Income variables have no significance whatsoever, but religion and family factors remain the dominant force. One additional set of influences that deserves note is that age continues to be negatively related to offense levels, even for persisters, and sex differences become insignificant at this point. Surprisingly, some variables associated with moral compliance appear to have greater impact on persisters in this group than they do on the general population of non-persisters. A positive attitude toward family sharing is a highly significant influence, as are having a religion and following it.

It is not surprising that prior stops ceased to be significant when individuals with more than 3 were deleted from the sample, since it is likely to be the *difference* in behavior between those with frequent stops and those with one or two that makes that effect significant. As can be seen from Table 5, this result was consistent for persisters with 3 or fewer stops no matter whether moral compliance variables were included or not. Including moral compliance variables for this same population subset did cause

TABLE 5
Effects of Earned and Supplemental Income on Frequency of Offenses When Other Variables Are Excluded

Dependent Variable	Data Set: 1. DESISTERS & PERSISTERS	Data Set: 2. PERSISTERS Not incl. PS > 3
PS0	-.129*	-.036
	(4.57)	(0.62)
PS1	-.104*	.002
	(3.79)	(0.04)
PS2	-.046**	.050
	(1.79)	(1.02)
EINC	-.097*	-.059**
	(4.42)	(1.88)
SINC	-.052**	-.066**
	(2.39)	(2.12)
R^2	.019	.013
F	8.92	2.68
	5,2090	5,1031
N	2096	1037

* Significant at the 1% level (1-tailed test)
**Significant at the 5% level (1-tailed test)

the income variable to lose significance, as well, suggesting that the effects of income in reducing involvement in crime are associated with the distinction between heavy involvement in crime (and many prior stops) versus minor involvement (few prior stops).

Conclusion

What these results seem to suggest is that the economic model of a rational decision process can explain a significant amount of crime at the margin. However, it appears that the expected cost of sanctions has a greater impact than lack of realized economic opportunities. In fact, the availability of income from any source ceases to be significant when other factors perhaps representing forces for moral compliance, i.e., the influence of religion and family attitudes, are taken into account.

Since this analysis does not take into account the probability of obtaining legitimate income, (e.g., unemployment rates) it would not be appropriate to argue that the availability of legitimate economic opportunities is not important. It does seem reasonable, however, to suggest that something like the stability associated with a moral background and family responsibility influences both the ability and/or responsibility to seek and obtain legitimate income and to desist from criminal activity.

II. CRIME, YOUTH, AND THE LABOR MARKET: A MICRO STUDY BASED ON INDIVIDUAL DATA

The preceding work has dealt with one dimension of our objective to explain crime as a rational choice process: the influence of family and moral influences on youth. At the same time, we were investigating the effect of economic opportunities on the individual's choices among school, crime, and work. This was a topic we had pursued in earlier work. Phillips, Votey, and Maxwell[8] showed crime for youth to be strongly related to labor market conditions. Subsequent research (1981) has shown that school enrollment had a strong bearing on the proclivity to be involved in crime for income. Because those studies relied on aggregate analysis, the NLS data provide a unique opportunity to test these ideas about the influences on individual choice using individual data.

Dropping out before completion of high school has been shown to be associated with greater delinquency.[9] But the effect of delinquency upon subsequent labor force behavior remains unclear. Are crime and delinquency competing income-generating activities? What happens to minors after they drop out of school? Which ones fare well in the labor market? Do illegal gains affect future employment? This section investigates the effect of labor force experience during 1979 upon the probability of employment in 1980, controlling for the fraction of support gained through illegal activities in 1979. Behavior is compared for three groups: those who dropped out of school in 1979, those who were enrolled during 1979 but had dropped out by 1980, and those who remained enrolled in school in 1980. The data source continues to be the youth cohort of the National Longitudinal Survey.

There is information about individual behavior at two points, and over one interval, in a time span. Whether the individual is employed or not at the time of the 1980 interview is the behavior to be explained. Employment status, yes or no, at the time of the 1979 interview is an explanatory variable. In addition, the fraction of weeks worked and the fraction of income earned illegally, during the interval between interviews, are used to explain employment in 1980. The idea is to compare the effect that past employment and criminal experience have on current employment for three groups: dropouts, those on the verge of dropping out, and those who continue in school.

This analysis focuses on minors, and since the labor force data in the NLS is collected for those sixteen and older, the sample we need to examine for this study is 3,047 sixteen and seventeen-year-olds, of which 2,779 provided information about their labor force experience in 1979. These 2,779 individuals may be divided into three subgroups: 153 who were not enrolled in regular school after the 1979 interview, 269 who were enrolled at some time after the 1979 interview but were not enrolled in 1980, and 2,387 who remained enrolled at the 1980 interview.

Joan Crowley[10] has used the Youth Cohort data to investigate delinquency and employment. However she excluded school dropouts under the age of eighteen, the focus of this study, and separately analyzed two groups: (1) high school students sixteen years and older, and (2) adults, ages eighteen through twenty-three, who were not enrolled in school and were civilians. She did not find a significant relationship between the fraction of support from illegal sources and the proportion of weeks worked between the 1979 and 1980 interviews for high school students. She does report that illegal income was significantly associated with fewer weeks worked for nonenrolled adult men.

A conceptual approach is developed in this work to relate the probability of employment at the time of the 1980 interview to whether an individual was enrolled or not at the time of the 1979 interview, and to the fraction of weeks employed between the two dates, on average 50 weeks apart. Each person is presumed to form some expectation of the fraction of weeks he or she will be employed, conditional upon whether he, or she is employed or not at the time of the 1979 interview. Employment at the time of this interview is presumed to raise expectations. If, between the interviews, the person actually experiences a fraction of weeks in employment that is less than the expectation, then it is presumed he or she chooses some activity other than employment. Thus, the expectation can be viewed as a minimally acceptable threshold for work experience. The possibility the minor engages in remunerative illegal activity during the interval prior to the 1980 interview is measured by the fraction of support from illegal sources. This illegal alternative for income is presumed to raise the expectations threshold for legal employment.

The predetermined variables of the probability of employment in 1979, measured as zero or one, and the proportion of weeks worked between the 1979 and 1980 interview dates, capture the influence of conditioning individual characteristics. The latter, for example, race, sex, and age, do not significantly affect the probability of employment in 1980, conditional upon the predetermined variables, although they do significantly affect the probability of employment in 1979. Thus the competing influences of illegal activity and legal work experience upon the probability of employment in 1980 can be investigated within a fairly streamlined formulation. This procedure is important to making rapid forward progress in the analysis, but the roles of race and sex will remain proxied until the final stages of the research are reached and employment status in 1979 is explained rather than taken as given. The strong dependence of employment status in 1980 upon that in 1979 suggests state dependency for labor force experience. Robert Meyer and David Wise[11] reach the opposite conclusion from their study of labor force experience for the four years following high school graduation.

Since the distribution of the fraction of weeks worked differs between those employed in 1979 and those not employed, a separate variable of fraction of weeks worked is included for each group. The equation for the probability of employment in 1980 is estimated using a linear probability model and a probit model.

The Employment Experience of Sixteen and Seventeen Year Olds

Employment status in 1980 for the three groups classified by enrollment experience is listed in Table 1. Note that the minors who are school dropouts are not entering the armed forces. A large fraction are in the civilian force and a considerable fraction are pursuing the activity labelled "other," which evidently includes crime.

The fraction of individuals employed at the two interview dates, and the fractions for weeks worked, weeks unemployed, and weeks outside the labor force during the interval between the interviews, are listed in Table 2 for the three groups classified by enrollment experience. Although a person from the group of 1979 dropouts is most likely to be employed in 1979, he, or she, is least likely to be employed in 1980. This is also the

TABLE 1
The Employment Status In 1980 For Three Groups Of Minors Classified By Enrollment Experience

	'79 Dropouts	'80 Dropouts	'80 Enrolled
Employed			
Working	54	99	877
Job, Not At Work	0	2	32
Unemployed	44	69	441
Keeping House	27	26	4
In Active Forces	1	2	0
Other	22	30	48
Unable To Work	1	0	0
Going To School	4*	11*	984
Total	153	239	2387
Average Probability Of Working In 1980	54/153=.353	101/239=.423	909/2387=.381

*These respondends had indicated that they had dropped out of regular school, which raises some question about the meaning of these responses.

group with the highest fraction of individuals reporting a quarter or more of their support came from illegal activities, namely 11.4%. This raises the question of whether their higher involvement in illegal activities is affecting their lower relative probability of employment in 1980. For the sixteen and seventeen-year-olds who dropped out in 1979, the probability of employment increases only 17% between 1979 and 1980, while for those who had dropped out by 1980, the increase is 65%, and for those still enrolled, it is 44%.

Although the fraction of weeks employed between the 1979 and 1980 interviews is similar for the three groups, classified by enrollment experience, the fraction of weeks unemployed is quite different. Those who dropped out in 1979 experienced almost twice the fraction of time unemployed as those who were still enrolled in 1980. Young people who drop out of school while still minors do not experience less employment than their friends in school, but may become more discouraged because of unemployment. They are less likely to drop out of the labor force because they are no longer in school.

The probability of employment in 1980 was chosen as the dependent variable, rather than the labor force participation rate, since the unemployment rate is such a significant factor for youth, and is a valid separate factor for explanation. In this work, the more complex task of explaining,

TABLE 2
Labor Force Experience Between 1979 and 1980 and the Probability of Employment at Interview Dates—Classified by Enrollment Status

Status	Probability of Employment 1979 Interview	Weeks Em-ployed	Weeks Unemp-ployed	Weeks Outside Labor Force
'79 Dropouts	.301	.353	.171	.475
'80 Dropouts	.255	.367	.144	.490
'80 Enrolled	.264	.347	.090	.563

Status	1/4 or More Support From Illegal Activities-Year Prior to 1980 Interview	Probability of Employment 1980 Interview
'79 Dropouts	.114	.353
'80 Dropouts	.105	.423
'80 Enrolled	.045	.381

jointly, the probability of employment and the probability of unemployment, was deferred to the future. An explanatory variable, in this case the predetermined variable, fraction of weeks worked, can affect the probability of employment and the probability of unemployment in countervailing ways, confounding its influence on the participation rate. This is illustrated in Figure 1.

Theory

The focus of this study is the probability of employment in 1980 and how it is influenced by (1) the fraction of weeks worked between the interview dates of 1979 and 1980, (2) earning a quarter or more of support from illegal activities in the twelve months prior to the 1980 interview, and (3) employment status in 1979. The influences of substantial illegal

FIGURE 1
Effect of Work Experience on the Probabilities of Employment and Unemployment in 1980

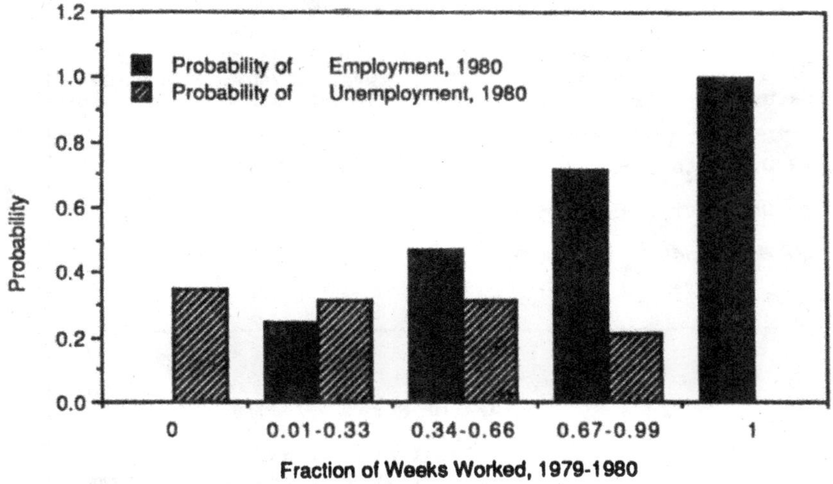

earnings and employment status in 1979 are presumed to operate on the probability of employment in 1980 by affecting expectations of a minimally satisfactory threshold for fraction of weeks worked. This threshold can be thought of as a reservation level of employment experience, obtained by dividing a particular level of (reservation) earnings for a given period, for example, 52 weeks, by the weekly reservation wage. It is possible the threshold will not be satisfied if the individual is underemployed. The interpretation is that the probability of employment is reflecting a choice between employment and some other activity, dependent upon satisfying the threshold or not. In the case of the influence of substantial illegal activity, it could be a choice between crime and legal work. Of course, it is possible that the individual continues to do both. Since data on illegal activity is only available for 1979 and not for 1980, this possibility can only be inferred if illegal activity in 1979 does not decrease the probability of employment in 1980.

Supplementary information is also available on the correlations among the three predetermined variables. If earning a quarter or more of support from illegal activities is negatively correlated with fraction of weeks worked, this can be interpreted as substitution of time between legal and illegal work. A number of considerations may affect the magnitude of this substitution effect. First, Travis Hirsch[12] has suggested that most delinquent activities are not very time intensive. Second, to the extent that minors are underemployed, they would be willing to moonlight, including possibly, illegal activities, even at a wage lower than the legal wage. This would not diminish the fraction of weeks worked. The latter tends to be much lower, on average, for those not employed in 1979, hence this group may be much less likely to show a significant negative substitution effect than those who were employed in 1979 unless their desired employment level is also commensurately lower, i.e. the substitution effect is likely to be conditional upon employment status in 1979.

A Model Of The Probability Of Employment In 1980: Econometric Considerations

The model can be viewed from the perspective of discriminant function analysis where, if there is some minimally satisfactory threshold, f*, then there should be a difference in the means of the distributions of labor force experience between those who end up employed in 1980 and those who do not, as illustrated in Figure 2. If the model were correct and if f* were not a stochastic threshold, varying with each individual, then the threshold would be a perfect discriminator and the distributions of labor

FIGURE 2
The Threshold For A Minimally Satisfying Employment Experience

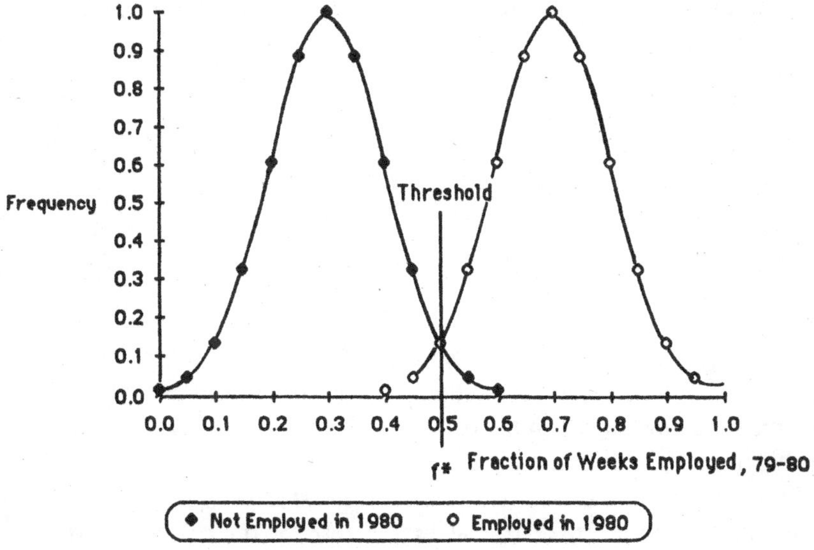

force experience for the employed and for those not employed would not overlap.

Some support for this approach can be gained by comparing the means of the distributions for fraction of weeks worked for those minors who dropped out from school in 1979. For those who end up employed at the interview date in 1980, numbering 54, the mean is 0.693, while for those who are not employed at this date, numbering 99, the mean is 0.197. The means are significantly different.

Discriminant function models for dichotomous outcomes can also be formulated in terms of the probability of choosing among outcomes. At the time of the 1979 interview, a young person is assumed to have formed some expectation of what would be a minimally satisfactory employment experience for the next year, that is, the interval until the next interview in 1980. This experience is measured as the fraction of weeks employed, f.

The expectation of a minimally satisfying experience, f*, will likely vary from person to person and, in the simplest formulation, is a constant, α, plus a stochastic term, u, which captures the individual variation in the threshold:

$$f^* = \alpha + u \tag{1}$$

If a person's labor force experience, f, exceeds expectations, f*, then he, or she, remains employed at the time of the 1980 interview, i.e.

$$P_E(80) = 1, \quad \text{if } f >= f^* \tag{2}$$

otherwise, he or she drops from the labor force, i.e.:

$$P_E(80) = 0, \quad \text{if } f < f^*. \tag{3}$$

The dependence of the probability of employment in 1980, $P_E(80)$, upon the fraction of weeks worked between the interview dates, f, can be estimated using regression, i.e., a linear probability model, or using a probit model.

In the linear probability formulation, the probability of employment in 1980, $P_E(80)$, which takes the value of zero or one, is equal to the difference between the fraction of weeks worked and the threshold.

$$P_E(80) = f - f^*, \quad (4)$$

and substituting for f^* from Eq. 1,

$$P_E(80) = f - (\alpha + u). \quad (5)$$

where the intercept for the regression is the constant α, the slope coefficient on the explanatory variable, fraction of weeks worked, f, is equal to one and the random error term for each individual is u.

The model was estimated in this simplest of formulations for the 153 individuals who dropped out in 1979. In addition, another factor that could affect the threshold for a minimally satisfactory employment experience, f^*, was incorporated: whether the individual was employed or not in 1979, $P_E(79)$. If the minor is employed in 1979, at the time the expectation is formed, and has some knowledge of the labor market or not, then expectations may be more realistic.[13] The estimated regression results for these two formulations are displayed in Table 3. Note that the coefficient on the fraction of weeks employed is not significantly different from one, as was postulated for the coefficient on f above.

The threshold, f^*, can be inferred from these estimated probability models as the value of fraction of weeks worked, f, where the corresponding estimated probability of employment in 1980 is one half, i.e. on the boundary between those who are employed in 1980 and those who are not. For the simpler model, the inferred value of a minimally satisfactory employment experience is 0.45 of the weeks of the interval. This expectation is approximately 0.5, the midpoint of the range for f, consistent with an uninformed estimate. For the more complicated model, which controls for whether the individual was employed in 1979 or not, the threshold, or acceptable number of weeks worked, is 0.44 for those not employed in 1979 compared to 0.63 for those who were employed.

Various modifications were explored to test the robustness of the estimates for the simpler model. First, the variables were weighted to correct for the heteroscedasticity in the errors for a linear probability model. The conclusions were not affected. Second, since the fraction of weeks worked is one minus the sum of the fraction of weeks outside the labor force, f_o, and the fraction of weeks unemployed, f_u, these latter two variables were used instead of f to check whether further distinguishing the nature of labor force experience added to the explanation of behavior. Once again the results were consistent and the goodness of fit did not improve. Third, the probit technique was used instead of linear regression.

TABLE 3
Estimates of the Probability of Employment in 1980:
Experience and Prior Employment Formulation—Not Enrolled Since 1979

	Linear Probability $\hat{P}_E(80)$	Linear Probability $\hat{P}_E(80)$
Constant, -	0.050 (1.14)*	0.053 (1.21)
Probability of Emploment in 1979: $P_E(79)$: -ß		-0.184 (-2.22)
Fraction of Weeks Employed, f:1	0.858 (9.60)	1.01 (9.08)
Minimally Acceptable Fraction of Weeks Worked: f*	0.45	
Not Employed in 1979:		0.44
Employed in 1979:		0.63
Coefficient of R^2 Determination	0.38	0.40
Percent Correct Predictions		
Number of Observations	153	153

*t-statistics in parentheses

Equations 1, 2, and 3 can be used to specify a likelihood function, where the probability that an individual is employed in 1980 is:

$$\text{Prob}[P_E(80) = 1] = \text{Prob}[f - f^* >= 0] = \text{Prob}[u \leqq f - \alpha] = F(f - \alpha), \quad (6)$$

where F denotes the cumulative distribution function of the stochastic term u, and the probability an individual is not employed in 1980 is:

$$\text{Prob}[P_E(80) = 0] = \text{Prob}[f - f^* < 0] = \text{Prob}[u > f - \alpha] = 1 - F(f - \alpha), \quad (7)$$

and the likelihood function, L, is

$$L = \prod_{P_E(80)=0}[1 - F(f - \alpha)] \prod_{P_E(80)=1} F(f - \alpha) \quad (8)$$

FIGURE 3
Distribution Of Fraction Of Weeks Worked By Employment Status in 1979

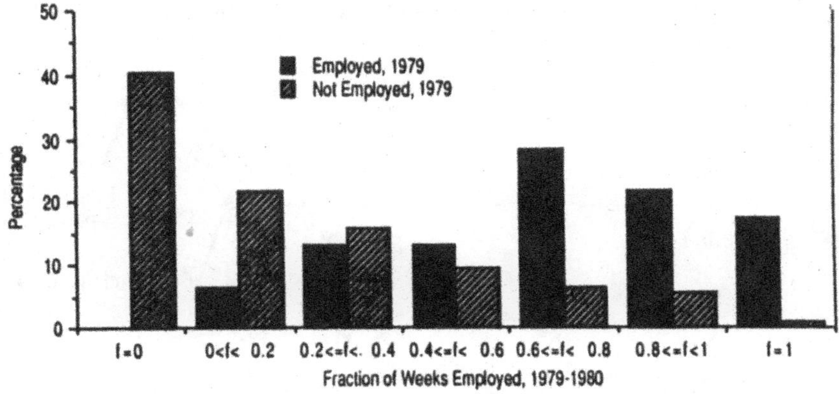

If we assume that the stochastic terms are normally distributed with cumulative distribution function Φ, then the parameters can be estimated using the probit technique.[14] The results from the probit model support all of the conclusions drawn from the linear probability model. The expected minimally satisfactory employment experience thresholds are similar to those obtained from the regression estimates. The employment experience in 1980 is correctly predicted for approximately 80% of the individuals.

Whether a school dropout from 1979 is employed or not at the time of the 1979 interview is an important consideration. It not only affects the probability of employment in 1980 but also affects the distribution of the fraction of weeks worked between the 1979 and 1980 interviews. This is illustrated graphically in Figure 3. A two-way contingency table analysis, using the seven categories for F as defined in Figure 3, shows that the probability of employment in 1979 is a highly significant determinant of fraction of weeks worked.

The importance of employment status in 1979 was explored by introducing separate variables for the fraction of weeks worked into the linear probability model, one for those employed in 1979, f_E, and one for those not employed in 1979, F_N. The estimated thresholds remained similar to those reported in Table 3, as did the goodness of fit. For those who were not employed at the 1979 interview, it is noteworthy that the coefficient on fraction of weeks worked is smaller than, but not significantly different from, one. In contrast, for those who were employed at that time, the coefficient is larger than one, bordering on being significantly so. Esti-

FIGURE 4
Probit Estimates Of The Probability Of Employment In 1980 As A Function Of Work Experience and Employment Status In 1979

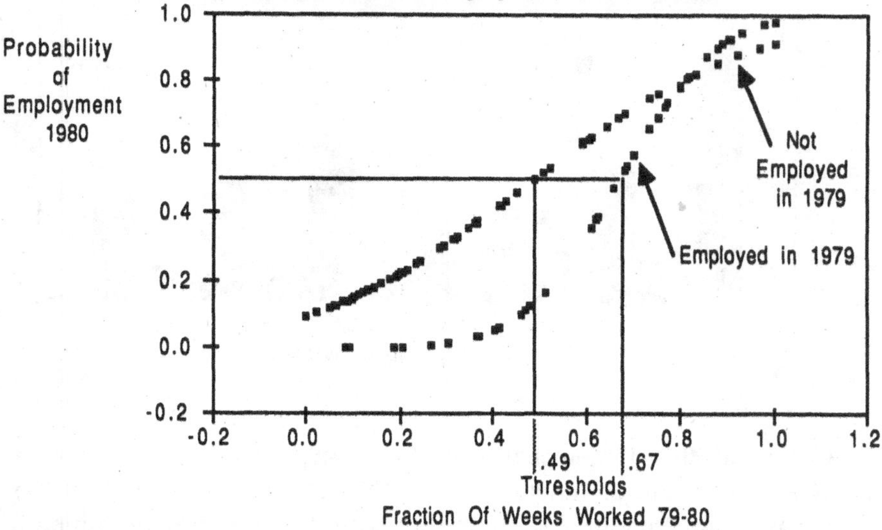

mates were also obtained using the probit procedure. Once again, these probit estimates supported the findings from the regressions.

The fitted values for the probability of employment in 1980 obtained from the probit model are plotted against fraction of weeks worked in Figure 4 and the inferred threshold values, classified by employment status in 1979, are illustrated. The shape or form of the dependence of the probability of employment in 1980 upon fraction of weeks worked is influenced by employment status in 1979, as dramatically revealed in Figure 4. The relationship is nearly linear for those not employed in 1979 but much more s-shaped or sigmoid for individuals who were employed. For the latter, it is only after the fraction of weeks worked exceeds one half that the probability of employment rises sharply with the fraction of weeks worked. This appears to reflect the well-formed expectations of those with prior work experience.

In sum, all of the estimations for the school dropouts who were not employed in 1979 indicate their expectations were considerably below those who were employed at that interview date. Nonetheless, they were still overly optimistic since the mean of their distribution of fraction of weeks actually worked was 0.22. In contrast, the threshold of 0.67 for the group of school dropouts who were employed at the time of the 1979 interview is equal to the mean of their distribution of fraction of weeks worked. Their expectations were realized or rational. That this finding is attributable to familarity with the labor market, implied by employment status in 1979, seems reasonable.

Incorporating The Effect of Illegal Income Into The Model

The focus of this study is the competing influence between legal and illegal work experience on the future likelihood of employment. Introduction of illegal income generating activity is the last modification to the model. Information was available on the fraction of income each individual obtained from illegal activities for the twelve months prior to the 1980 interview, with categories of: zero, very little, about 1/4, about 1/2, about 3/4, and almost all, for 140 of the 153 dropouts. The probability of obtaining substantial income from illegal activities, $P_I(79\text{-}80)$, was measured as zero if the category was zero or very little, and was measured as one otherwise. If an individual obtained a substantial amount of support from illegal activities, this presumably raised the threshold for a minimally satisfactory employment experience, f^*.[15]

This model was estimated and the results are reported in Table 4 for the linear probability model and the corresponding probit model. For comparison, estimates are presented for all three groups of individuals, classified by enrollment status: (1) 1979 dropouts, (2) 1980 dropouts, and (3) 1980 still enrolled.

Minors Who Dropped From School In 1979

As expected, the coefficient on illegal income is positive, and just significant at the 5% level using a one tailed t-test. The estimates of the other coefficients are similar to those found previously. The estimated probabilities of employment in 1980, and their dependence on the fraction of weeks worked, are illustrated in Figure 5, for the probit model from Table 4.

Thus there is evidence that illegal income generating activities are an alternative to legal ones, although the statistical relationship is not strong. Furthermore the interrelationships are complex. There is a strong positive relation between the probability of employment at the time of the 1979 interview, $P_E(79)$, and the probability that a substantial fraction of support between the 1979 and 1980 interviews is illegal, $P_I(79\text{-}80)$. This is consistent with an individual who is engaging in both legal and illegal activities having a low reservation wage. There is no relationship between the frac-

FIGURE 5
Estimated Probabilities Of Employment In 1980, Probit Model, 1979 Dropouts

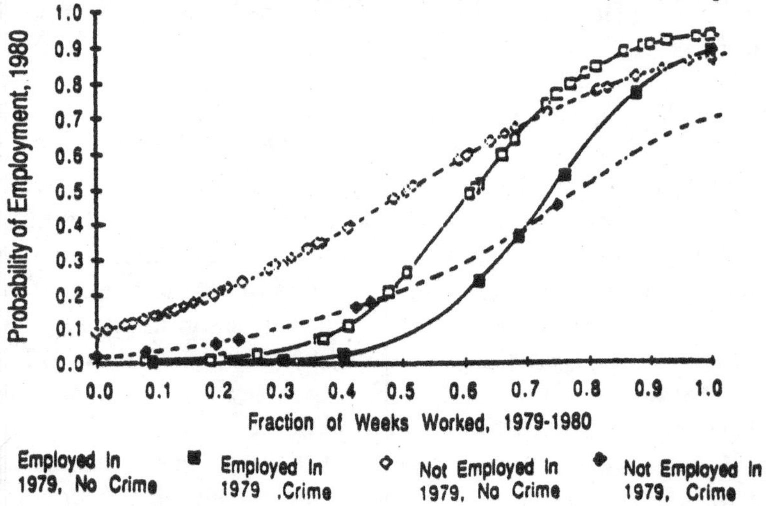

tion of weeks employed between the intervals, f, and the probability of obtaining a substantial fraction of support from illegal activities, P_I(79-80), although it is negative for those employed in 1979. This is consistent with Joan Crowley's similar finding for high school students, not including dropouts, age sixteen and older.[16] Focusing on this relationship alone, as she did, gives the appearance of no relationship between legal and illegal activities. This seems to be true in a contemporaneous sense and needs to be explained. However, behavior over time tells a different story. Early employment experience increases the probability that some school dropouts become involved in both the legal and illegal markets, but involvement in crime tends to decrease the probability of future employment. Of the sixteen dropouts who reported that a quarter or more of their support came from illegal activities, half were employed at the 1979 interview, but only a quarter remained employed in 1980. These patterns between legal and illegal employment experience are illustrated schematically in Panel A of Figure 6, for comparison with those who dropped from school later or remained enrolled.

Minors Who Dropped From School In 1980

Most of the features that characterized the situation for minors who dropped out in 1979 are also present for those who dropped out by 1980.

TABLE 4
Comparison of Linear Probability and Probit Estimates of the Probability of Employment in 1980

Explanatory Variables	Not Enrolled, 1979		Dropout by 1980		Enrolled in 1980	
	Linear Probability	Probit	Linear Probability	Probit	Linear Probability	Probit
Constant ($-\alpha$)	0.083 (1.77)*	-1.34 (6.07)	0.065 (1.55)	-1.54 (7.38)	0.049 (4.75)	-1.56 (26.8)
Probability of Employment ($P_E(79)$: $-\beta$)	-0.333 (2.10)	-2.37 (1.89)	-0.124 (0.94)	-0.231 (0.40)	-0.186 (4.60)	-0.595 (2.90)
Illegal Income 1/4 or Greater of Support ($P_I(79\text{-}80)$: $-\gamma$)	-0.168 (1.73)	-0.792 (1.63)	-0.088 (1.08)	-0.398 (1.08)	0.021 (0.63)	0.117 (0.76)
Fraction of Weeks Employed (f_E:1)	1.30 (6.38)	6.10 (1.72)	0.960 (5.68)	3.02 (4.05)	1.06 (22.5)	3.54 (14.4)
Fraction of Weeks Not-Employed (f_N:1)	0.851 (6.56)	2.76 (4.91)	1.20 (11.15)	4.33 (7.70)	1.07 (36.2)	3.76 (23.3)
Threshold: Acceptable Fraction of Weeks Worked (f*)						
Not Employed '79 - No Crime	0.49	0.49	0.36	0.36	0.43	0.44
Not Employed '79 - Crime	0.69	0.77	0.44	0.45	0.41	0.41
Employed '79 - No Crime	0.58	0.61	0.58	0.58	0.60	0.57
Employed '79 - Crime	0.67	0.74	0.67	0.72	0.58	0.54
R^2	.459		.444		.522	
% Correct Predictions		84		68		85
N	140	140	229	229	2288	2228

* Absolute Value of t-statistic in parentheses ( ).

FIGURE 6
The Pattern of Relationships Between Legal and Illegal Work

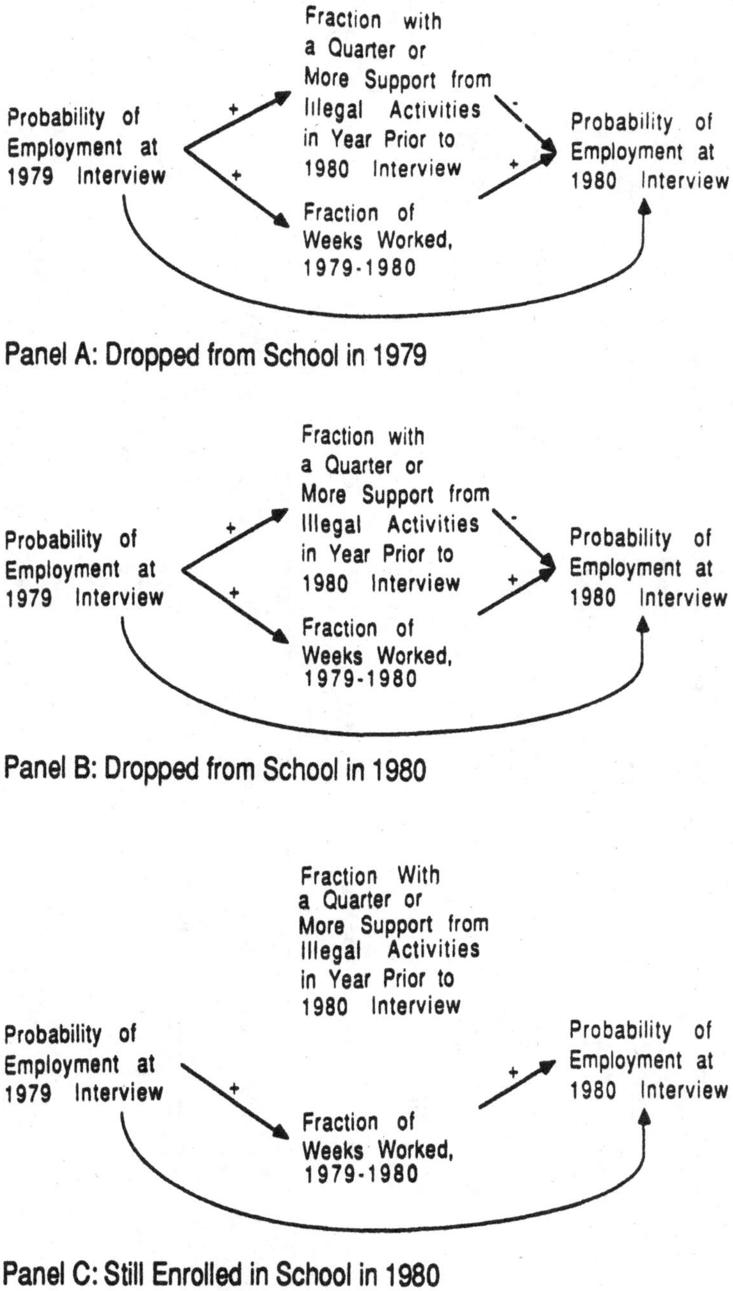

The fraction of weeks worked is an important determinant of the probability of employment in 1980. Employment status in 1979 affects the distribution of the fraction of weeks worked between the interviews in a fashion similar to that illustrated in Figure 3 above. The principal differences are in the relationships between labor force experience and the fraction of income earned illegally. The latter still has a negative impact on the probability of employment in 1980 but it is not significant. The probability of employment in 1979 is no longer a significant determinant of the probability that a substantial fraction of income will be earned illegally. The latter is significantly and negatively related to the fraction of weeks worked between the interviews, which was not the case for those who dropped out in 1979. The correlation is a larger negative number for those who were employed in 1979 than for these who were not, consistent with the hypothesis that the latter group was more likely to be underemployed. These relationships are illustrated schematically in Panel B of Figure 6.

Earning a quarter or more of support illegally did not affect the future probability of employment in 1980, as indicated by the estimates in Table 4. However, there was a significant and negative contemporaneous association with fraction of weeks worked for those who dropped out of school in 1980. These patterns are just the opposite of those observed for the minors who dropped out in 1979 and consequently were allocating no time to school.

Minors Still Enrolled In School

Once again, the features that characterized the other two groups persist for this group, with the exception of the relationships between earning a quarter or more of support illegally and the variables measuring employment experience. Employment status in 1979 is a significant determinant of fraction of weeks worked between the interview dates and of the probability of employment in 1980. Fraction of weeks worked is a significant determinant of the probability of employment in 1980. But earning substantial support illegally is not related to the measures of legal labor market activity, past, current, or future.[17] These relationships are depicted schematically in Panel C of Figure 6 and the estimates from the linear probability model and the probit model are presented in Table 4.

Conclusions

A comparison of the difference in significant relationships among minors who were out of school by 1979, those who dropped out in 1980, and those who remained enrolled, is facilitated by Figure 6. For sixteen and seventeen-year-olds, the impact upon the probability of employment in 1980 from earning a quarter or more of their support illegally is −.17 for those who were not enrolled in school since the 1979 interview, is −.09 for those who had dropped out by 1980, and is .02 for those still enrolled. The standard errors are −.097, −.081, and .021, respectively, and decrease as expected with the square root of the number of observations. These estimates are from the linear probability model.

From the perspective of substitution between activities, the pattern seems clearest for dropouts. For those who dropped out in 1979 and were no longer in school between the interview dates, prior employment in 1979 increases the probability of substantial illegal work, and involvement in the latter decreases the probability of future employment in 1980. The only puzzle is why there is no relationship between illegal work and fraction of weeks worked between the interview dates. One explanation is that for this group, the decision is more one of career choice between legal versus illegal rather than allocation of time between competing work activities. Another possibility for this group that is no longer in school is that they are underemployed in the legal market and are moonlighting in the illegal market and that, over time, some of them drift out of the legal market into crime as their career.

For those who dropped out in 1980, school continued to be a factor between the interview dates. For them, there is a significant substitution effect between fraction of weeks worked and illegal support. Since this group was still in school, career choice was less of a consideration but allocation of time included school as well as legal and illegal work. Furthermore, since this group was on the verge of dropping out, they may have needed considerable time for school, making allocation of time an important factor.

The group that remained enrolled in school in 1980 also has to consider allocating time among school, legal and illegal activity. However they are more productive with their time in school and may feel they can substitute among school, and legal and illegal activity, rather than between the latter two. Furthermore, since they are still investing in education they may not yet be at a career decision point between legal and illegal work. This could explain the apparent lack of connection between the variable measuring substantial illegal support and the three variables measuring past, contemporary, and future legal labor market involvement.

From the perspective of social welfare, it would appear there is no major loss of gross national product due to diversion of legitimate employment into crime. For this youth cohort sample, 14.1% had dropped out of school by adult age and 5.4% reported that one quarter or more of their support came from illegal activities, yet the estimates depicted in Figure 5, for example, show that only three out of the 140 minors who had not been enrolled in school since 1979 were diverted from employment in 1980 because of substantial criminal activity. Since only dropouts are apparently being diverted, at most 0.3% of this entire sample of sixteen and seventeen-year-olds is being diverted from legitimate work to exclusive criminal careers.

Bachman, O'Malley and Johnston[18] conclude that while dropouts tend to be the most criminal group, there is no evidence that dropouts become more criminal after leaving school. They suggest there is some factor causing failure in school as well as delinquency. Elliot and Voss[19] found that self-reported delinquency measures, especially for serious crimes, fell after the dropouts left school. The evidence from the National Longitudinal Youth Survey raises a question about the latter finding. The minors who were no longer in school after 1979 were the group with the highest fraction reporting substantial support from illegal activities, with the next highest being for those who dropped out by 1980. This evidence indicates serious criminality continuing unabated after dropping out. Furthermore, although we have developed no evidence that their criminality is increasing in an absolute sense, in a relative sense, dropouts are the only group being diverted into crime as a full-time career for these age groups below eighteen.

For most minors, earning a substantial fraction of support from illegal activities appears to be not so much a matter of career choice as of taking on another activity. Perhaps in time, for some individuals, legitimate work becomes more attractive than crime, a possibility deserving further investigation. For others, crime may continue as a moonlighting activity.

To the extent that the career criminal is a long-term problem and is a substantial source of crime over the lifetime of a cohort, policies and programs that target school dropouts are necessary. Greenwood and Zimring[20] survey intervention strategies for juveniles. However, focusing on school dropouts to the exclusion of those who remain enrolled would ignore 72% of the minors reporting substantial earnings from crime.

Employment status in 1980 depends heavily upon the fraction of weeks worked and employment status in 1979. For dropouts, age, sex, race, and the highest grade attained in school are not significant factors. The importance of individual characteristics is limited to determining the probability of employment in 1979. A more thorough estimation of this important employment equation is a project for the future. The evidence from this study suggests a great deal of inertia in labor force status, given initial conditions, and hence it is important to understand what determines those initial conditions.

III. ECONOMIC OPPORTUNITY, PARENTAL SUPPORT AND CRIMES BY YOUTH

In this research, key results of the analysis of the two previous sections are brought together to provide a more complete and more satisfying explanation of the choice by youth among legitimate work and crime for income. The form and substance of the econometric modeling builds on the labor-theoretic formulation of the previous section, accounting for the roles of work experience, educational attainment, and work availability on the choice to work. It also incorporates into the model the influence of family and religion in creating moral constraints on the temptation to be involved in crime that was explored in the first section. The focus continues to be on juveniles, sixteen and seventeen years of age. The objective continues to be a rigorous set of explanations that respond to economists' notions of how choices are made while responding to the assertions of sociologists and criminologists that family influences and moral forces can intervene in such a way that the usual economic models yield incorrect results.

The analysis of the supply of labor is developed within a framework established by Gronau.[21] The supply of weeks worked is viewed as depending on potential earnings which, in turn, are affected by years of school completed, experience, and may vary as well by sex and race. If the value of the labor supply function exceeds some threshold value, as determined by the reservation wage, then labor supply is positive and can be measured by a continuous variable or, alternatively, by a qualitative indicator taking the value one. If the supply is below the threshold value, then the indicator will be zero. The threshold value can be expected to vary among individuals and is influenced by the value of time in nonmarket pursuits, such as household production, and, more generally, by tastes.

The supply of effort to illegal activities is formulated in a parallel fashion, varying with potential illegal earnings. The latter is postulated, once again, to vary with sex, race, schooling, and experience. The supply of illegal effort will be positive if it exceeds the threshold value. The latter may be influenced not only by the value of time in other pursuits, which may vary by sex and race, but in this analysis also by moral constraints, as proxied by whether the individual was raised in a religious faith, professes one now, and is an active practitioner.

Of course other considerations may affect the supply of effort to illegal activities, including past delinquent behavior, and previous contact with the criminal justice system as developed in the first section, but the focus of this section is on two social institutions, the home and religion, since these latter two influences may be the antecedents that affect the evolutionary history of delinquent behavior and misbehavior in school.

A complex issue on which this analysis expands is the possible connection between the supply of effort to illegal activities and to work. We recognize that there is a group of individuals who participate in neither crime nor work, presumably because the return to either pursuit is below the corresponding reservation wage.

There is a second group involved in crime who do not work. It includes those for whom the reservation wage for work exceeds the return. This group may also include some for whom the wage exceeds the reservation wage, but who can earn a higher illegal than legal wage. This group could even include some for whom the legal wage exceeds the wage in crime, but who would be overemployed in legal work, and hence would choose crime.

A third group works but is not involved in crime. Similar considerations apply to this group as to the second one, but with the situation of crime and work reversed.

Lastly, the fourth group includes individuals who both work and supply effort to crime. For all of these individuals, both for work and for crime, the wage exceeds the reservation wage. They are receptive to supplying effort to both work and crime if, for example, the wage for work exceeds the wage for crime, but they are underemployed in work, or *vice versa*. Furthermore, for some, work and crime may be contingent complements, i.e. work provides the opportunity for crimes, such as embezzlement, pilfering, selling drugs to co-workers *etc.* Alternatively, crime may provide the financial basis for expanding effort into legal activities, including laundering money through legal fronts.

Data

The results reported in this section are based on information from questions asked at the 1979 and 1980 NLS interviews of 2,278 individuals, aged sixteen and seventeen (in 1980), who remained enrolled in school at the time of the 1980 interview. The measure of schooling is the highest year of school completed by the 1980 interview. The measure of experience is whether the individual was employed at the time of the 1979 interview. This may not only be a measure of experience prior to the interval between the interview dates, but also a basis for forming expectations about the probability of finding work.

The Model

Evaluating the determinants of the supply of effort to legitimate work and to crime depends upon identifying the thresholds at which participation in either or both take place. This requires two parallel derivations. The modeling takes advantage of what has been learned in the preceeding section regarding the determinants of supply. Thus, in this model, an individual is presumed to supply effort to work, measured in our data by the fraction of weeks worked between the 1979 and 1980 interview dates, h_L, if this effort exceeds the threshold, η_L. In the formulation we develop here, the supply of effort depends upon schooling, s, experience, x, race, r, and sex, g. The threshold is presumed to depend upon the reservation wage, which reflects the value of time in non-market activities, such as the household, and is specified to be a function of race (black: 1, white: 0) and sex (male: 1, female: 0). Thus for labor supplied to legitimate work, h_L, we have:

$$h_L = a_L + b_L s + c_L x + d_L r + k_L g + e_1 = X'\beta_L + e_1, \tag{1}$$

and for the threshold, η_L, we can write:

$$\eta_L = m_L + n_L r + q_L g + e_2 = Y'_L \gamma_L + e_2 \tag{2}$$

where $h_L > 0$ if $h_L > \eta_L$, i.e. if $X'\beta_L + e_1 > Y'\gamma_L + e_2$,
or defining $e_L = e_1 - e_2$,

$$h_L > 0 \text{ if } e_L > Y'_L \gamma_L - X'\beta_L . \tag{3}$$

In a similiar fashion, we can model h_I, the supply of effort to crime, measured in our study by the level of support obtained illegally (none, very little, about 1/4, about 1/2, about 3/4, almost all) between the 1979 and 1980 interview dates. It will be positive if it exceeds the threshold, η_I.

Once again, the supply effort is presumed to depend upon potential earnings, as determined by schooling, experience, race, and sex, so that:

$$h_I = a_I + b_I s + c_I x + d_I r + k_I g + e_3 = X'\beta_I + e_3 . \quad (4)$$

In this case, the threshold depends upon the reservation wage for engaging in illegal behavior, which may be a function of moral constraint, as well as the value of time in non-market activities. It is specified in this study as depending upon sex, race, whether the individual was raised in a faith, f_1, whether the individual has a current religious affiliation, f_2, and the frequency of church attendance (not at all, infrequently, once per month, 2-3 times per month, once per week, more than once per week), f_3, thus:

$$\eta_I = m_I + n_I r + q_I g + t_I f_1 + u_I f_2 + v_I f_3 + e_4 = Y'_I \gamma_I + e_4 \quad (5)$$

where $h_I > 0$ if $h_I > \eta_I$, i.e. if $X_I + e_3 > Y'_I \gamma_I + e_4$,
or defining $e_I = e_3 - e_4$,

$$h_I > 0 \text{ if } e_I > Y'_I \gamma_I - X'\beta_I . \quad (6)$$

Econometric Considerations

Equations 3 and 6 can be used to estimate the supply of effort to work, and to illegal activities, respectively. For example, taking Equation 3, participation could be estimated using a logit or probit specification, and the fraction of weeks worked could be estimated using a tobit procedure.

The indicator variable, ρ_L, for participation in work or not will be one if $h_L > 0$, i.e., $e_L > Y'_L \gamma_L - X'\beta_L$, and zero otherwise, as illustrated in Fig. 1 for the distribution of e_L. The likelihood function will be:

$$L = \Pi \, F(Y'_L \gamma_L - X'\beta_L) \, \Pi \, [1 - F(Y'_L \gamma_L - X'\beta_L)], \quad (7)$$

where the type of distribution, F, assumed for e_L, will determine whether the specification for the marginal probabilities is probit or logit. The objective is to estimate which of the variables significantly determines the precise point in the distribution at which the threshold exists.

If we consider the two decisions to participate in work and in crime jointly, then we can proceed in two ways. Assuming that the errors, e_L and

FIGURE 1
The Marginal Probit (or Logit) Distribution and the Participation Threshold

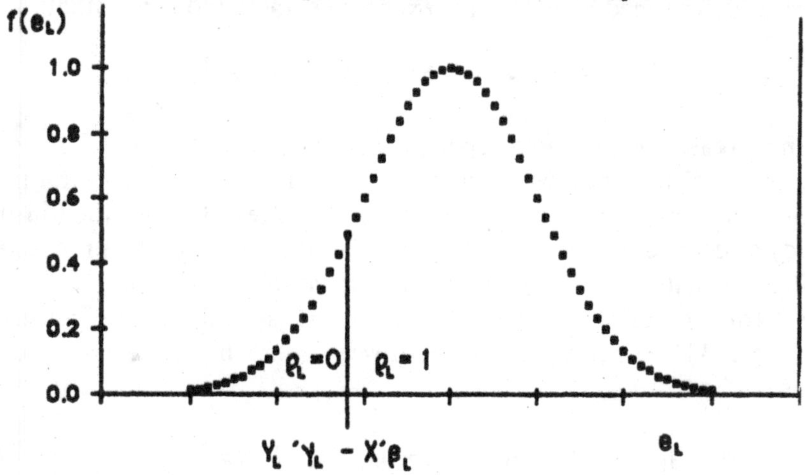

e_I, have a bivariate normal distribution, a bivariate probit model can be estimated, which takes into account the possible correlation between the error terms e_L and e_I. As discussed in Amemiya[22] this procedure keeps the simple probit form for the specification of the marginal probabilities. A second specification, also discussed by Amemiya, is to make the joint probabilities the focus and to use a multinomial logit model for the four alternatives, indexed by j, of:

(1) not participate in either work or crime, $j = 0$,
(2) participate in crime but not work, $j = 1$,
(3) participate in work but not crime, $j = 2$, and
(4) participate in both, $j = 3$.

This procedure specifies a simple logit form for the joint probabilities. These four choices, as illustrated by the marginal and the joint probabilities, are illustrated in Fig. 2. This is a plot of the joint distribution of the error terms, e_L and e_I, for equations 3 and 6. The threshold for participation in legitimate work, $Y'_L\gamma_L - X'\beta_L$, is represented vertically and that for crime, $Y'_I\gamma - X'\beta_I$, horizontally. The distribution of the errors for the population of individuals is represented by the concentric ellipses. As represented in Figure 2, the bulk of the population is participating in legitimate work ($\rho_L = 1$) and not in crime ($\rho_I = 0$). The smallest population subset is in crime only ($\rho_I = 1$, $\rho_L = 0$). The objective of the multinomial

FIGURE 2
The Joint Vs. the Marginal Probabilities For Participation in Work and Crime

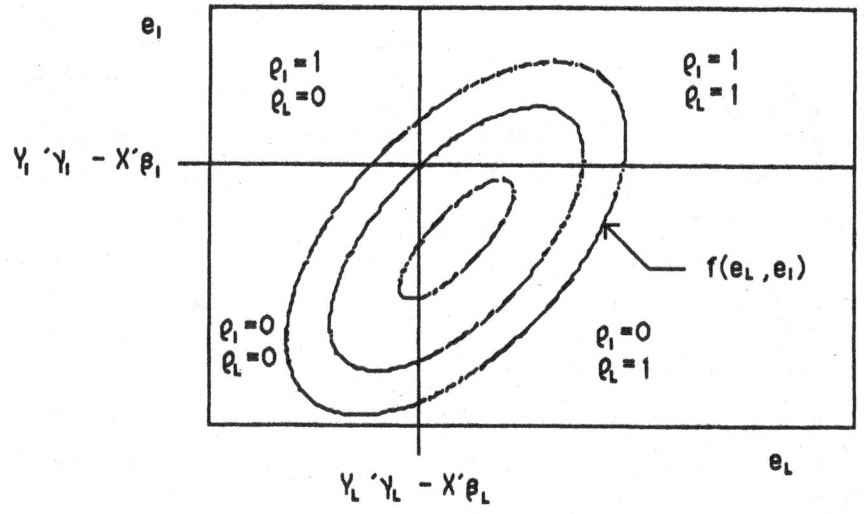

estimation procedure is to estimate, jointly, the determinants of this outcome.

Note that Y_I includes the variables in Y_L. The vector Z' is defined in terms of the vectors X' and Y_I', $Z' = X'$: Y_I', and the indicator variable y_{ij} is defined as taking the value one if the ith individual is in the jth group, as determined by participation in work and crime, and zero otherwise. The logarithm of the likelihood function for the multinomial model is:

$$\ln L = \Sigma\Sigma\, y_{ij} \ln P_{ij} \tag{8}$$

where

$$\ln P_{ij} = \exp(Z_i'\delta_j)/\Sigma \exp(Z_i'\delta_j), \quad \text{and } \delta_0 = 0. \tag{9}$$

Estimation

The potential power of the human capital and demographic variables in explaining the decision to participate in work is revealed in a simple fashion by comparing the list of means of the explanatory variables for the 783 individuals who did not work between the 1979 and 1980 interview dates with the corresponding list of means for the 1,495 people who did

TABLE 1
Mean Values of Schooling and Other Variables for Those Who Worked and Those Who Did Not

	Not Working		Working	
Explanatory Variable	Mean	Standard Deviation	Mean	Standard Deviation
Schooling (Years)	9.57	.93	10.02	.87
Sex (M=1, F=0)	.42	.40	.54	.50
Race (B=1, W=0)	.39	.40	.20	.40
Experience (Empl. in 79=1)	.001	.036	.49	.41
Number of Observations	783		1495	

work. The standard deviations, as well as the means, are exhibited in Table 1.

The group who worked had a higher mean number of years of schooling completed than those who did not. The working group was composed of 54% males and 20% blacks, compared to 42% males and 39% black, for the other group. Of those working between the interview dates, 49% had been employed at the time of the 1979 interview, while for those not working during the interval, only 0.1% had been employed at that date.

The participation equation for work was estimated using a linear probability model, as well as the probit and logit specifications. The results are reported in Table 2. Not surprisingly for a model well developed in the literature, the human capital model of potential earnings and participation in work produces satisfying results. Schooling and experience both have a positive impact on participation. Males are more likely to participate than females and blacks are less likely to participate than whites. As indicated by the linear probability model, 24% of the variance is explained, a level sufficiently high that the probit and logit models have some power in classifying (or discriminating between) those who work and those who do not. As indicated by the figures at the bottom of Table 2, 72% of the individuals are correctly classified by the model. Of course, if the individuals were classified perfectly by the model, the marginal distribution totals of 783 and 1,495 would lie along the diagonal of the cross-classification table with zeros for the off-diagonal entries.

The human capital and demographic variables, even though augmented by the proxies for moral restraint, do not have much explanatory

TABLE 2
Estimated Models of Participating in Work

Explanatory Variable	Linear Probability	Probit	Logit
Constant	-.307	-3.04	-5.07
	(3.4)*	(-8.6)	(-8.5)
Schooling	.087	.315	.525
	(9.0)	(8.9)	(8.8)
Sex	.101	.369	.609
	(5.8)	(5.8)	(5.9)
Race	-.130	-.420	-.683
	(-6.5)	(-6.2)	(-6.2)
Experience	.404	2.80	6.19
	(19.9)	(9.0)	(6.1)
Coefficient of Determination, R^2	.240		

*t-statistics in parenthesis

Classification	Predicted: ρ_L=0	ρ_L=1	Totals
Actual: ρ_L=0	332	451	783
ρ_L=1	192	1303	1495
Totals	524	1754	2278

power in distinguishing those individuals who commit economic crimes from those who do not. The means and standard deviations of these variables are listed for those two groups in Table 3.

The differences between the means for schooling, experience, and race are much smaller in the case of the decision to participate in crime or not than was the case of the decision to participate in work. However, the difference in the means for the variable sex is greater.

The participation decision for crime was also estimated with a linear probability model, as well as with the probit and logit specifications. The results are reported in Table 4. An important finding of this study is that the human capital model of potential earnings is not nearly as effective in explaining the decision to participate in crime as it was in explaining the decision to participate in work, even after accounting for the effect of moral constraint on the reservation wage. The striking fact is that schooling has even less explanatory power in explaining the decision to participate in crime than experience does. The measure of experience, indicating as it does that the individual was working at the time of the 1979 inter-

TABLE 3
Mean Values of Schooling and Other Variables for Those Who Commit Crime and Those Who Do Not

Explanatory Variable	Do Not Commit Crime Mean	Do Not Commit Crime Standard Deviation	Commit Crime Mean	Commit Crime Standard Deviation
Schooling (Years)	9.88	.92	9.81	.91
Sex (M=1, F=0)	.46	.50	.66	.48
Race (B=1, W=0)	.26	.44	.32	.47
Experience (Empl. in 79=1)	.26	.44	.30	.46
Raised In Faith (Yes=1)	.96	.20	.93	.25
Have Current Faith (Yes=1)	.92	.28	.88	.32
Church Attendance (Ordinal: None=1, ...>Once/Wk.=6)	3.69	1.72	3.26	1.72
Number of Observations	1850		428	

view, may in fact, have little relevance to experience in crime. But why is schooling not significant? Is schooling irrelevant to earning power in illegal activities, or is the schooling measure a poor index of the human capital accumulated by those individuals that go into crime? The fraction of variance explained by this crime participation model is only 3.6%, too small for the model to have any power in classifying individuals correctly, although since 1,850 individuals do not commit crime, 81% are correctly classified, as indicated by the figures at the bottom of Table 4. Nonetheless, the model predicts that no one will commit crime compared to 428 who do. Males are much more likely to participate in crime than females, and the estimated coefficients for the sex variable for this model are similar to those estimated for the model to participate in work. Blacks are more likely to participate in crime than whites. Moral restraint has some impact in raising the reservation wage for participating in crime, particularly the frequency of church attendance.

Expanding the specification of the supply of effort to crime to account for expectations of sanctions, as well as involvement in other kinds of misbehavior, such as suspension or expulsion from school and status offenses, may increase the explanatory power. Nonetheless, there is a

TABLE 4
Estimated Models of Participating in Crime

Explanatory Variable	Linear Probability	Probit	Logit
Constant	.307	-.476	-.856
	(3.1)*	(-1.3)	(-1.3)
Schooling (Years)	-.008	-.035	-.053
	(-0.9)	(-1.0	(-0.9)
Sex (M=1, F=0)	.109	.419	.747
	(6.7)	(6.6)	(6.6)
Race (B=1, W=0)	.056	.209	.367
	(3.0)	(3.0)	(3.0)
Experience (Empl. in '79=1)	.036	.134	.244
	(1.9)	(1.9)	(2.0)
Raised in Faith (Yes=1)	-.059	-.183	-.314
	(-1.2)	(-1.0)	(-1.0)
Have Current Faith (Yes=1)	.006	.030	.047
	(0.2)	(0.2)	(0.2)
Church Attendance (Ordinal: None=1, ...>Once/Wk.=6)	-.018	-.068	-.121
	(-3.6)	(-3.5)	(-3.5)
Coefficient of Determination, R^2	.036		

*t-statistics in parenthesis

Classification Predicted:	$\rho_I=0$	$\rho_I=1$	Totals
Actual: $\rho_I=0$	1850	0	1850
$\rho_I=1$	428	0	428
Totals	2278	0	2278

dramatic contrast in the variance explained by the participation formulation applied to work versus that for crime.

Turning next to the two-way classification of individuals by whether they participate or not in work and crime, the residuals from the marginal probit models for work and crime were found to be significantly and positively correlated with a coefficient of 0.17, indicating some tendency to participate in both or neither. To provide insight, the means and standard deviations of the explanatory variables are listed in Table 5 for the four groups.

The individuals with the most education and work experience and are not involved in crimes for income, while those with the least education

TABLE 5
Mean Values of Schooling and Other Variables for Joint Participation (or not) in Work and Crime

Explanatory Variable	Neither Crime Nor Work Mean	Crime Not Work Mean	Work Not Crime Mean	Both Crime And Work Mean	All Individuals In Samples Mean
Schooling**	9.60 (.92)*	9.39 (.98)	10.05 (.87)	9.94 (.85)	9.87 (.92)
Sex	.40 (.49)	.56 (.50)	.50 (.50)	.69 (.46)	.50 (.50)
Race	.38 (.49)	.44 (.50)	.18 (.39)	.28 (.45)	.27 (.44)
Experience	.001 (.038)	.000 (.000)	.41 (.49)	.39 (.49)	.27 (.44)
Raised in Faith	.97 (.17)	.89 (.31)	.95 (.21)	.94 (.23)	.95 (.21)
Current Faith	.92 (.27)	.87 (.33)	.92 (.28)	.89 (.32)	.91 (.28)
Church Attendance	3.72 (1.72)	3.39 (1.74)	3.67 (1.72)	3.32 (1.72)	3.60 (1.73)
Number of Observations	680	103	1170	325	2278

*Standard deviation of the variables in parenthesis
**For Units, See Table 4.

and experience are involved in crime and do not work. Females constitute 60% of the group that do not participate in either work or crime, while males account for 69% of the individuals who participate in both. Blacks are least represented in the group that works and does not participate in crime, and are most represented in the group that does not work but does participate in crime for income. Those involved in crime, whether they work or not, tend to attend church less frequently, and 11% of the individuals who participate in crime, but do not work, were raised in a religious faith.

In order to take account formally of the fact that the individual really faces a four-way choice, the joint probabilities of participating or not in work and crime were estimated with a multinomial logit model. The estimated parameters are reported in Table 6. Recall that the estimated parameters for the individuals who participate in neither work nor crime are normalized to zero. As before, schooling and experience are important variables in explaining participation in work. Males tend to participate more in both work and crime than females. *The most important finding is that race is not a significant explanatory variable for the group who participate in crime but not in work. At a minimum, for individuals*

TABLE 6
Multinomial Model for Joint Participation (or not) in Work and Crime

Explanatory Variable	Crime Not Work	Work Not Crime	Both Crime And Work
Constant	.665 (.6)*	-4.53 (-6.5)	-5.23 (-5.8)
Schooling (Years)	-.174 (-1.6)	.519 (8.1)	.441 (5.3)
Sex (M=1, F=0)	.570 (2.6)	.512 (4.5)	1.25 (8.2)
Race (B=1, W=0)	.200 (.9)	-.791 (-6.5)	-.219 (-1.4)
Experience (Empl. in '79=1)	-5.80 (-.1)	6.05 (6.0)	6.07 (6.0)
Raised in Faith (Yes=1)	-1.52 (-2.7)	-.710 (-2.0)	-.505 (-1.2)
Have Current Faith (Yes=1)	.438 (.9)	.115 (.5)	.032 (.1)
Church Attendance (Ordinal: None=1, ...>Once/Wk.=6)	-.062 (-.9)	.015 (.4)	.129 (-2.8)

*t-statistics in parenthesis

Classification: Actual:	Predicted: $\rho_L=0,\rho_I=0$	$\rho_L=0,\rho_I=1$	$\rho_L=1,\rho_I=0$	$\rho_L=1,\rho_I=1$
$\rho_L=0,\rho_I=0$	354	1	325	0
$\rho_L=0,\rho_I=1$	57	0	46	0
$\rho_L=1,\rho_I=0$	211	0	959	0
$\rho_L=1,\rho_I=1$	80	0	245	0

who are not working, this means that there is no significant racial differential for those in crime versus those who are not. The major difference for blacks is that a much smaller proportion work than is the case for whites, as reflected by the significant negative coefficient on race for the group that works but is not involved in crime. Lastly, consistent with Table 5, being raised in a faith significantly decreases the probability that an individual will participate in crime but not work. The frequency of church attendance only decreases the probability of participating in both work and crime. Fifty-eight per cent of the individuals are correctly classified among the four groups.

The Effect of Dropping Out of School on Work and Crime

The sample was expanded by 228 observations to include those individuals at the same ages who dropped out of school between the 1979 and

TABLE 7
Participation in Work or Crime Conditional on Enrollment in 1980

	Neither Crime Nor Work $\rho_L=0, \rho_I=0$	Crime Not Work $\rho_L=0, \rho_I=1$	Work Not Crime $\rho_L=1, \rho_I=0$	Both Crime And Work $\rho_L=1, \rho_I=1$	Total
Dropouts by '80	18.0	5.7	49.1	27.2	100%
Enrolled in '80	29.8	4.5	51.4	14.3	100%
Total	28.8	4.6	51.2	15.4	100%

1980 interviews. A dummy variable was added to the multinomial estimations to indicate whether the person was still enrolled as of the 1980 interview. In treating the variable as exogenous, we are presuming that the decision to drop out is based on achievement in school, or the lack thereof, as determined by a cumulative process over time, and is not influenced by the decision to participate in work or crime. Of course, some of the young people enrolled in school are involved in crimes for income before they enter the labor force. Modeling the decision to stay enrolled in school as jointly endogenous with the decision to participate in work and crime is an alternative for future analysis.

Examining the decisions to participate or not in crime or work, conditional upon classification by whether the individual was still enrolled or not as of 1980, shows that dropouts were more likely to participate in both crime and work than enrollees, and less likely to not participate in both activities. The conditional distributions are reported in Table 7.

The results of the multinomial model, estimated for the enlarged sample and with the additional variable indicating enrollment status as of the 1980 interview, are reported in Table 8.

The individuals who remain enrolled in school have a significantly lower probability of participating in crime or work, or both. Fifty-seven percent of the individuals are correctly classified among the four groups, although with the additional information on enrollment status the model classifies some individuals in the group that participates in both work and crime. The evidence from this study is consistent with the notion that dropouts are more involved in crimes for income than those who remain in school. Further analysis is needed to ascertain whether a dropout becomes less criminal after leaving school.

Principal Findings

The decision to participate in work is explained satisfactorily by a model of individuals comparing their potential earnings, as determined

TABLE 8
Multinomial Model for Joint Participation Given School Enrollment Status in 1980

Explanatory Variable	Crime Not Work	Work Not Crime	Both Crime And Work
Constant	.707	-3.67	-3.62
	(.7)*	(-5.7)	(-4.6)
Schooling (Years)	-.135	.473	.373
	(-1.3)	(8.0)	(5.1)
Sex (M=1, F=0)	.188	.548	1.29
	(3.0)	(5.0)	(9.0)
Race (B=1, W=0)	.188	-.774	-.288
	(.9)	(-6.6)	(-1.9)
Experience (Empl. in '79=1)	-5.69	6.08	6.01
	(-.1)	(6.0)	(6.0)
Raised in Faith (Yes=1)	-1.26	-.475	-.233
	(-2.4)	(-1.5)	(-0.6)
Have Current Faith (Yes=1)	.466	.113	.125
	(1.0)	(.5)	(.4)
Church Attendance (Ordinal: None=1, ...>Once/Wk.=6)	-.798	.022	-.111
	(-1.3)	(.7)	(-2.6)
Enrollment in '80 (Yes=1)	-.635	-.688	-1.33
	(-1.8)	(-3.3)	(-5.7)

*t-statistics in parenthesis

Classification:	Predicted: $\rho_L=0, \rho_I=0$	$\rho_L=0, \rho_I=1$	$\rho_L=1, \rho_I=0$	$\rho_L=1, \rho_I=1$
Actual:				
$\rho_L=0, \rho_I=0$	365	1	349	6
$\rho_L=0, \rho_I=1$	62	0	52	2
$\rho_L=1, \rho_I=0$	227	0	1045	10
$\rho_L=1, \rho_I=1$	82	0	297	8

by their human capital, with their reservation wage, as influenced by alternative uses of their time and their tastes. Applying the same framework of analysis to the decision to participate in crime is not as successful, in terms of the fraction of the variance explained, notwithstanding that 76% of the individuals in the sample who are involved in crimes for income also work. Nonetheless, this approach provides some insights.

Parents who instill moral values in their children, measured in this study by being raised in a religion, are less likely to see their children involved in crimes for income. Youth who practice their faith through church attendance are less likely to participate in crime. These findings are consistent with moral values raising the reservation wage for participating in crime.

An important finding is that race affects neither the probability of participating in crime but not work, nor the probability of participating in both crime and work. Controlling for human capital and moral values within the framework of the model is important to this result, since 44% of the individuals who participate in crime but not work are black, compared to their average of 25% in the NLS sample.

Blacks are significantly less likely to participate in work but not crime, controlling for potential earnings and sex. This suggests that either blacks face a handicap in finding jobs, or that there are unmeasured factors affecting the reservation wage that are associated with being black.

Dropouts are twice as likely to participate in both crimes for income and work than are persons who remain in school. The young people who are involved in both work and crime account for over three-fourths of those involved in crimes for income and have levels of schooling nearly as high as those who only work. Recent dropouts account for one sixth of this group. In contrast, the individuals involved in crime, but not in work, are a less educated group. They may be handicapped by lack of education in their efforts to find a job.

SUMMARIZING THE RATIONAL CHOICE MODELS

At this point, it may be useful to the reader to summarize what we believe we have learned about the role of race in determining the choice among leisure, work, and crime. Race was not considered directly in the first section, which focused on an extensive list of environmental, attitudinal, and family characteristics as they influence the choice process. One should recognize that these characteristics may vary with race, so that, in some sense, race differences are accounted for, but not explicitly recognized. Recall that in the second section, the approach was to explain the probability of employment in 1980 in terms of two predetermined variables: the probability of employment in 1979 and the fraction of weeks worked between 1979 and 1980. Although race and sex affect these predetermined variables, given the predetermined variables, race and sex do not significantly affect the dependent variable, the probability of employment in 1980. Thus, the use of the predetermined explanatory variables captures the effects of race and sex.

In the third section, the use of the intermediary predetermined variables is dropped and the decision is expanded from solely employment to the joint decision to participate in work and/or crime. This is explained in terms of individual characteristics that affect the earnings potential of human capital and the shadow price of time, both of which are expected to vary with race and sex. The model is formulated to allow us to investigate the differential effect of race on the four-way choice among working or not and engaging in crime or not. Controlling for moral compliance and economic conditions, we find that *race is not a factor in determining whether individuals engage in crime or not, given that they are not working*. We obtain this result notwithstanding the fact that blacks are disproportionately represented in the group not working, but engaged in crime. *In contrast, controlling for education and experience, we do find that race still significantly explains that blacks are less likely to be working but not in crime. There appears to be a labor market effect of race, but not a criminal effect.*

We view these results as a confirmation of the appropriateness of the approach we have followed and substantial support for the hypothesis that differences in crime participation for income between blacks and whites reflect differences in economic opportunities. We regard the fact that there is no difference in the intercept between races with respect to crime involvement in the multinomial logit estimates as a valid test. The result is reinforced by the very significant difference we find between blacks and whites regarding participation in legitimate work.

The implications of these results should certainly be pursued further. For example, it would be desirable to estimate the final relationships separately for race and sex as was done in other work of ours.[23] The fact that taking account of educational attainment, family influences, and employment opportunities eliminates race as an explanation for crime doesn't rule out the possibility that there are interaction effects between these variables and race. Blacks may suffer in terms of educational opportunities relative to whites, but this may be explained, at least in part, by diminished opportunities in education. Differences in family factors may be important for blacks, as earlier writers have suggested. These questions could be investigated further using the approach we have presented here as a point of departure.

NOTES

The authors wish to acknowledge support for this research from the Law and Social Science Division of the National Science Foundation and from the University of California-Santa Barbara Academic Senate Committee on Research. The first two sections have benefited from constructive criticism at our session of the Western Economic Association International Annual Meetings, San Francisco, July 1986. The third has benefited from comments at a similar session at the Allied Social Sciences Association Meetings in New Orleans, December 1986.

1. Phillips, L., H.L. Votey, Jr. and D. Maxwell, "Crime, Youth and the Labor Market," *Journal of Political Economy*, 80, 3 (1972): 491-504.

2. Phillips, L. and H.L. Votey, Jr., "The Influence of Police Interactions and Alternative Income Sources on the Dynamic Process of Choosing Crime as a Career." *Journal of Quantitative Criminology*, Vol. 3, No. 3 (1987): 251-273.

3. Blumstein, A., D.P. Farrington, and S. Moitra, "Delinquency Careers: Innocents, Desisters and Persisters," in M. Toury and N. Morris (eds.), *Crime and Justice: An Annual Review of Research*, Vol. 6, (Chicago: University of Chicago Press, 1985).

4. Phillips and Votey, *op. cit.*

5. Shapiro P. and H.L. Votey, Jr., "Deterrence and Subjective Probabilities of Arrest: Modeling Individual Decisions to Drink and Drive in Sweden." *Law and Society Review*, 18, 4 (1984): 583-605.

6. Phillips and Votey, *op. cit.*

7. Phillips and Votey, *op. cit.*

8. Phillips, Llad, Harold L. Votey, Jr. and Darold Maxwell. *Op. cit.*

9. Bachman, Green and Wirtanen report on findings from a nationally representative panel of over 2000 adolescent boys. Their evidence indicates that delinquent behaviors precede dropping out from school. Their twenty-six item list of self-reported delinquent behavior included five behaviors in the class of economic crimes or crimes against property. The authors found the strongest association between educational attainment and interpersonal aggression and delinquent behavior in school. Elliot and Voss studied 2617 junior high and high school students from California. Their ten-item list of self-reported delinquent behaviors included four economic crimes. They found that dropouts, both male and female, had four times more police contact than graduates and also reported more delinquent behavior. However, they also find that after the dropouts leave school, police contact and self-reported delinquency decline to the point that they are substantially below those for graduates. See Bachman, J., S. Green, and I. Wirtanen, *Youth in Transition* Vol. III *Dropping Out: Problem or Symptom?* (Ann Arbor, MI; Institute for Social Research, University of Michigan, 1977) and Delbert Elliot and Horwin Voss, *Delinquency and Dropout* (Lexington, Massachusetts: Lexington Books, 1974).

10. Crowley, Joan. "Delinquency and Employment." In Michael Borus, ed., *Youth and the Labor Market* (Kalamazoo, Michigan: W.E. Upjohn Institute for Employment Research, 1984).

11. Meyer, Robert and David Wise. "High School Preparation and Early Labor Force Experience," in Richard Freeman and David Wise, ed., *The Youth Labor Market Problem*. (Chicago: University of Chicago Press, 1982).

12. Hirschi, Travis. *Causes of Delinquency*. (Berkeley: University of California Press, 1969).

13. Of course the probability of employment in 1979 $P_E(79)$, is an imperfect measure of labor market knowledge, and other factors may affect the expectation as well, and these considerations are represented by the constant, α, and the error term, u. The modified formulation of Eq. 1 is:

$$f^* = \alpha + \beta P_E(79) + u \quad ,$$

and the linear probability model becomes,

$$P_E(80) = -\alpha - \beta P_E(79) + f - u \ .$$

If being employed in 1979 raises the expectation of a minimally satisfactory employment experience, which seems plausible, then β will be positive.

14. Following Maddala, if the probit parameters are divided by 2.5, first adding 1.25 to the constant term, then they are comparable to the linear probability model. See Maddala, G.S. *United Dependent and Qualitative Variables in Econometrics* (Cambridge: Cambridge University Press, 1983).

15. Illegal, as well as legal, work experience should affect expectations about a satisfactory fraction of weeks worked:

$$f^* = \alpha + \beta P_E(79) + \gamma P_I(79\text{-}80) + u \quad ,$$

where $\gamma > 0$, and the linear probability model becomes,

$$P_E(80) = -\alpha - \beta P_E(79) - \gamma P_I(79\text{-}80) + f - u \ .$$

16. Crowley (1984), *op. cit.*

17. Once again, having one quarter or more of illegal support is negatively correlated with fraction of weeks employed between the interview dates for those who were employed in 1979, indicating some weak evidence of substitution, but for those employed in 1979 the correlation is significantly positive, and for the two groups combined the correlation is positive and insignificant.

18. Bachman, Jerald, Patrick O'Malley and Jerome Johnston. *Youth In Transition, V., VI. Adolescence to Adulthood-Change and Stability in the Lives of Young Men.* (Ann Arbor: Institute For Social Research, University of Michigan, 1978).

19. Elliot, and Voss, *op. cit.*

20. Greenwood, Peter and Franklin Zimring. *One More Chance.* (Santa Monica: The Rand Corporation, 1985).

21. Gronau, Reuben. "Wage Comparisons-a Selectivity Bias," *Journal of Political Economy*, 82, (1974) pp. 1119-1143.

22. Amemiya, Takeshi. *Advanced Econometrics*, (Cambridge, Mass.: Harvard University Press, 1985).

23. Phillips and Votey, (1987), *op. cit.*

UNEMPLOYMENT AND RACIAL DIFFERENCES IN IMPRISONMENT

Samuel L. Myers, Jr. and William J. Sabol

Conventional wisdom about the criminal justice system suggests that extralegal factors such as race or employment status should not affect sentencing outcomes. In this paper we examine an alternative model of the relationship between imprisonment and unemployment and race. The model suggests that penal practices are shaped by the labor market conditions of a system of production and that prisons, as part of a larger set of institutions providing support for economically-dependent populations, help to regulate the most superfluous group of workers in the industrial economy of the Northern states of the United States—unemployed black workers who comprise a large fraction of the pool of "reserve" workers necessary for price stability and economic expansion. We find support for the structural model that links black imprisonment (and Northern imprisonment in general) to manufacturing output and black unemployment.

THREE VIEWS ON EMPLOYMENT AND CRIME

Theoretical and empirical efforts have long been directed toward investigating the relationship between unemployment and crime. From Bonger[1] to Becker[2] economists, sociologists, and others have attempted to understand this intuitively appealing relationship. For economists in particular there are three roots of the fascination with efforts to discover the linkages between crime and labor markets. First, in an era when the nation's prisons are bursting at their seams with thousands of unemployed, mostly black young males, there is a suspicion that low wages, high unemployment, and the disadvantage created by segmented labor markets might be causally linked to criminal behavior. The microeconomic wisdom has it that as the relative attractiveness of illegal pursuits increases so too will the rational offender's allocation of time to crime. Since high unemployment, low wages, and unpleasant working conditions can be expected to enhance the attractiveness of illegitimate activities, a logical connection between crime and unemployment arises in this Beckerian-type world.[3] Unfortunately, tests of this straight-forward hypothesis have yielded mixed if not inconclusive results. Consequently, policy-relevant analyses that demonstrate the efficacy of improved employment opportunities in reducing crime have been discredited.[4]

A second line of thought adopts an explicitly macroeconomic perspective. The long-term fluctuations in economic activity are assumed to be causally related to the growth and decline of crime rates. Thus, an era of economic expansion is expected to be associated with a slowing in the growth of crime, while depressions and recessions are expected to be associated with an increase in crime. The reasons for this anticipated cyclical pattern of crime vary from writer to writer. But the theories offered are related remotely to the structure of opportunity models familiar to sociologists.[5] Here, the causal mechanism connecting illegitimate pursuits and lack of employment is less a function of rational choices of self-interested, individualistic, utility maximizers and more a function of the structure of rewards and means for attaining them in a market economy, or to paraphrase Merton, the interaction between deviants and the larger society is symptomatic of a divergence between culturally determined aspirations and the socially structured avenues available to achieve those goals.[6]

Within this broader, macroeconomic or macrosociological approach to labor markets and crime, the resurgence of interest in business cycles has helped fuel heated debate about the existence of a counter-cyclical pattern of crime and economic prosperity. Harvey Brenner,[7] one of the most influential and controversial proponents of the view that unemployment causes crime and related social ills, has offered detailed evidence of a strong correlation between homicide rates and unemployment rates. This correlation does not admit to a simple cyclical relationship because in some periods economic growth is found to drive *increases* in homicide rates rather than the expected reductions. Even these impressive findings have been challenged, however. In several papers Cook and Zarkin[8] contend that the widely cited Brenner conclusions are suspect on various methodological and data suitability grounds. Those authors, unable to replicate the Brenner results, contend that it is too soon to adopt significant policy initiatives based on the presumption of a business cycle effect on crime. They conclude:

> The major movements in crime rates during the last half century cannot be attributed to the business cycle. Recessions have caused relatively small increases in some types of crime (robbery, burglary) but have reduced auto theft and had negligible influence on murder rates.[9]

Finally Richard Freeman's[10] dated review summarizes the emerging "conventional wisdom" among economists as it relates to this macroeconomic view: (1) Although there is a cyclical pattern to the crime rate, with crime rising over the cycle with unemployment, it rises only weakly so that changes in crime rates are dominated by other factors. (2) The widely different crime rates of various cities and states are loosely linked to labor market conditions. (3) In studies that include measures of criminal sanctions and labor market factors, criminal sanctions tend to have a greater impact on criminal behavior than do labor market factors.[11]

The third perspective on labor markets and crime stems from the classic political economy literature on crime and punishment. It offers quite another perspective of the role of economic fluctuations. It looks at the interaction between the response to criminal activity, punishment, and alternating periods of economic growth or decline. Stemming from the now famous statement of the political economy of punishment, Rusche and Kirchheimer's *Punishment and Social Structure*,[12] this perspective suggests that imprisonment, as a form of punishment, does more than just punish offenders. Specifically, it suggests that in capitalist economies prisons perform a regulatory function that helps to drain off the excesses from the labor markets that lead inevitably to surpluses due to the tendency of capitalist economies to overproduce.

Rusche and Kirchheimer's theory was among the first to break the putatively inextricable bond between crime and punishment by demonstrating how penal policies were shaped by economic and political forces. Their theory, which begins with the proposition that every system of production tends to discover punishments that correspond to productive relations, implies that in addition to the usual functions of deterrence and retribution, systems of punishment fulfill other functions required by the productive system of the society at large. They show, for example, how punishment has been utilized, via coercion of convict labor, to counteract chronic labor shortages, say in pre-capitalist Germany, or conversely, in industrial societies with chronic unemployment, how the form of punishment was changed from labor coercion to idle imprisonment.

The Rusche/Kirchheimer theory does not deny that judges or other individuals involved in sentencing or conviction decisions believe themselves to be reacting to the severity of the offender's crime (which they do); nor does their initial proposition deny that punishment practices or penal philosophies reflect a serious concern for criminal behavior and the level of criminal activity (which they do); nor finally does their theory deny that punishment is a necessary consequence of crime (which it is). Rather, they state that punishment practices and punishment theories reflect prevailing ideologies which themselves are a function of the economic requirements of the system of production which are reflected in labor market conditions. Imprisonment, as a system of punishment, is merely one mechanism situated within a larger system of production that is geared to fulfill the material requirements of that system of production and consumption. Since that system, i.e., advanced capitalism, is characterized by labor surpluses, punishment is related to the labor market via this regulatory function. Hence, imprisonment levels and differences in levels between different groups in different economic regions of the country are best understood by breaking the connection between crime and punishment and investigating the relationship between labor markets, systems of punishment, and variations in levels of punishment.

For example, in the United States, in the era since the mass migrations of blacks to the urban North, prisons appear to have operated in this regulatory fashion. The prisons are of course too small and imprisonment is too costly for the state to incarcerate the entire labor surplus. Instead, the prisons seem to siphon off the most superfluous class of workers, such as young black men who are increasingly becoming marginalized members of society. Thus our thesis is that the missing link in the business cycle, employment, and crime nexus is race. Like Rusche and Kirchheimer, we recognize the importance of *punishment* as the correlate with economic conditions, and like Brenner, we discover a strong effect of unemployment, although only after examining the impacts separately for blacks and whites.

Current policy debate over what to do about our blackening prisons and over how to contain the explosive potential inherent in overcrowded and increasingly violent jails and penitentiaries has overlooked completely the economic link between race and punishment. That link suggests that the worsening labor market condition of blacks has influenced the rapidly changing demands on the prison system, a system that has seen a doubling of its incarcerated population in the past decade. We contend that this reliance on the prisons as a labor market regulatory device is by no means a novel or accidental feature of current policy making on crime and punishment. Indeed, we argue below, that labor market conditions have historically shaped penal policies in America, particularly as those policies have affected differentially the incarceration rates of black and white workers.

BUSINESS CYCLES AND TRENDS IN IMPRISONMENT

Advanced industrial economies characteristically exhibit secular growth overlaid by short-term cycles in economic activity. Whether the patterns can be described precisely as "cycles", or whether such a thing as the "business cycle" actually exists, is of course a disputed matter. However, no one can deny the persistence of fluctuations and deviations from the underlying trends in just about every economic series imaginable.

In a similar fashion prison populations, while exhibiting growth, also are overlaid with shorter-term cycles or fluctuations in size. If they are conceptualized as a series, then even though the series itself may be stable or trendless, the oscillations around the trend rarely are stable.[13] In fact, the oscillations in prison admissions correlate strongly with the oscillations in unemployment.

In a recent paper[14] we analyzed the long-term differences in black and white incarceration rates between the North and the South in the United States. Pooling observations across states (14 in the North and 17 in the South) and over time, we estimated trend models of the rates of growth of punishments for each group from 1870 to 1980. We discovered, corroborating sociologist Darnell Hawkins findings[15] for male prisoners in the U.S. in 1979 and for North Carolina's imprisonment rates from 1870-1980, that Northern blacks were incarcerated at much higher levels than any other group in either region, and their higher level of incarcerations persisted throughout the post-1940 northward migration. The average black incarceration rate for the North (740 per 100,000 black population) was more than twice that of the South, and despite that much higher level, the northern black incarceration rate was the least stable of any of the incarceration rates series. (See Tables 1 and 2)

The usual theories of crime and punishment are unable to explain these differences. First, the so-called stability of punishment hypothesis implies that there should be less variation in the punishment rates than actually is

TABLE 1
North-South Incarceration Rates (Average incarceration rates per 100,000 population)

	North			South		
Year	Total	White	Black	Total	White	Black
1850	30.19	26.23	289.81	14.80	18.62	8.34
1870	86.83	80.65	507.36	70.54	42.56	120.35
1880	119.38	112.09	558.98	101.90	51.00	192.26
1890	130.74	121.38	718.10	122.33	55.17	251.85
1900	106.48	94.91	771.86	94.20	39.16	206.88
1910	114.48	102.36	773.11	116.55	48.80	287.31
1920	93.21	77.25	734.30	95.88	49.64	217.07
1930	137.83	117.00	722.29	173.05	117.66	351.87
1940	200.57	162.98	1132.42	264.95	175.66	553.09
1950	149.98	108.68	867.16	184.70	123.19	408.57
1960	148.28	97.83	822.04	214.12	142.45	493.07
1970	121.73	71.83	611.09	181.46	113.46	460.73
1980	161.66	84.41	671.96	292.58	145.72	631.12

Sources: Census documents and Myers and Sabol (1986).

Incarceration rates for 1860 were omitted since no racial breakdowns were given in the Census Reports in that year.

observed, especially for the total incarceration rate.[16] Second, traditional explanations that relate the level of crime to the level of punishment do not fit since the level of black punishment in the South from the post Civil War period through much of the 20th century was more a function of Southern whites' attempts to re-enslave freed blacks through the adoption of peonage, sharecropping, the black codes, and the aforementioned convict-lease system rather than a function of the true level of criminal activity.

We contend that an alternative explanation must address the differing labor market conditions in the North and South, and the different types of regulations that prison systems in those two regions adopted in response to the needs and requirements of their economies. Such an expla-

TABLE 2
North/South Disproportionality Ratios*

Year	North (1)	South (2)	North/South (3)=(1)/(2)
1850	11.05	0.45	24.56
1870	6.29	2.83	2.22
1880	4.99	3.77	1.32
1890	5.92	4.56	1.30
1900	8.13	5.28	1.54
1910	7.55	5.89	1.28
1920	9.51	4.37	2.18
1930	6.17	2.99	2.06
1940	6.95	3.15	2.21
1950	7.98	3.32	2.40
1960	8.40	3.46	2.43
1970	8.56	4.06	2.11
1980	7.96	4.33	1.84

Sources: Census documents.

*Disproportionality is the ratio black to white incarceration rates. Incarceration rates were calculated from the total number of persons in federal, state, or local prisons, jails, or reformatories on the date that the Census was conducted. The details of the procedures used to calculate the disproportionality measures as well as the average incarceration rates in Table 1 are discussed in Myers and Sabol (1986).

nation must go beyond a simple demonstration of differences in incarceration that result from disparities in employment; the explanation must establish why the pattern of punishment and employment differed between the North and South.

Business cycle theory may help to shed some light on the different patterns of punishment and different structures of employment. It explains development in terms of secular trends which are overlaid by shorter-term upswings and downturns in economic activity. Longer trends, which indicate the tendency of a movement, are generally monotonic movements. The cyclical components of the movement, consisting of the fluctuations lasting from three to eleven years, are the periods of expansion or contraction. Seasonal components of the cycle last for a year or less. Finally, the random component of the movement of the series covers non-recurrent changes, such as sudden shifts in the level or "trend breaks" due to a large number of random causes. It is useful, in order to establish whether and why regional variations in punishment arise, to focus initially on these longer-term components.

Different types of economies move along different trends at different rates and are overlaid with cycles of varying intensity and duration. Industrial economies, such as the industrial North, grow at a faster rate (i.e., the trend) than agricultural economies, such as the South, even though their trends are associated with more severe swings in the cycles, i.e. the amplitude and damping factors. Arthur Burns[17] describes the "typical" pattern for a relatively mature industrial economy quite well. We discuss it briefly here as a "model" for the North. Aggregate production fluctuates at a wider range than aggregate sales; durable goods fluctuate more widely than non-durables. Industrial production usually fluctuates more than the level of industrial wholesale prices, which generally fluctuate more than retail prices or wage rates. Cyclical fluctuations in hours worked are larger than the fluctuations in the number employed, and fluctuation in the number employed is much larger in commodity-producing industries than in service trades. This last point is especially pertinent for our purposes.

Agricultural production, although exhibiting stronger seasonal variations in employment, fluctuates less than industrial production. Fluctuations in employment are dependent upon the growing season and mobility of labor. In short, business cycle theory indicates that in an industrial economy one should observe wider fluctuations in a variety of factors, but especially employment, than in an agricultural economy with a year-long growing season. This model describes, relatively aptly, the North-South context in the United States.

Extending this perspective a bit further, business cycles tend to operate by their own processes. In other words, they are internally driven. To maintain a relative degree of stability, in light of the persistent fluctuations, certain requirements must be met. One prominent requirement, as articulated by Burns, is the proposition that a degree of unemployment is not only personally desirable (as when workers experience frictional unemployment when looking for new jobs) but is also socially necessary. Burns states matters succinctly: "not all unemployment is evil, and some unemployment actually serves a useful function from the viewpoint of the individual or that of society."[18]

Burns first justifies his argument by the ideology of freedom and equity, i.e., workers should be able to change jobs whenever they like, and in order for them to have that freedom there should be some frictional unemployment, or conversely, employers should be free to fire incompetent workers. However, his main contention is that zero unemployment is actually destabilizing to an economy characterized by cyclical activity. In order to maintain price stability by keeping the growth in aggregate demand manageable for the capacities of the economy, some unemployment is necessary lest the labor market produce constant shortages which lead to increases in wages and subsequently prices, and ultimately shortages in commodities as more dollars chase after the fewer goods that can be produced with older equipment and less experienced workers. Thus on the one hand, zero unemployment is inherently inflationary.

On the other hand, zero unemployment retards economic expansion. If the economy is moving along at a relatively stable rate with zero unemployment but a technological innovation in production comes along and is met with the requisite capital to build a new factory, then the labor to meet the demand to operate the equipment will be in short supply. Expansion, or the amplitude of the cycle, will be dampened more quickly than if there were a reserve of unemployed workers ready to fill the new job openings. If, on the other hand, the new factory opens and the owners hire workers from other industries by paying higher wages, then shortages appear and the inflationary cycle is fueled. As Burns puts it, "Just as stocks of raw materials help to insure the continuity of production, so does the existence of a certain number of people seeking work help to insure the continuity and efficiency of production, thereby also contributing to the stability of total employment itself."[19]

The necessity of a class of unemployed workers is also a Marxian notion.[20] Marx wrote of this class, and although his rhetoric was perhaps a bit more vituperative, his analysis was essentially the same. Marx argued that capitalist economies need to maintain a permanent reserve of surplus labor which could be called upon in periods of growth to produce for newly invested capital. According to Marx, wealth is created by labor power applied to the production process. The capitalist expropriates a portion of the wealth or value created (surplus value) which generates profits. Capital-to-labor ratios increase in maturing industries which helps hold down the cost of circulating capital (or wages). In turn, this dries up the source of wealth, i.e., labor power, since less is necessary to produce the same quantity of commodities as previously. Still, capital must circulate to reproduce itself in the production process. With sources of profits drying up as labor-saving machinery is introduced, new areas of investment must be found. The best sources of profits are those investments which initially are highly labor intensive. Hence, new investments require that same reserve army for the same function that Burns described. Without a class of unemployed workers to employ in new methods of production, wealth creation and profit maximization would decrease.

Additionally, the reserve army also places limits on the demands which employed workers can make. The surplus army of reserve labor provides the "stick" to discipline unruly labor and to help depress wages. Low wages help to keep prices low. Moreover, the existence of the surplus precludes labor shortages and helps to obviate the inflationary spiral even before it can get started.

Finally, the general condition of this "necessary" class of unemployed workers, regardless of the Marxist or non-Marxist interpretation, is prolonged unemployment. As a consequence they have no visible means of support, either selling their labor power for wages to meet material needs or living off expropriated surplus value. This class is completely dependent upon the state for its survival since it must be maintained for the productive requirements of a capitalist economy. State support generally comes in the form of social welfare expenditures and other state-sponsored services. It also comes in the form of the criminal justice system. Imprisonment, one of the major features of the criminal justice system, helps to regulate the size of this reserve class of "socially necessary" unemployed persons.

Since business cycle theory teaches that the size of that class expands and contracts with industrial expansion and contraction, particularly with durable goods and non-durable goods sectors (in that order), then we expect to find larger prison populations during downturns. In the case which we wish to examine, the secular growth in imprisonment is examined in relation to the secular growth in the size of this reserve army of unemployed workers and the growth rate in manufacturing output.

EMPIRICAL EVIDENCE

This theory suggests a number of testable hypotheses. The most immediate is that imprisonment levels and unemployment levels co-vary. Greenberg's[21] correlation coefficients between the unemployment and prison admissions series in the U.S. from 1960 to 1972 of 0.91 for first admissions into federal prisons and 0.86 for first admissions into state prisons suggest a strong relationship. Jankovic's[22] multivariate analysis confirms this relationship. Jankovic tested two labor market and imprisonment hypotheses. First, since deterrence policies are pursued more aggressively during economic downturns, he hypothesized that imprisonment and unemployment co-vary directly, or that increases in unemployment lead to increases in imprisonment. Second, convinced that this regulatory aspect of imprisonment operates in two directions, not only removing but also reducing the size of the pool of unemployed workers, Jankovic tested the hypothesis that increased imprisonment reduces unemployment. Using data from the *National Prisoner Statistics* and controlling for the level of crime (number of arrests), Jankovic confirmed the first hypothesis but rejected the second. He interpreted the lack of evidence for the second in terms of the size differential between prison stocks and unemployed persons. However, a better conceptualization of the type of regulatory mechanism should include the number of welfare recipients and other participants in state-sponsored social welfare programs.

More recently and more rigorously, Inverarity and McCarthy[23] re-ran Jankovic's regressions. Using the same data source, but correcting for the simultaneity of crime and imprisonment and correcting Janovic's autocorrelated errors, they found strong support for prisons as regulators. Specifically, they distinguished between unemployment in the monopoly and unemployment in the competitive sectors, the latter reflecting more volatile and less protected unemployed workers. Controlling for the level of crime, they found the strongest relationship between imprisonment and competitive unemployment.

While these findings provide impressive support for the punishment and social structure model, they do not address the issue of racial disparities in imprisonment, nor do they address the regional variations in imprisonment. In a recent article Myers[24] addresses racial disparities in punishment as a result of the effects of the business cycle. There, a strong relationship between black imprisonment and black unemployment is uncovered. For example, Myers observes, with the exception of the Depression years, a strong, positive, and unambiguous correlation between unemployment and the *flow* of blacks out of the noninstitutionalized civilian population and into the nation's prisons and reformatories. Black prison admissions rose to meet the increasing unemployment of the late 1920s. Similarly, falling black imprisonment during the war years of the early 1940s accompanied declining unemployment. With the subsequent rise in unemployment after World War II, black flows into the prisons again increased. The long-term pattern has been one of the significant positive association between the rate of removal of blacks from the work world and into the institutionalized world of prison.

The model of the relationships among imprisonment, unemployment and regional variations in growth which we sketched briefly above suggests a number of testable hypotheses about secular trends for investigating racial disparities in imprisonment. These monotonic movements in the series imply the following. First, given the predominance of industry in the North (compared to the South), prison populations are expected to vary inversely with the movements in manufacturing output. Since manufacturing, particularly durable goods manufacturing, produces the widest swings in employment, or conversely, generates the largest fractions of increase or decline in the pool of the unemployed, prison populations should decrease when manufacturing output increases and increase when it decreases. These effects should be stronger in the North than in the South.

Second, Northern black employment stems historically from migration into an industrial economy that coincided with labor shortages brought about by World War I and the restrictions on immigration. Northern black workers never fully enjoyed the same protections of union membership as did white workers, and their position in the industrial workforce was particularly precarious. Additionally, the more recent (ie., post World War II) gains in black earnings and employment grew out of their participation in industrial employment. Consequently, the movement in black manufacturing employment (or, conversely, the secular movement in the size of their unemployed labor force) should be a stronger predictor both of their imprisonment rates and of total imprisonment rates than that of white manufacturing employment. Stating this in another manner, we expect that the effects of the movement in manufacturing output should be inversely related to black imprisonment rates, or as opportunities in manufacturing have decreased, relative to other sectors of the economy, black imprisonment rates should have increased.

Third, since blacks contribute disproportionately to the unemployed work force, their contribution should be felt in the prison populations. Specifically, we hypothesize that the movement in the size of the black unemployed population varies directly with total and black imprisonment. We also expect that the movement in the black pool of unemployment should vary inversely with white imprisonments, or as the black unemployment increases, white imprisonments should decrease, controlling for white unemployment. We do not expect the movement in white unemployment to produce a significant change in imprisonment rates.

Finally, we expect substantial regional variation in the effects of the size of the pool of unemployed persons; however, we hypothesize that the effects of the growth in manufacturing will have the largest impact on imprisonment in both regions.

To test these hypotheses we estimated a series of equations with the dependent variable alternating among the total prison population, the white prison population, and the black prison population, in natural logarithms. Explanatory variables include the value added due to manufacturing and the value of farm products sold, which are stock measures (in natural logs). As such, they are best suited for examining the longer-run trends in imprisonment and economic fluctuations. Additional explanatory variables include measures of the number of unemployed males, which was defined as the difference between the total number of males in the workforce and the total number of employed males[25] and dummy variables to code for the year in which a state practiced probation and parole policies.[26]

Observations on all the variables were taken by state by decennial census period. Thirty states and the District of Columbia were included in the analysis; seventeen of those were the Southern states corresponding to the South Atlantic, West South Central and East South Central census divisions. The Northern states were those belonging to the New England, Middle-Atlantic and East North Central regions.

We estimated two equations for the total imprisonment model (results reported on Table 3) and two equations each for the white and black imprisonment models (results in Table 4). The models followed the general form:

$$\ln T = \beta_0 + \beta_1 \ln X_{1t} + \beta_2 \ln X_{2t} + \beta_3 \ln X_{3t} + \beta_4 \ln X_{4t} + \gamma_1 Z_{1t} + \gamma_2 Z_{2t} + e_{it}$$

Where T = number imprisoned
X_1 = population
X_2 = unemployed pool of males
X_3 = manufacturing output
X_4 = agricultural output
Z_1 = dummy variable for the years a state practiced parole
Z_2 = dummy variable for the years a state practiced probation
e_{it} = The error term.

We assumed cross-sectionally heteroskedastic and timewise autoregressive errors. According to Kmenta[27] this amounts to a GLS estimation process.

For the white and black equations, the dependent variable, population (X_1) and unemployment (X_2) were race-specific.

Considering first the general relationship between unemployment and imprisonment in Column 1 of Table 3, we find support for the first hypothesis outlined above, that is, that imprisonment helps to regulate the supply of unemployed persons by "mopping up" so to speak, some of the excess. The relationship between the growth in the unemployment pool

TABLE 3
GLS Estimates for Northern States, 1890-1980

DEPENDENT VARIABLE: NATURAL LOG OF THE TOTAL PRISON POPULATION
(t-statistics in parentheses)

	(1)	(2)
Total population	0.66	0.70
	(3.01)	(2.94)
Total unemployment	0.51	--
	(2.78)	--
White unemployment	--	0.13
		(0.59)
Black unemployment	--	0.19
		(2.60)
Manufacturing output	0.002	-0.09
	(0.02)	(-1.00)
Agricultural output	-0.04	0.01
	(-0.49)	(0.17)
Parole	-0.30	-0.17
	(-2.00)	(-0.93)
Probation	0.16	0.25
	(1.18)	(1.51)
Constant	-7.33	-3.87
	(-6.80)	(-2.06)
R-squared	0.92	0.89

Note: All variables except "Parole" and "Probation" are in natural logs. Parole and Probation are dummy variables representing the years in which states had parole or probation policies in operation.

and the growth in imprisonment is stronger in the North than in the South. The effect on prison populations of the size of the economically productive labor force that is not employed, measured as a logarithm, is positive and statistically significant. This association is less strong in the South than in the North. The South's agricultural dominance, for much of its economic history, provided more informal employment opportunities than did the structure of the northern industrial economy. In other words, if the formal labor markets did not offer employment, workers may have migrated back to the farms of family or friends and found at least part-time work. Or to put it in different terms, rural, agricultural societies do not have the same productive requirements as industrial economies.

The respective effects of the black and white unemployment on total imprisonment in the North are different as Column (2) of Table 3 indicates, and as hypothesized above. In contrast to black unemployment, which exerts strong influences on the imprisonment rate, the effects on white unemployment diminish. Thus increasing Northern imprisonment appears to be the result of increasing black imprisonment and increasing growth in the pool of unemployed blacks regardless of white unemployment or white imprisonments. This finding offers tentative support for the second and third hypotheses that the growth in the stock of unemployed blacks exerts a downward influence on the white imprisonment process.

Other conclusions emerge from this statistical exercise. We find that as the relative contribution of manufacturing to total output has fallen (particularly in recent years) and as the relative share of manufacturing jobs has fallen, the growth rate of the pool of unemployed, particularly the black unemployed, has put increased pressure on imprisonment rates. Thus, not only have Northern incarcerations increased, but Northern black incarcerations have done so at a much faster rate. When the dependent variable is the black or white incarceration rate, respectively, as in Table 4 this conclusion is reinforced further. Black imprisonment rates are negatively related to manufacturing output. No such effect is found for white imprisonment. Hence, the relative decline in manufacturing output in the North has played a more important role in influencing black imprisonments than in influencing white imprisonments. Northern blacks apparently became an integral part of the structure of the industrial economy there. They played the role, which both Burns and Marx described, of providing that necessary reserve to help to maintain price stability and to prevent labor shortages from disrupting the circulation of capital in an expanding economy.

This finding is consistent with the anecdotal evidence on the nature of black employment in the North. The Department of Labor,[28] for example, reprinted a series of studies on black migration and industrial employment in the early 1920s. The results of those studies indicated that industrial capitalists in some Northern cities (like Cleveland) generally

TABLE 4
GLS Estimates for Northern States, 1890-1980

DEPENDENT VARIABLE, COLUMNS 1 AND 2,
NATURAL LOG OF THE WHITE PRISON POPULATION

DEPENDENT VARIABLE, COLUMNS 3 AND 4
NATURAL LOG OF THE BLACK PRISON POPULATION

(t statistics in parentheses)

	(1)	(2)	(3)	(4)
White population	0.82	0.85	--	--
	(4.79)	(3.75)		
Black population	--	--	0.89	0.94
			(10.57)	(9.06)
White unemployment	0.34	0.32	--	--
	(2.37)	(1.75)		
Black unemployment	--	--	0.17	0.15
			(2.47)	(1.98)
Manufacturing output	-0.03	-0.08	-0.12	-0.18
	(-0.60)	(-1.09)	(-2.58)	(-2.57)
Agricultural output	-0.11	-0.07	0.08	0.09
	(-1.57)	(-0.81)	(1.67)	(1.25)
Parole	--	-0.21	--	0.12
		(-1.21)		(1.76)
Probation	--	0.23	--	0.17
		(1.55)		(1.28)
Constant	-5.82	-5.85	-4.42	-3.63
	(-6.37)	(-5.19)	(-6.42)	(-3.72)
R-squared	.85	.87	.93	.93

Note: As in Table 3 all variables are in natural logs except "Parole" and "Probation."

made little effort to place black workers in secure jobs. The Labor Department reports, "They [employers] have taken on Negroes when they were hard pressed for help and put them out at what might be termed turnover work—work not fitted to the man's training, and upon which there would be a constant change of employees."[29] Surveys of the steel industry in Pittsburgh in the early 1920s also indicated similar findings. Employers there stated that the greatest increase in black employment occurred in 1923 due to business prosperity (expansion) coupled with a shortage of white labor, either foreign or native. In those years, black imprisonment in the North was low, and employment, particularly in manufacturing, was growing. Today, however, in the recent era of plant closedowns, deindustrialization, and flight of industry from the frost belt, black employment is declining and black imprisonment is growing. Northern black workers have typified the class of industrial reserve labor.

The results for parole, as Tables 3 and 4 indicate, show the expected signs for the total and white imprisonment rates, but parole did not significantly reduce the black imprisonment rate. Probation had no effect. The parole results are interesting in their own right, because one need not jump to the conclusion that the absence of an effect of parole on black imprisonment is the result of discrimination or prejudice. If, as hypothesized, black workers in the North had poor employment histories and if preprison employment and the likelihood of post-prison employment are used as predictors of parole success, then by virtue of their disproportionate involvement in unemployment, black males would have lower parole rates. Thus, while we have not tested here the existence or persistence of discrimination in imprisonments in the North, we do find that conditions for social discrimination or membership in disadvantaged groups have been present in the North. In short, this result further helps to point out that the disproportionate representation of blacks in northern prisons is embedded in the social structure of that region.

In the South these findings are not replicated.[30] The general relationship between the growth in the stock of unemployed workers and imprisonment is not significant. Rather, the strongest factor predicting the growth rate in imprisonments is agricultural output. Overall, the increase in the imprisonment rate in the South is explained by the declining, relative to manufacturing, employment opportunities in Southern agriculture. In other words, much of that informal sector which was concomitant to the agricultural society of the South, disappeared as the South industrialized.

Again, the complexities of the Southern case defy easy descriptions.

Imprisonment there after the Civil War and Reconstruction, operating through the notorious convict-lease system, was caused by severe labor shortages and the necessity to maintain slave-like labor for the profitability of the plantation economy. The absence of an industrial structure like that of the North and the chronic labor shortage resulted in a different form of punsihment from that of the North. Starting around the first world war and culminating in the massive post–World War II northward black migration of the 1940s, 50s, and 60s the South underwent a tremendous transformation. A major portion of the labor force left the region. Industrialization and mechanization in agriculture left the post–second world war South a mere shadow of its former image in terms of economic relations. Hence, it is not surprising that its imprisonment process followed a pattern different from that in the North. The absence of a relationship between the reserve supply of unemployment, and imprisonment in the South does not refute the proposition we are testing. Rather, it emphasizes the social structural differences between the two regions, which apparently resulted in different systems of punishment. Nevertheless as Tables 1 and 2 indicate, since the 1960s the disproportionality gap between the two regions has narrowed due to increasing black incarcerations in the South. The South is beginning to look more like the North.

CONCLUSION

Recently scholarly debate has broached the subject of the black underclass in America. The phrase describes a class of blacks, usually young males between their teens and early 30s, who face such scandalously poor conditions and social circumstances that policy makers, academicians, and interested parties are at a complete loss to solve the problem, although not for lack of proposed solutions. Most writers on the subject discuss its emergence as a comparatively recent phenomenon, dating to the 1960s fair-housing legislation and the movement of jobs out of the city centers which permitted middle-and working-class black families to leave the ghettoes and enjoy more dignified surroundings. The urban underclass, largely unemployed, was trapped behind. From there bad conditions deteriorated rapidly.

Those analyses of the origins of the underclass are not to be faulted but for the dates of the nascence of this contemporary crisis. The results of the investigation here show that the conditions precipitating the contemporary situation were locked into and hidden in the structure of the relationship between the necessity of a class of unemployed workers for price stability and expansion in industrial societies and the growth of imprisonments. The results for the North are beyond dispute. That relationship which linked the growth in black unemployment to the prisons is older than the 20 or so years since the so-called origins of the black underclass. In short, what these results tend to demonstrate is that the origins of the black underclass, particularly in the urban and industrial North, are located in the development of the black labor market in that region of the country. Further, the marginalization of black men is less the result of failed government policies or cultural differences and more the logical consequence of the necessity of unemployment in capitalism.

NOTES

1. Willem Adrian Bonger, *Criminality and Economic Conditions,* translated by Henry P. Horton, (Boston: Little, Brown, and Company, 1916).
2. Gary S. Becker, "Crime and Punishment: An Economic Approach," in Gary S. Becker and William M. Landes (eds.) *Essays in the Economics of Crime and Punishment.* (New York: National Bureau of Economic Research, 1974).
3. Samuel L. Myers, "Do Better Wages Reduce Crime?" *American Journal of Economics and Sociology,* Vol. 43, No. 2 (April, 1984) p.p. 191-196; W. Kip Viscusi, "Market Incentives for Criminal Behavior," in R.B. Freeman and H.J. Holzer (eds.) *The Black Youth Employment Crisis,* (University of Chicago Press, 1986), pp. 301-346.
4. Early efforts to establish the desirability of adopting employment strategies to fight crime include L. Phillips, H.L. Votey, Jr., and D. Maxwell, "Crime, Youth and the Labor Market," *Journal of Political Economy,* Vol. 80, May-June 1972 p.p. 491-504.
5. Richard A. Cloward and Lloyd E. Ohlin, *Delinquency and Opportunity: A Theory of Delinquent Gangs,* (New York: Free Press, 1960).
6. Robert K. Merton, *Social Theory and Social Structure,* revised, (Glencoe: Free Press, 1957).
7. Harvey M. Brenner, "Assessing the Social Costs of National Unemployment Rates" (formal statement submitted before the Subcommittee on Domestic Monetary Policy of the U.S. House Committee on Banking, Finance and Urban Affairs Committee, U.S. Congress, August 12, 1982. Or see "Estimating the Social Costs of National Economic Policy: Implications for Mental and Physical Health, and Criminal Aggression," prepared for the Joint Economic Committee, U.S. Congress, Oct. 26, 1976.
8. Phillip J. Cook and Gary A. Zarkin, "Homicide and the Business Cycle," *Journal of Quantitative Criminology,* Vol. 2, No. 1. (March 1986) pp. 69-80.
9. Phillip J. Cook and Gary A. Zarkin, "Crime and the Business Cycle," *Journal of Legal Studies,* Vol. 14, No. 1, (January 1985) p. 128.
10. Richard B. Freeman, "Crime and Unemployment," in James Q. Wilson (ed.). *Crime and Public Policy,* (San Francisco: ICS Press, 1983), pp. 89-106.
11. Note, however, the contrary evidence provided by Samuel L. Myers showing that the employment effects outweigh the criminal sanction effects. Myers, "Estimating the Economic Model of Crime: Employment vs. Punishment Effects," *Quarterly Journal of Economics,* Vol. 98, (February 1983) pp. 157-166.
12. Georg Rusche and Otto Kirchheimer, *Punishment and Social Structure,* (New York: Columbia University Press, 1939).

13. For empirical evidence on the dynamics of prison populations see Alfred Blumstein and Soumyo Moitra, "An Analysis of the Imprisonment Rate in the States of the United States: A Further Test of the Stability of Punishment Hypothesis," *Journal of Criminal Law and Criminology*, Vol. 70 (Fall 1979) pp. 376-390. Or Alfred Blumstein, Jacqueline Cohen, Soumyo Moitra, and Daniel Nagin, "On Testing the Stability of Punishment Hypothesis: A Reply," *Journal of Criminal Law and Criminology*, Vol. 72, No. 4 (Winter 1981) 1799-1808. David F. Greenburg, "The Dynamics of Oscillatory Punishment Processes," *Journal of Criminal Law and Criminology*, Vol. 68 No. 4 (December 1977) pp. 643-651. Also David Rauma, "Crime and Punishment Reconsidered: Some Comments on Blumstein's Stability of Punishment Hypothesis," *Journal of Criminal Law and Criminology*, Vol. 72 No. 4, (Winter 1981) pp. 1772-1798.

14. Samuel L. Myers, and William J. Sabol, "The Stability of Punishment Hypothesis: Regional Differences in Racially Disproportionate Prison Populations and Incarcerations, 1850-1980," Paper presented at the Annual Law and Society Association Meetings, Chicago, IL, June, 1986.

15. Darnell Hawkins, "Beyond Anomalies: Rethinking the Conflict Perspective on Race and Criminal Punishment", *Social Forces*, Vol. 65, (March 1987) pp. 719-745; and "Trends in Black-White Imprisonment: Changing of Race or Changing Patterns of Social Control?" *Crime and Social Justice*, No. 24, (December, 1985) p.p. 187-209.

16. For sources on this hypothesis, see the sources in footnote 13 and Richard A. Berk, David Rauma, Sheldon L. Messinger, and Thomas F. Cooley, "A Test of the Stability of Punishment Hypothesis: The Case of California, 1851-1970," *American Sociological Review*, Vol. 46 (December, 1981) pp. 805-829.

17. Arthur F. Burns, *The Business Cycle in a Changing World*, (New York: National Bureau of Economic Research, 1969).

18. Ibid., p. 83.

19. Ibid., p. 185.

20. Marx, Karl, *Capital: A Critique of Political Economy*, Vol. 1, (New York: International Publishers, 1967).

21. David F. Greenberg, "The Dynamics of Oscillatory Punishment Processes," *Journal of Criminal Law and Criminology*, Vol. 68 No. 4, (December 1977) pp. 643-651.

22. Ivan Jankovic, "Labor Market and Imprisonment," *Crime and Social Justice*, (Fall-Winter, 1977) 17-31.

23. M. Inverarity, and J. McCarthy, Punishment and Social Structure, Revisited." A paper presented at the annual Law and Society Association Meetings, Chicago, Illinois, June 1986.

24. Samuel L. Myers, "Imprisonment and Unemployment," *Urban League Review*, (Fall 1986) pp. 98-105.

25. Previous research, e.g., Greenberg (1977) and Jankovic (1977) has used the unemployment rate or the number unemployed as the measure for the reserve. However, official unemployment rates omit a significant number of persons who are not working but would like to be working and could be defined as members of the labor force if economic conditions became favorable enough to draw them into the ranks of the employed or "officially unemployed." Further, by most counts the official unemployment figures grossly underestimate the extent of unemployment, particularly among black males. Since we wished to include persons who could participate in the labor force in our unemployment concept, the measure that we used is better than unemployment rates. It does, however, overestimate the true size of the "reserve" since it includes persons who are incapable of working. This probably results in a regression coefficient that is biased downward, which means that the reported coefficients are underestimates of the true effects.

26. Parole and probation were included in the analysis to determine the effects of changes in penal sanctions on imprisonment. As was described in the text, the theory that we tested grants that criminal justice officials believe that they are responding primarily to the severity of crime and not to levels of employment or unemployment in meting out sentences or releasing convicts. Further, since no measures of crime or crime rates exist for the entire period that we covered, we used parole and probation as proxies for criminal conditions or the effects of crime on imprisonment. If criminal justice officials are influenced by crime rates in sentencing offenders, then we expect to find a negative coefficient on the probation variable. If crime levels are exceedingly high, then the sentencing provided by probation discretion should reflect the tendencies of judges and to combat crime. Use of probation should decrease when crime increases, causing imprisonment rates to increase since judges would be more prone to sentence offenders to prison than, for fear of recidivism, to release them. At the other end, even though parole boards might share in the same reluctance as judges to release offenders early, parole is an effective means to alleviate overcrowded prison conditions. Thus the sign on parole cannot be predicted without ambiguity even though the Berk, et. al. work cited earlier suggests that it should be negative.

27. Jan Kmenta, *Elements of Econometrics,* (New York: Macmillan Publishing Co., Inc., 1971).

28. The data on prison populations came from the Census Bureau reports on institutionalized persons. Since 1850, the U.S. Bureau of the Census conducted special enumerations of those populations for every decade except 1930. That year's report was replaced by the *National Prison Statistics of Prisoners in State and Federal Prisons and Reformatories* (NPS) an annual report that began in 1926. Data on population and occupation distribution over various years from 1880 to 1984 came from the Statistical Abstracts, U.S. Department of Commerce, Bureau of the Census. Contact the authors for exact dates and abstracts used for occupation and population as well as abstracts used for information on occupation, agriculture, and employment.

29. U.S. Department of Labor, Bureau of Labor Statistics, *Handbook of Labor Statistics, 1924-1927,* (Washington: U.S. Government Printing Office, 1927).

30. Because of this we have not reported the regression results.

POLITICAL BUSINESS CYCLES AND IMPRISONMENT RATES IN ITALY: REPORT ON A WORK IN PROGRESS

Dario Melossi

Sociologists have shown the presence of statistically significant associations between changing economic conditions and rates of imprisonment in a number of countries characterized by common law systems. Furthermore, these associations do not seem to be mediated by changing rates of criminal behavior. This article considers the possibility that the same relationships exist in a civil law society, Italy, for the period 1896-1965. It then goes on to highlight an hypothesis and possible test to explain the nature of these associations, based on the intervening role of public opinion.

Relationships between socioeconomic indicators and indicators pertaining to the criminal justice and correctional systems have been of interest to social scientists for a long time.[1] Attention has been rekindled recently, by reemergence of the previously almost unknown but seminal work of Georg Rusche and Otto Kirchheimer.[2] Statistical evidence of an association between change in economic indicators and change in imprisonment rates has been found in recent research, based mainly on North American and English data.[3] The question about the nature of such association is however still a question open to social scientists' research.

A powerful research strategy to test the systematic character of this association and begin investigating the reasons of it lies in international, cross-country comparisons. If, in fact, change in the demographics of imprisonment in countries which have developed highly diversified forms of criminal justice and corrections can be shown to be related to change in the indicators of their respective economies, we can come to the conclusion that those relationships are expressions of social processes which are not occasional to one country. Instead, such processes would seem to be stable, and characteristic of advanced industrial societies in general.

North American and British legal systems are, of course, highly diversified legal systems. They all belong, however, to the common law tradition and share language and parts of the same culture. My research program is directed toward comparing the strength and the nature of the association between the economy and imprisonment in common law countries to those of continental European countries, such as Italy. Italy is a Western, industrialized country, but its culture and legal system are very different from those of North America and the British Isles. If in Italy and other continental European countries the same kind of statistical associations hold true, we can indeed come to the conclusion that these associations are generally present throughout contemporary societies. The question that should then be addressed is the one concerning the specific articulation of these relationships.

A SOCIOLOGICAL THEORY OF THE "LAW IN ACTION"

The legal-sociological theory that inspires this study is grounded in a concept of positive law as the specific vocabulary that is socially and formally (legally) selected as a future guide to behavior in opposition to other, potentially conflicting, vocabularies.[4] The chosen constructs are provided with sanctions, which are determined by law and entrusted for enforcement to a specialized and legally identified staff. Each such sanction, positive or negative, is a motive provided by law. The strength of such a motive with reference to other motives, which may be socially provided with nonlegal sanctions, is socially and historically situated.

Legal coercion is nothing but the supposedly bona fide attempt of that part of the public which backs a certain legal proposition to furnish other sectors of the public with a motive (or an additional motive) for conforming to the behavior prescribed in that proposition. Other motives for compliance, different from "consensus" or "coercion," are of course possible. An abstract loyalty to a formalist conception of law as "positive" law can be a motive. A specific legal venue may also be a way, or "the" way, to account for behavior determined by motives of a nonlegal nature, as research on policing and plea bargaining has shown.[5]

Such use of the law in the books is essentially what "law in action" consists of.[6] Weber wrote:

> "[L]egal norms" and all the other products of the conceptual scheme of juristic dogmatics, viewed as "empirically existing" in historical reality,

> are conceived only as *ideas* present in the minds of men, as *one among other* determining grounds of their actions and desires.[7]

"Law in action," in sum, is seen in this perspective as the actual behavior of the officials who, in a given legal order, are supposed to make and "enforce" the positive law—as well as of the members of the "audience" toward which the law is directed. It is suggested that these actors actually use the law instead of enforcing or abiding by it and that the specific character of any such usage is the outcome of a situation determined by the input of vocabularies of motive other than the legal sanction spelled out by the law in the books. As long as the main rules of the game are respected—that is, as long as neither the whole legal order nor a part of it are rejected outright—such an outcome is likely to be expressed in the highly predetermined and formalized language of the law in the books on which the participants in the control game rely as a resource to be used.

IMPRISONMENT AND SOCIAL CONTROL: THE CASE OF ITALY (1896-1965)

This theoretical perspective can be applied to research in the sociology of criminal and penal law.[8] Let us consider the relationship between imprisonment and the business cycle. A structural equation model of Italian time-series data of the business cycle, and of the imprisonment, conviction, and crime rates, was tested for the period 1896-1965. As the model predicted, I found two associations, one independent from the other, between imprisonment and convictions on the one hand, and between imprisonment and a measure of the business cycle—per capita national income—on the other. More specifically, the results show that a change of one unit in the business cycle indicator is inversely associated with a change of .1692 in prison admissions. This is not trivial. It amounts to saying that a yearly increase of 100 lire (year 1938) per capita in the national income—a rather average year-to-year change—would be associated with a decrease of 16 prison admissions per 100,000 population. Given the current Italian population, this would amount to a decline of roughly 10,000 prison admissions in one year.[9]

These results are partially consistent with the results of the already mentioned research about other legal systems. A common finding of a statistically significant association between business cycle indicators and imprisonment indicators holds in these studies. Is it possible to use the ascertained associations in order to build a causal model of the same relationships? The common explanation, in fact, is based on the utilitarian premises of classical criminology. According to these premises, the ones who end up being labeled as "criminals" are seen as the "free-willing" victims of an inexorable machine: poverty causes crime, and crime causes imprisonment. Such common explanation, however, has been put in question in the cited literature as well as in my study. Italian crime rates do not seem to be the intervening variable between the business cycle indicator and imprisonment rates. In Italy, for the period indicated, the significant negative association between business cycle and imprisonment rates is not mediated through the official rate of general criminal behavior. Furthermore, a much stronger association between business cycle and imprisonment rate indicators than between business cycle and crime rate indicators has been shown before for other legal systems, such as the American federal and state prison systems.[10] The nature of the association between imprisonment and the business cycle remains therefore obscure.

Rather vague formulations, such as the need for social control, the needs of capitalism, and similar unsatisfactory accounts of a functionalist nature have been proposed. The state has typically been used as a shorthand for (or together with) such functionalist reasoning. Cohen and Scull have noted recently that "an emerging Marxist criminology and sociology of law" has developed the "social control" aspect of so-called labeling theory in a direction that "returned the state to the centre of the drama."[11] An example, as good as any of the premises on which such reasoning has been built, is given in the following passage:

> The punishment of crime is a political act. It represents the use of physical force by the state to control the lives of people the state has defined as criminal. Whether the main purpose of imprisonment is the "rehabilitation" of the criminal, the deterrence of certain kinds of behavior, or simply the vengeful punishment of the wicked, it is a political act, for the organized power of the state is imprisoning the offender.[12]

Here, an insightful and useful understanding of the *political* character of punishing behavior has been drowned in the invocation of the "artificial man." Leviathan in fact is the ideal stand-in for the real culprits in the script of conspiratorial functionalism. Thanks to the artificial man, analysts do not need to reconstruct the causal chain of typical orientations and actions that connect, for instance, changes in economic indicators with criminal and penal system management decisions and actual rates of imprisonment. They can have the *Deus ex machina* called state descend and take care of it all. This artificial Superman can be used as if it were representative of in-the-flesh men and women.[13]

Not only, therefore, do I claim that change in the crime rates is no explanation for the existing relationship between the business cycle and imprisonment rates, but I also claim that the state need not be invoked to explain variations in punishment for crime. Nor should speculations about the motives of individual agents of control be invoked. I believe the overall strategy that should be followed is a very different one. It consists of establishing a discursive chain between, on the one hand, the ways in which the social and political conflicts around the business cycle are rationalized and given account of, and, on the other, the vocabularies of motive which are available to the agencies of penal control as they account for their actions.

My hypothesis is that the observed association between change in imprisonment rates and change in economic indicators, an association which is not mediated by change in crime rates, depends on an intervening variable that—according to the theoretical perspective I have introduced above—I call vocabularies of punitive motive. Such vocabularies are specifications of pendulum-like movements in the moral climate of a society, movements which accompany the alternation of economic periods of expansion and recession. These oscillations are in turn the product of interactions among classes, groups and organizations—interactions which influence, for instance, the production of the economic indicators that make up what we call the business cycle (and that, for these reasons, should be more properly called a political business cycle). Within the (empirically determinate) boundaries designed by the vocabulary of the law in the books, the actual behavior of the public officials who are in charge of law enforcement, is determined by oscillating vocabularies of punitive motive. Therefore, such oscillations appear to be associated statistically with oscillations of economic indicators.

However, how could this hypothesis be tested? Measures of moral entrepreneurship, or of the moral climate of a society, in fact, can be devised by making a content analysis of crucial and authoritative texts defining the issues of crime and punishment at a certain point in time. This research design has been implemented successfully in political sociology, for instance, in order to measure the relation between changing political thematic concerns or issues and long-term economic cycles.[14] In the sociology of law, the role of authoritative definitions of the situation has been long recognized as important,[15] but nobody has ever put it in a systematic relation to changing economic conditions, nor has an empirical test of such relation been developed.

A first measure to be used in order to put this model to test, is constructed from the speeches of the highest-ranking prosecuting magistrates which traditionally have opened each so-called judiciary year in Italy. These—which have been noted by historians and jurists but never studied by social scientists—are authoritative statements of policy on criminal justice and penal policy matters, resembling the speech that the U.S. Attorney General delivers at the annual meeting of the American Bar Association. Such statements are authoritative insofar as, on the one hand, they constitute a summary of the moral climate characterizing the perception of criminal and penal matters in a given social context, and on the other they furnish the members of the criminal justice and penal systems with moral, political, and professional guidance. They are delivered in an atmosphere of great solemnity and are widely discussed, commented upon, and regarded as substantial (even if they may not be agreed upon) by the lay public as well as by the practitioners. Since their very inception after the unification of Italy in 1861, these public addresses have painted a comprehensive picture of the state of the criminal question in Italy. A classification of center-stage positions, recurring issues, and values in these speeches is being devised, and a scale constructed, measuring the magistrates' attitude, year by year, toward such matters as severity of punishment, penal reforms, crime waves, and so on. This measure can then be used as the indicator for a specific and very important contribution to the making of a vocabulary of punitive motives.

This is but one of the rings in a discursive chain that connects forms of behavior so far apart as doing business and doing punishment. Other indicators could of course be used in order to reconstruct this discursive chain. One needs only to mention content analysis of legislative statutes, media reports, specialized journals and magazines, and so on. The same strategy of research could then be comparatively extended to the correctional and legal systems of other countries. For the United States, for instance, I have already mentioned the speeches of the Attorney General. Furthermore, besides the indicators already mentioned, there is in the United States a wealth of public opinion polls on the issues of crime and punishment that can be related to change in the economy and imprisonment.[16]

This strategy of research is premised on what Arthur Bentley once called the "wave motions of the linguistic behaviors of men, advancing and receding across the centuries."[17] It tries to overcome the assumptions of neoclassical reasoning as well as those of mechanistic functionalism—both of which may come in either a left-wing or a right-wing version. The economistic imperialism of neoclassical thinking sees its hero, the economic man, as a free-chooser in an accountant's universe of costs and benefits—a sad lot that not even the criminal has the privilege to escape.[18] The functionalist instead portrays the criminal as a puppet, animated by those social forces which are nothing but the hands of the puppeteer herself. I would rather consider the sources and motivations of people's behavior as socially constructed in the interaction of individuals and groups. My view on the building of what I should call a nonreified theory in social sciences is that evidence of causal connections between so-called structural variables is to be based as much as possible in the expressed intentions of the actors themselves. The generous reliance of social scientists on the concept of unintended consequences of purposive social action has often masked, in fact, the substitution of the analysts' own intentions for those of the members of society who are the object of their analyses.[19]

NOTES

Paper originally presented at the ASSA Annual Meetings, New Orleans, December 1986.

1. Donald R. Cressey, "Hypotheses in the Sociology of Punishment," *Sociology and Social Research*, 39 (July-August 1955), pp. 394-400.

2. Georg Rusche and Otto Kirchheimer, *Punishment and Social Structure* (New York: Russell & Russell, [1939] 1968). On Rusche, see Dario Melossi, "Georg Rusche: A Biographical Essay," *Crime and Social Justice*, 14 (1980), pp. 51-63.

3. Ivan Jankovic, "Labor Market and Imprisonment," *Crime and Social Justice*, 8 (1977) pp. 17-31; James Inverarity and Daniel McCarthy "*Punishment and Social Structure* revisited: Unemployment and Imprisonment in the U.S. 1948-1981," paper delivered at the Law and Society Association Meeting, Chicago (1986); David F. Greenberg, "The Dynamics of Oscillatory Punishment Processes," *The Journal of Criminal Law and Criminology* Vol. 68, No. 4 (1977) pp. 643-651; Steven Box and Chris Hale "Economic Crisis and the Rising Prison Population in England and Wales," *Crime and Social Justice* 17 (1982), pp. 20-35.

4. The argumentation supporting this view is developed in Dario Melossi, *The State of Social Control* (Cambridge, England: Polity Press, 1988). The concept of "vocabulary of motives" is derived from C. Wright Mills, "Situated Actions and Vocabularies of Motive," pp. 439-452 in C. Wright Mills, *Power, Politics and People* (New York: Oxford University Press [1940] 1963).

5. Egon Bittner, "The Police on Skid-Row: A Study of Peace-keeping," *American Sociological Review* 32 (October, 1967) pp. 699-715; David Sudnow, "Normal Crimes," *Social Problems* 12 (Winter 1965) pp. 255-276; Arthur Rosett and Donald R. Cressey, *Justice by Consent*, (New York: Lippincott, 1976); Douglas Maynard, *Inside Plea Bargaining* (New York: Plenum Press, 1984).

6. Don H. Zimmerman, "The Practicalities of Rule Use," pp. 221-238 in J.D. Douglas (Ed.), *Understanding Everyday Life* (Chicago: Aldine, 1970).

7. Max Weber "Knies and the Problem of Irrationality," pp. 91-208 in *Roscher and Knies: The Logical Problems of Historical Economics* (New York: Free Press, 1905-1906), p. 146.

8. For a more complete explanation and for the technical aspects of this section, see Dario Melossi, "Punishment and Social Action: Changing Vocabularies of Punitive Motive Within A Political Business Cycle," *Current Perspectives in Social Theory* 6 (1985), pp. 169-197.

9. Ibid., pp. 174-178.

10. See literature cited in note (3).

11. Stanley Cohen and Andrew Scull (Eds.) *Social Control and the State* (Oxford: Martin Robertson, 1983) p. 7. This is but an instance of a more general theoretical move stressing the importance of what Sutherland and Cressey called the "politicality" of processes of formal social control, namely the fact that "only violations of rules made by the state are crimes." Sutherland and Cressey, however, hastened to add that it may indeed be difficult to recognize what a "state" is in a situation without a modern type of "legislative justice." Edwin H. Sutherland and Donald R. Cressey, *Criminology* (Philadelphia: Lippincott, 1978), p. 5.

12. Erik Olin Wright, *The Politics of Punishment*, (New York: Harper and Row, 1973), p. 22.

13. Dario Melossi "A Politics Without A State: The Concepts of 'State' and 'Social Control' From European to American Social Science," *Research in Law, Deviance and Social Control*, 5 (1983), pp. 205-222; Dario Melossi, *The State of Social Control*.

14. J. Zvi Namenwirth, "Wheels of Time and Interdependence of Value Change in America," *Journal of Interdisciplinary History* 3 (Spring 1973), pp. 649-683; Robert P. Weber, "Society and Economy in the Western World System," *Social Forces* 59 (June 1981), pp. 1130-1148.

15. George H. Mead "The Psychology of Punitive Justice," pp. 212-239 in *Selected Writings*, (Indianapolis: Bobbs-Merrill, [1918] 1964); Joseph R. Gusfield *Symbolic Crusade* (Urbana: The University of Illinois Press, 1963); Murray Edelman *The Symbolic Uses of Politics* (Urbana: The University of Illinois Press, 1964).

16. Arthur L. Stinchcombe *et al.*, *Crime and Punishment—Changing Attitudes in America* (San Francisco: Jossey-Bass, 1980).

17. Arthur F. Bentley, "Epilogue," pp. 210-213 in Richard W. Taylor (Ed.), *Life, Language, Law* (Yellow Springs (Ohio): The Antioch Press, [1953] 1957), p. 212.

18. Gary Becker, "Crime and Punishment: an Economic Approach," *The Journal of Political Economy* 76 (March/April 1968) pp. 169-217; for a critique of this general approach see Dario Melossi, "Overcoming the Crisis in Critical Criminology: Toward a Grounded Labeling Theory," *Criminology* 23 (May 1985), pp. 193-208.

19. Anthony Giddens, *The Constitution of Society* (Berkeley: University of California Press, 1984); Douglas Maynard and Thomas P. Wilson, "On the Reification of Social Structure," *Current Perspectives in Social Theory* 1 (1980), pp. 287-322.

COMMENTS

Llad Phillips

There is a complementarity among these studies. They offer new perspectives on an old question, the relationship between economic opportunity and crime. The tradition has been to look at the effect of unemployment, as a business cycle indicator, upon criminal behavior. The fresh perspective offered by the micro studies by Richard Freeman and by Llad Phillips and Harold Votey is to ask what effect involvement in crime has on subsequent employment. The fresh perspective offered by the macro studies by Samuel Myers and William Sabol, and by Dario Melossi is to link business conditions to imprisonment.

Controversy about identification and specification has been central to the evaluation of research on the economics of crime. A subtlety of the Freeman approach is to pose the fresh question of the impact of crime upon employment in a recursive framework. What effect did criminal behavior in the previous month (or year) have on the likelihood of working during the survey week?

I would like to raise four questions about conditioning effects or variables that may be important to the study by Professor Freeman. The *first* has to do with a puzzle that Professor Freeman has reviewed himself, namely the weak effect of unemployment upon crime.[1] Much of that evidence was based on aggregate data, either cross-section or time series. As one moves from the macro level to the micro level, *and* simultaneously reverses the focus to the effect of crime upon employment, it may be important to remember unemployment. Professor Votey and I have found that youths who had dropped out of school were not only more likely to be involved in economic crime but were also more likely to suffer longer stretches of unemployment.[2]

The second question has to do with the contemporaneous relationship between criminal behavior and employment. The impact of one variable on the other after a delay appears simpler than their contemporaneous relationship, but as Professor Freeman notes in his article, crime and work may be complementary.

The third question has to do with the youth group under study. Professor Freeman focuses on youths no longer in school. Is their behavior different from those still enrolled?

The fourth question has to do with age. How do these relationships between crime and employment change with maturity? Professor Freeman controls for age, but the structure of the relationships between the variables may be dfferent for sixteen and seventeen-year-olds than those twenty-one to twenty-two years of age.

The study by Professors Myers and Sabol is valuable in that it forces us to confront the facts of the blackening of prisons in the United States and the higher per capita rates of incarceration for blacks in the North than in the South. It also forces us to question why there is a much stronger correlation between unemployment rates and imprisonment rates than between unemployment rates and crime rates. This latter point is reinforced by a similar finding for Italy in the discussion by Professor Melossi who uses income per capita rather than unemployment as an index of the business cycle.

Professors Myers and Sabol argue that young black men are the marginalized members of our society who disproportionately make up a reserve of surplus labor. They also argue that support and regulation for this class comes from social welfare or other state-sponsored activities such as prisons.

One question is why, with welfare, must society resort to a more expensive alternative such as prison? The authors do not note, but could, that the figures for incarceration in their Table 1 show that incarceration rates have been falling for both blacks and whites in the North since 1940, coinciding with the rise in welfare support in this country. However, the trend is not so evident in the South, another puzzle.

The authors argue that the connection between unemployment and imprisonment is a feature of capitalism and race is the key to identifying who is in the reserve supply of labor. It would be interesting to look at other economies that make use of workers from different ethnic groups as a reserve, the Finns in Sweden or the Turks in Germany, to see if there is any evidence of a similar phenomenon in other societies.

Professor Melossi suggests an alternative explanation for the connection between the business cycle and imprisonment rates, a variation in moral climate over the business cycle. Certainly public attitudes change over time. We witness changes in attitude about driving while intoxicated, the death penalty, the severity of sentences and other phenomena. The possibility that these may be related to the business cycle, as well as representing secular and episodic change, is an interesting possibility.

NOTES

1. Richard B. Freeman, "Crime and Unemployment" in James Q. Wilson (ed.), *Crime and Public Policy* (San Francisco: ICS Press 1983).
2. See Phillips and Votey, Section II, in this volume.

CRIME AND EMPLOYMENT RESEARCH: A CONTINUING DEADLOCK?

Richard McGahey

These remarks discuss issues raised in four articles in this volume which were originally presented at a 1986 session of the American Economic Association meeting: Phillips and Votey,[1] Freeman, Myers and Sabol, and Melossi.

I must confess to some frustration with my assignment. All of the articles are interesting and provocative. However, they are so diverse in approach, theory, and methodology that it is almost impossible to comment on them as a group. Taken as a whole, they reproduce many of the binds that economic analysis of crime has encountered since it took off in the late 1960's fueled by the work of Becker, Phillips and Votey, and others.[2] We remain confronted with paradoxical and hard-to-resolve findings, findings which are further complicated by diversity in theoretical approach. And the studies seem rather far away from any attempt to synthesize findings or develop a common vocabulary through which these diverse theoretical claims or empirical findings can be related or compared to each other.

In this short commentary, I discuss the problem briefly, show how it emerges from the four articles, and then indicate where the field might go in the future in trying to move beyond the current impasse.

The problem which continues to face economic analyses of crime is that the most familiar, well-developed and testable (and in my view the least rich) theory, the individual choice model of crime which draws on models of individual labor supply, often continues to produce little or no empirical evidence in support of that theory. The Phillips and Votey work is no exception. The Freeman analysis does find empirical support for a crime-employment relation, but without the theoretical architecture of many other analyses, which limits the interpretation that he can provide.

Conversely, attempts to link macroeconomic and social conditions with macro indicators of crime, such as the other two articles (Myers-Sabol and Melossi) find stronger empirical links between economic and crime or criminal justice indicators, but have a much weaker theoretical structure, especially in terms of individual variations in criminal behavior.

This theoretical problem is compounded by using measures of criminal justice system activity, such as imprisonment, in place of or in addition to measures of criminal activity. It may be that criminal justice system activity is tied to economic activity in ways that are relatively independent of actual variations in criminal behavior, a possibility that is not fully explored by Myers and Sabol and is explicitly asserted by Melossi. This problem makes communication among the authors and their work even more difficult.

Taking the Phillips and Votey study first: this is an excellent example of individual economic choice approaches to crime, and it illustrates the problems that the neoclassical approach has encountered. It draws on a well-developed theoretical structure of time allocation and individual labor supply, adapting that model to criminal behavior, and the analysis attempts to test the implications of that model econometrically. Its conclusions are also consistent with this literature, including work that I conducted as part of the Vera Institute of Justice's Employment and Crime project: human capital theory provides relatively robust explanations of legal work and earnings, but no statistically significant explanations of criminal behavior.[3]

There are some specific issues which might be addressed. First, the model treats crime as work, rather than leisure. This makes the analysis more tractable theoretically, but may be problematic. What if crime is a social or personally enjoyable activity, done without regard to earnings? Can the implications of treating crime as leisure, rather than labor, or (even worse) both be examined? On the empirical side, I have some questions and suggestions. On tabular data, chi-squares would be useful. In the analyses, age should be tested as a variable, for age will clearly be associated with years of schooling and work experience, especially for teenagers, and age may be working in some of the variables that are presented and analyzed. As the sample is rather substantial in size, it might be better to test race-sex specific combinations, rather than treating race and sex only as separate independent variables.

The labor market experiences of men and women vary substantially, even as teenagers, and this is further complicated by race. Black and Hispanic male teenagers have different and worse labor market experiences than other groups, and these differences may not be adequately captured in the structure of this analysis. Perhaps separate equations should be run for subpopulations to test the robustness of the argument, as some of Myers' earlier work did with striking differences by race. Finally, the analysis of schooling and work experience strikes me as somewhat circular in places; non-working individuals by definition have no work experience, so saying that work experience is positively related to labor force participation seems perhaps tautological.

Further analysis in the context of other literature would also be useful. For example, the analysis cuts against the work of Viscusi on the NBER sample,[4] but reaches conclusions strikingly similar to the Vera Institute research, especially on the inability of the individual choice model to explain very much about criminal behavior.[5] It may be that Phillips and Votey, like the Vera study, use actual labor market experiences and criminal participation data, where Viscusi's work used expectations about returns from crime. Such expectations seem to be consistently overreported by everyone, including those who participate in crime.

In short, this study, while very professionally conducted, underscores the fairly dismal record of the individual choice model in explaining variations in criminal behavior as a function of legal labor market experiences. The model explains 3.6 percent of the variance in crime participation, and as the authors note, "... the model predicts that no one will participate in crime." But, of course, people do. This inability to account for criminal behavior has been the experience of most empirical studies testing the individual labor-supply model, and we may have more to gain by shifting the terrain of the discussion and analysis.

Richard Freeman's article offers an interesting variation in analysis. Rather than analyzing crime as the dependent variable in terms of employment, Freeman inverts the usual analysis and studies employment as the dependent variable in relation to crime. Freeman provides a nice, common-sense discussion of the ways in which crime might influence and reduce employment. These possibilities take into account the ambiguous nature of crime as work or leisure, and also the geographic issue of local labor market constraints in poor neighborhoods.

Unlike Phillips and Votey, Freeman's analysis (using the NBER data set on inner-city poor youth) finds "a substantial inverse relation between crime and employment." Freeman's findings here parallel and support those of Viscusi[6] whose analysis also found this type of evidence, using the same data set. Further, Freeman finds that the "crime-employment tradeoff is significant in the presence of diverse control variables."

Perhaps the most intriguing finding is that variables which affect employment in Freeman's analysis (such as education and church attendance) had little or no direct relationship to self-reported crime. That is, employment itself seems related inversely to crime, but those factors which are positively associated with employment are not directly associated with crime. The analysis might have benefited from either a recursive or simultaneous structure to help address these puzzles. Still, Freeman provides a note of clarity by showing that crime and employment, while related, are not "mirror images." His careful use of empirical results (discussions of "associations" rather than "causes," for example) is welcome as well.

But the analysis is still frustrating. Freeman does not develop the more elaborate theoretical framework of neoclassical labor economics, but his analysis still concentrates on individual "tradeoffs" without a theoretical or other interpretive framework. Although reference is made to the potential influence of local labor market conditions, little is done to test for such effects. Like Viscusi, in using the NBER study, Freeman must rely on youths' assessments of gains from illegal opportunity, which may be highly overstated. In summary, Freeman's cautious empirical approach is a good one, but leaves his conclusions somewhat disconnected from larger theoretical and policy issues.

The other two articles provide a shift in terrain, but they do it in part by changing the questions—implicitly in Myers and Sabol, and explicitly in Melossi. These two studies come from an entirely different theoretical perspective than Phillips and Votey or that implied in Freeman's analysis. Indeed, in Melossi's case, the theoretical structure bears almost no relation to neoclassical economic analysis. However, these latter articles encounter their own substantial theoretical problems, both in terms of linking economic changes to criminal behavior, and to the related problems of explaining the functioning of criminal justice institutions in relation to the economy.

Myers and Sabol take up the issue of crime and economy in a different context—the relationship of imprisonment to macroeconomic cycles, and the variations by race in imprisonment ratios. This approach draws on a rather different theoretical structure than the individualized labor supply model used by Phillips and Votey, the Marxian criminological analysis of Rusche and Kirschiemer,[7] which related different punishment styles to different stages of capitalism. Myers and Sabol argue that a general Marxian analysis of the functions of the reserve army of labor is similar to a neoclassical account of business cycles, an observation that seems provocative but not easily supported, except at a very general level. There also are intricacies in the various Marxian theories of business cycles, and the reserve army of labor is not primarily linked to business cycles in Marx's analysis. Likewise, Rusche and Kirschiemer use a "mode of production" analysis which has been sharply criticized in recent Marxian literature.[8]

Myers and Sabol want to address two issues—the relationship between imprisonment rates and business cycles, which they see as validating the reserve army of labor thesis, and the variations in race-specific imprisonment rates, which would presumably show how the reserve army issue plays out in the racially divided and discriminatory case of the United States.

What is simultaneously striking and troublesome about their approach is that they do not use any measure of criminal activity—overall crime rates, economic-specific crimes, racially-specific offending rates—in their analysis. The article does not address the issue of whether the business cycle and economic conditions cause changes in crime, both in level and type, which in turn have an effect on imprisonment and punishment. Although this failure to use crime rates may be tied in part to insufficient data, it may also indicate the need to take up the issue more directly. What is the hypothesized relationship of economic conditions to criminal behavior? Following that, what is the relationship of criminal behavior to punishment and imprisonment, both in the aggregate and in the context of racial discrimination in courts, labor markets, and regions?

In its opening, the article provides a very clear account of different theoretical approaches to the problem of relating punishment and economic conditions, but the authors seem insufficiently cautious about the problem of examining long historical periods with econometric analyses. Analysis of subperiods for robustness would improve the analysis. Structural labor market change in the United States, North and South, and for blacks and whites, have been rather substantial between 1890 and 1980. Do the same relations obtain before the Depression as in the post-World War II period, for example? It seems unlikely that they could, given that virtually all of the other relationships in the economy and society underwent substantial changes in those years, so the search for a stable econometric relationship over that entire period seems rather daring. Second, for whatever time period it is possible, the analysis needs to explicitly take up the question of criminal behavior and its role (or lack of a role) in influencing changes in imprisonment. This could be analyzed for different types of crime, and for different groups of offenders, especially blacks and whites.

This second concern raises a basic theoretical problem, one which is common to Marxian-oriented analyses—the theoretical problem of agency. Who's acting here? How do macroeconomic and social conditions play out their effects in the society? Do individual variations in behavior matter? In short, how are the links between these cyclical fluctuations and structural transformations carried out, either by potential criminals or by criminal justice system actors? Or doesn't the problem of agency matter? Explicit attention to this issue would clarify the study and the intent of the authors.

The problems of criminal behavior and its impact on punishment, and the theoretical problem of agency, are addressed directly by Melossi, in an article that employs an entirely different theoretical approach than either neoclassical or conventional Marxian analyses. Melossi's article is a report on work in progress, and takes up a series of theoretical concerns. But he is explicit on several points that Myers and Sabol do not address. For example, Melossi sees no role for crime and criminal behavior in explaining how the economy influences imprisonment. We are thus left with the provocative problem of how economic cycles influence the activities of courts and legal institutions without reference to actual changes in criminality, either in type or volume.

Second, Melossi takes up the agency problem explicitly. He provides a nice critique of Marxian instrumentalist approaches, which rely on vague references to "the state" as the locus of changes in law and punishment. Melossi insists that we must examine how the effects of economic conditions on punishment take place, without using either changes in criminality, or an instrumentalist explanation based on "the state" (or by implication on "the reserve army labor" and "the needs of capitalism," unlike Myers and Sabol).

So far, so good, at least as a theoretical critique. But Melossi's alternative theoretical strategy seems very problematic to me. It is one that is quite unfamiliar to economists, or most other American social scientists, involving a blend of sociological content analysis with a semiotic and structuralist approach to social theory. Melossi proposes to classify speeches by prosecuting magistrates to create a scale of their expressed attitudes on punishment and crime issues, and use that scale as a measure to be correlated with changes in the economy. To use his example, it would be like taking the annual address of the U.S. Attorney General to the American Bar Association, developing a scale to measure the addresses' attitudes on crime and punishment, and examining that in relation to the business cycle, and to actual changes in punishment.

Out of the frying plan, into the fire! In taking on the problem of agency, Melossi would take speeches in a political forum by different individual Attorneys General and score them. What about the relation, perhaps problematic, between speeches and actions? (After all, President Reagan says every year that he wants to cut the federal deficit.) At least in the United States, crime is a local phenomenon, and laws and punishment vary by states and regions, both formally and in actual practices of enforcement. At a more theoretical level, the adaption of a semiotic-like strategy (using the "texts" or speeches) creates enormous (and to my mind currently insoluble) problems for empirical analyses. The approach is parallel to structuralist Marxian accounts of economic and social theory, which promise to explain empirical phenomena, but never can get there. Melossi's theoretical account and critique are extremely provocative but probably "overdetermined;" that is, they promise to explain too much. It seems to me that his proposed empirical enterprise cannot be carried out, or would be not very meaningful if it is.

Summing up is very difficult; in reviewing these four articles, the problems at the Tower of Babel come to mind. The four studies are not speaking the same language, theoretically or empirically. And it is hard to imagine on what grounds they can communicate with each other. Neoclassical economic theory simplifies some questions for empirical work, although I continue to question if the theoretical invocation bears any necessary relation to the empirical work. But studies like Phillips and Votey continue to find little or no explanatory power relative to crime. Freeman's empirical work does argue for a relationship between the two, but without a theoretical structure that can elaborate and guide interpretation of the findings. The Marxian account of the reserve army of labor and the needs of a capitalist economy as used by Myers and Sabol, with the specific problem of race in the United States, suffers from a lack of linkages between macro conditions and the behavior of individuals and institutions. And the theoretical strategy of Melossi, while avoiding some of the more deterministic problems of the older Marxian accounts, seems to me unworkable for empirical research that has any clear interpretation.

Future research in this area should begin to explore, theoretically and empirically, bridges between individual behavior (as in the neoclassical economic account) and larger socioeconomic forces (as in the Marxian-oriented analyses). One possible locus for such work is more intensive analysis of urban areas and neighborhoods, particularly those poor urban neighborhoods where most street crime takes place.[9] Attention to such issues might help explain a seeming paradox in Freeman's analysis: crime and employment are related, but do not have the same determinants.

Analysts in the future might concentrate much more in the future on how economic changes influence critical social and non-market institutions (school, family, neighborhood organization), and how those institutions in turn influence crime.[10] Implications for public policy would then have to reconsider both short-term employment programs and more severe punishments, which both rely in part on the individualized model of crime and employment tradeoffs for their potential policy impact. This direction for future research may help break the deadlock which now seems to characterize much of the research on crime and employment, and it might at least shed some new light on what now seem to be rather incompatible modes of analysis and empirical conclusions.

NOTES

1. The comments refer specifically to section three of the Phillips and Votey article which appears in this volume. The opinions expressed here are solely those of the author.
2. These issues are discussed in more detail in Richard McGahey, "Crime, Criminal Justice, and Economics: A Review Essay," *American Bar Foundation Research Journal,* no. 4, (Fall 1984), pp. 869-887.
3. Richard McGahey, "Labor Market Segmentation, Human Capital, and the Economics of Crime." Ph.D. dissertation, New School for Social Research, 1982.
4. W. Kip Viscusi, "Market Incentives for Criminal Behavior," in *The Black Youth Joblessness Crisis* edited by Richard Freeman and Harry Holzer, (Chicago: University of Chicago Press, 1986).
5. Richard McGahey, 1982, *op. cit.* and Michelle Sviridoff with Jerome E. McElroy, "Employment and Crime: A Summary Report," Vera Institute of Justice, New York, 1984 (mimeo).
6. Vicusi, *op. cit.*
7. Georg Rusche and Otto Kirschiemer, *Punishment and Social Structure,* (New York: Columbia University Press, 1939).
8. Heilbroner provides a very useful introduction to and discussion of some of the theoretical complexities in current Marxian thought. See Robert L. Heilbroner, *Marxism: For and Against,* (New York: Norton & Co., 1980).
9. Recent work in this vein can be found in Albert J. Reiss, Jr. and Michael Tonry (eds.), *Communities and Crime,* volume 8 in the series *Crime and Justice: A Review of Research* (Chicago: University of Chicago Press, 1986).
10. This argument is developed in Richard McGahey, "Economic Conditions, Neighborhood Organization, and Urban Crime," in Reiss and Tonry, *op. cit.*